BEECH BOAT

JANINA KOSCIALKOWSKA

BEECH BOAT

TRANSLATED BY

ANNA MARIANSKA

READERS INTERNATIONAL

The title of this book in Polish is *Lódz bukowa*, first published in 1988 by the Polish Cultural Foundation Ltd, London.

First published in English by Readers International, Inc., Columbia, Louisiana, and Readers International, London. Editorial inquiries to the London office at 8 Strathray Gardens, London NW3 4NY, England. US/Canadian inquiries to RI Book Service, PO Box 959, Columbia LA 71418-0959, USA.

The editors wish to thank the National Endowment for the Arts, Washington DC, the Arts Council of Great Britain, London, and the Central and East European Publishing Project, Oxford, for their support.

Cover design by Jan Brychta.
Printed and bound in Malta by Interprint Limited.

Library of Congress Catalog Card Number: 93-83084
British Library Cataloguing-in-Publication Data:
A catalog record for this book is available from the British Library.

ISBN 0-930523-95-4 Hardcover
ISBN 0-930523-96-2 Paperback

To Waclaw, my husband

1

"It was you who wrote these minutes, comrade? You don't deny it?"

"I did."

On the back wall, right next to the window, a cage with a little bird was dangling. There were two people in the room, one of whom was pushing some greenery between the bars of the cage. I hadn't met these people until now. I'd never seen them in the factory, but I knew they were both delegates from the Congress of Trade Unions. One was a Russian who didn't speak any Polish, the other spoke it fluently. For me that was the worst thing possible. He immediately started shouting.

"How dare you not write in the local language? These minutes are worthless. The official language is Ukrainian. Don't pretend you don't know, there can be no discussion about it. Your duty was to take minutes in Ukrainian."

And so on, and on, constantly shaking the papers which I recognised as the reports I had written. I was astonished to note a factual mistake; I was sure I hadn't made any.

So I said as calmly as I could that I didn't know Ukrainian. I wrote in Polish and no one objected.

But this was no excuse for them. A row was brewing from the moment when, shrugging my shoulders, I raised my voice as well.

"So I won't be doing it any more of course. Give these papers to whoever will be doing it from now on, but sign that you've taken these minutes away from me. Signature, seal, date. Then you can give them to someone to translate, that's your business."

Not for a moment did it enter my head that I could, that I should, be arrested on the spot. The tone of the whole incident was becoming increasingly fierce, perhaps because the younger of these two strangers wanted to demonstrate his zeal as a defender of the new system in front of the Russian, who didn't say a single word. Good-looking, tall, and tidy in a very shiny black leather jacket, he seemed rather bored with the whole scene. Yet evidently he must have understood something of what I said because at a certain moment he nodded his head and with a careless movement took my papers out of the other man's hands. Arbitrarily I decided that this closed the matter so I went out of the office. But someone in the factory management must've been fully informed because from the next day I was assigned to the spinning shop. They'd managed to get six benches going a few days earlier; I was transferred to one of them. From that moment I was on the register of workers, with the right to canteen food as well as food rations. You do understand what it meant to get hold of food at that period.

I was relating what had happened during 1939 to Wlodzimierz Solowij in London in 1945, and of course he could not fully grasp the relevance of the question of food that winter. He had spent that winter and the year prior to the war in London.

Mr Solowij was the first person I had met and come to know more closely in London. He was from Lwów; he had known my parents. "I often danced with your mother at soirées in olden times, that means in very olden times now."

Both of us laughed at the fact that different times like that had really existed and the word 'soirée' no longer existed in the vocabulary of young people of my generation. Mr Solowij was worried about his wife; he was expecting her arrival from Poland from week to week. He talked about it a lot, perhaps to allay his doubts. He told me what he had bought for her when she came, and walking along the streets of London together, we used to stop in front of jewellers' shops. Our ensuing discussions always finished with a cup of tea in the nearest tearoom. In an obvious and almost automatic way views of the past would emerge. Photographs of streets tucked away in smart black leather cases. The Royal Arsenal, Prince Lew's Castle Hill, Woloska's Orthodox church, the Orthodox church of Saint Jura, the seat of the Stauropegion, the Armenian Cathedral, the Basilian monastery. This predominance of photographs of the Ukrainian monuments in my city did not surprise me. Wlodzimierz Solowij was one of the main leaders of Ukrainians in exile. He had chosen the Ukrainian nation as his own, just as his own brother Tadeusz had chosen the Polish nation.

The remarkable thing about the Solowij family was the marriage of the brothers to two sisters, Poles. These women and their families - rooted for centuries in one country - became a political 'problem', a 'question'. And this is exactly what Mr Solowij said to me, as he was putting away the photographs: "As you can see, I am part of 'the question'."

He kissed my hand. After that we never talked about the Cause or the Question any more. I was held by tentacles from beyond the grave of Poland's partitions and its wanderers; he was oppressed by his awareness of what had happened during the German occupation and by his unfulfilled dreams of his own country. In 1945 it was not yet time to settle any accounts from the past nor form perspectives for the future. Entombed by the present, we drank tea.

Of course he asked about my family. Only my brother

Bogumil had been arrested and deported. At first I used to travel to Sambor, where he was imprisoned, with parcels for him, and I remember those journeys, each one an epic in its own way. My contorted attempts at wheedling his freedom from the prison authorities revealed a new breed of Russian to me. Had I never realised before what kind of people they were? But I couldn't convey the pathos of it all; too much had been buried by the commonplace and the banal.

I also remembered how in Aldous Huxley's novel *Point Counter Point*, the protagonist, familiar with all the horrors of war, confesses that what he missed most in the trenches and under fire was not a woman, not home, but a small group of friends who, whisky glasses in hand, would tell their own and other people's adventure stories. Stories that were invented and no more than digressions. There is nothing more pleasant, nothing more real than digressions. My knowledge of English literature helped me as well. The power of the armchair is England's strength.

"As for the rest of the family, they remained where they were. I avoided arrest by vanishing from the house - I escaped from Lwów aboard a special train for refugees called the 'Malopolska'. I was the only one named in the charge, although in similar cases they usually deported whole families. They arrested Bogumil in Krasiczyn, not in Lwów. The charge against me was serious."

"Probably not 'bourgeois origin' only," smiled Mr Solowij, "probably something even worse."

"You've guessed it. Something far worse."

In fact it concerned something funny; initially everything looked so amusing that even in London the memory of it made me smile.

"You must've known the engineer Zygmunt Harland, director of the State Institute of Fine Arts? After all, who in Lwów wouldn't have known him."

"Yes, of course. Rather superficially, but I did know him. His first wife was an excellent artist."

"I'd done my diploma there in June of that year, and it was this Mr Harland who had directed me to the then emerging Textile Industry Union, and more precisely, to the Weavers' Union which was being formed at that time. Among its members were refugees from Lódz, Bielsko Biala, and also weavers in and around Lwów; there were a lot of them in the area. So Harland instructed me to keep an eye on the design of the materials so that they weren't 'unaesthetic'. Of course it's hard not to laugh at it today, but at that time it seemed natural to me. So that was how I came across this Union. In fact it wasn't even a union then; they were just in the process of organising themselves. They'd found themselves a factory in the old Langer building on Janowska Street. Do you know where it is?"

"More or less. Somewhere in the area behind the Grand Theatre, isn't it?"

"Yes. It turned out that any production at all was still out of the question. They were only quarrelling about who should be in the union's managing body. The fact that they quarrelled is understandable. But do you remember what language those workers used? Those people from the factories of Lódz, Bielsko and Zyrardow?"

"Yes, I do. Simply a jabber."

"Neither Yiddish nor German nor Polish, not to mention any correct sentence structure. But I understood them. And for no reason at all, just for my own interest and out of curiosity really, I used to write down the course of those meetings. Once I took the floor in order to declare that one of the speakers had mistakenly quoted the motions from the previous meeting. And that's how I became their minute-taker. And because of it I became an important person. Even very important as it turned out. At every meeting I would read out what had been proposed, agreed and carried at the previous meeting. Of course it was all very short sentences, simple, in the most commonplace words, but sentences with a subject and predicate, clear and honestly faithful to what had been said. And I learnt then about the power of the word.

"When one of the workers - they were nearly all Jewish - spluttered some muddled meaning, labouring and losing himself to find the right expression, and then heard at the next meeting the clear complete sentence from my lips: 'Brigade leader Katz suggests replenishing missing needles when the shops are already at a standstill, or having some of them repaired in the city's machine repairs workshop' - then quite simply this selfsame Katz felt proud. It sounded serious, to the point, it was true. And at that time there were already nearly eight hundred people like Katz or whatever their names were. The workforce was growing from day to day.

"The poverty of these people is simply hard to imagine; it was the first time I'd seen poverty like that at close quarters. The fact that they'd been Communists for ages and ages didn't surprise me either. The majority had a few years of Polish prison behind them and they constituted a sort of elite. The way they reasoned, their proposals for sharing out the work, investment costs, the governing body - in a word, the organisation - had the appearance of an excellent cooperative, but it was dependent on the Congress of Trade Unions. And that's exactly it, the whole truth of the matter."

"But what kept you there in company like that? As far as I know, the factory wasn't obliged to give you work."

"What kept me there? That question had already been put to me then, in Lwów, whenever anyone took the time to think about someone else's affairs. I used to reply that I worked there, which was only part of the truth. What kept me was my interest in what it looked like in practice, this 'building a new system', seeing it at the very bottom. I had known the faces of these people, these or others, only from the thin strips of police photographs published in the papers with the caption 'Communist cell'. But now this black strip turned around before my eyes, the photographs separated themselves from one another, behind each of them stood a living person. They were enemies of the Republic, but you should get to know your enemies better, and there seemed to be a mechanism at work inside me, a rocket launcher of a moral missile. I suspected even then that missiles were the most fallible weapons, but to avoid the experience - and never try to get to grips with people who had different opinions - seemed to me something close to desertion.

"The minutes I wrote were already a kind of documentation for me, psychological above all, although they looked like administrative notes, and in the course of those November days they kept getting thicker and longer. Under my fingers grew a veritable wood of snippets of information."

"I'm surprised at you," said Mr Solowij, closing his cigarette case with evident disapproval. Like all Polish gentlemen of pre-war times, he carried a silver cigarette case, with an engraved coat of arms or monogram, which emitted a quiet, characteristic click when being shut. Excellently dressed, elegant in every movement, he seemed a living embodiment of those times. But those times existed in a different world, although it was only six years previous.

Out of courtesy rather than real interest he asked how this situation of mine had finally ended.

"It finished up badly, as you correctly surmise. Not only for me, it ended worse for those idealist Communists. But we're talking about me just now."

2

In the summer of 1945 I left Switzerland and came to
England. I settled in London, but today it seems to me
that the place where I really lingered during this time was
a small-town cemetery in Jaslo in the Lower Carpathians
where my grandparents had once lived. Yet on my part it
was not a nostalgic expedition, quite the reverse.

The cemetery, like most similar places in Poland, lay in
wooded verdure but never seemed to me to offer any
kind of isolation. Neither for the dead, because I visited
them often, nor for the living, because I used to meet
many people I actually knew there and others I knew
only by sight. An atmosphere of discreet contemplation
reigned here, the dignity of huge trees and small shrubs,
and my familiarity with the scene always caused me to be
in a visiting mood, not so much mourning or ceremonious
as ordinary and social, between five and six in the
afternoon. In addition, nowhere do you feel so strongly
that you are young and healthy as when visiting the long
dead.

Walking towards the graves of my grandparents on my
father's side and my great-grandfather Jordan Witt and
his siblings, I used to pass the graves of former exiles.
From the sides of the quiet, neatly maintained paths,
streamed surname after surname furnished with the word
'exile' as if it were an academic title or a family coat of
arms. An 'exile, director of the Polish School in France'
was buried there. A few steps further you were again
informed or reminded in gold letters that someone else
had been an exile. Without a doubt in this cemetery one

could see that it was an honourable title, meant to arouse special respect, and it never entered my head to voice out loud the thought that these particular dead people seemed to me a little less dead than the others, a bit like usurpers, like subtenants of consecrated ground.

I had known since childhood that they were worthy and honourable men, something like heroes, indeed better; but in fact they seemed exactly the opposite. Who can really know if they had to, or perhaps wanted to, live abroad? The very word 'exile' contained something slightly embarrassing, in contrast to the word 'traveller'. A traveller is an explorer and a scholar, a lord by his own choice and decision, but an exile exudes a smell of martyrdom and compels later grandchildren to admire his sad, or simply tragic, situation. Happy people do not make exiles, so why carve on their graves of marble, stone or granite, often generously gilded, the fact that they were wretchedly unfortunate?

I was pleased, quietly and privately, that it had not been written alongside the name of my grandfather Wladyslaw Wegrzynski, although he was an insurrectionist and exile. It was only later, on the hundredth anniversary of the November Insurrection, that the word which he so rightly deserved was carved, and his grave, like those of other insurrectionists, was visited because of it by an official delegation of local worthies and schoolchildren. In the former grammar school building a meticulous and almost magnificent exhibition of the warriors' mementoes was organised, and a large stained glass window was placed there glorifying their actions. Justice was finally done to them.

Yet in my former pre-war and unjust youth what counted most was the sunset when leaving the cemetery gate. The approaching evening and then night became impregnated with greater intensity. They, the dead, deserved a farewell at the ending of the day, but we deserved all the delights of the world which had always liked to enjoy itself in the evening most of all. Coffin lids for some, youth for others. The cemetery seemed to understand this perfectly; it was neither excessively sad nor sinister, almost a park except for its stone angels.

So the insurrectionists perished, and the exiles lay in their graves on native soil at last; history took care of them all. But if the servants' superstition about the dead rising from the grave and frightening decent folk turned out to be true, who would this returning spectre be if not these very people who had left so much of themselves in strange lands and unknown adventures?

The servants sensed this well. My grandmother's servants, carrying lights on the evening of All Souls', would quickly pass the ones 'who had died leaving us so far behind'. It was a strange sentence, a bit uncanny. While still alive the exiles were orphans of their own homeland, and that cannot be altered. So why did Wikcia Tabor or pious Maria Drakowna say about them that they had left us so far behind when they died? They had returned to their homeland after all. Could they have been brought here after they died?

My grandfather returned. Entangled in a long property dispute over his native Chlebna, he married a young girl twenty years his junior and settled with her in the country at Jasiony. Numerous photographs from those days survived. Today they are family souvenirs, but before the war they bored me. Grandfather pretended to farm, he hunted a lot, but overall everything bored him to death in the country. So much so that he decided to break off with it and move to town, to my grandmother's deep regret. The town attracted him, meetings with people, conversations, social life, work in the community, he called it 'positivist' and believed in it passionately. Jasiony was like an umbilical cord binding him to the landed gentry, and he cut it once and for all by selling it. "He dispossessed himself," as was said in the family, who blamed his political desires fanned during his long stay abroad. In Paris he held the post of tutor to the young Branickis for a while, and after his return to Poland he was reproached with having lived at a nobleman's court while in exile, which was considered a worse humiliation than the usual nomadic penury. As a child I unwittingly made a note of the fact that being an exile was first and foremost poverty and privation or humiliation, in other words only awful things.

Or else completely incomprehensible, like that conversation in the drawing room in Rajowice which I particularly remembered for long years of my childhood and which nailed me to the spot in astonishment. It was the height of summer. I was visiting with my widowed grandmother; the company of grown-ups were having a wonderful time in the corner, and through an open door the way led along the hall and the steps to the garden. I had run in from the garden having remembered that I must have lost a silk net for balls there. Halfway across the hall I was struck by one of the women's words reaching me from the drawing room, a fragment of a sentence, and what I heard was its amused and high-pitched tone: "Then I'd rather kiss a pug dog under its tail than the Pope on his sandal", which was covered by the laughter of everyone present. Something immobilised me for a moment. The bravado and cadence of the words, the excellent flow of the phrases, the cavalier aristocracy of the utterance. But what could words so singular mean, what could be the sense of them? They had to mean something after all. I was a taciturn child and attentive although discreet, and I never asked anyone about what I heard then, maybe for fear that it should be thought that I was the sort of child who listens in to her elders' conversations, which was not a fault of mine. I knew there was a custom of kissing the Pope's sandal which contains a relic, but the rest of the sentence remained a mystery or a prank.

It was only several years later and by chance, looking through a book of eighteenth-century engravings I saw a print showing the ceremony of women being received into a Masonic lodge. A beautiful woman in a rich dress, two semicircles of bare breasts bursting from a tight bodice, held her flower-like hands with obvious and bewitching ostentation far from her body. She was sitting on a stool, stretching forward her face with its curls - completely charming. Directly in front of her stood a young man in an embroidered dress coat and a white wig. He was handing the beautiful woman a little toy dog, a little pug dog with its tail lifted up, which her parted and smiling lips were touching. The caption explained that this kiss implanted on the chamois-leather dog completed the initiation ceremony and symbolised submission and humility.

At the time in Rajowice that woman's words were considered a scandal, and the scandal was talked about for a long time. My grandmother declared that she would never set foot in that house again, although many worthy people were received there. Anyway, this was already 'once, long ago'.

Grandfather kept in touch with them after he settled in Jaslo, where he bought a large house with a garden. "From the Baligrodzki", my grandmother always added when the subject came up, probably in order to stress that people who live lavishly always end up badly - by selling large, medium or even small properties.

Grandmother did not like exiles. She looked unfavourably on her husband's contacts with his former companions in exile abroad although she could not and dared not oppose them. She showed some photographs of a tall slim man in a dark frock coat, rather hunched, with his beard parted in the middle - apparently an old comrade of grandfather's - who, she explained in an unfriendly way, visited him "rarely, fortunately". Might it have concerned financial support? Or obligations of a different nature? Shared reminiscences that my grandmother did not favour? Was she afraid of plans for the future, or was it perhaps a simple dislike in her of people who had not been successful? Against a background of plush door curtains, a cabinet with shells, a glass-fronted bookcase and a bronze lamp, the former friend and companion had the appearance of an old person, though he was said to be only forty-five, and this contributed to my lasting image of him as someone branded and pushed to the sidelines of life.

I did not know my grandfather at all. He died long before I was born, and grandmother never passed on his stories and experiences abroad. But he did enjoy the sincere interest of his pupils when he undertook to teach history and Polish in the local grammar school. The professor, who was a former insurrectionist and exile, was a classic figure of that epoch and the pattern was frequently repeated at the time. Men of merit, working for the nation.

Yet surely nobody suspected them, nobody imagined that they could be, that they would turn out to be, so vengeful: that they would arise and catch up with me in London in the year 1945. I do not know if it was with a just, but castigating, hand.

Probably a just one, because the feeling of punishment overcame me so completely that I did not try to resist. Quite the opposite. But what were they actually taking revenge for? It was not because of the fact that at home they were sometimes given the name 'circular patriots', meaning people who had travelled round the whole world and returned to the same place. Could that have wounded them so much? It would not be reason enough. But I was to blame for something else which I remembered very well, and if I had not remembered, it now lit up in my memory like the clear light of day. For on a clear day and in a spacious classroom in our grammar school I distinctly said certain words which must have offended the spirits of the insurrectionists. When my professor of Polish asked me: "What was the most important role played by Romantic literature?" I replied that I knew what role it had played, but I did not want to discuss Romantic literature.

That is, Polish literature after the partitions of Poland in the eighteenth century.

Dixi. Nothing happened to me. I was a very good pupil, one of those who are 'very promising', so I could allow myself to say it, I could afford to. I added no further explanations, but it was clearly evident that I was turning my back on that colossal pain, so excellent and fertile from the literary point of view. I diminished nothing in word or thought, I just did not want to have anything more to do with it. Not any more. I had the right to have 'violets in my head' or 'spring and wine',* a right to a different page of history.

In the meantime, as it turned out, I did not have this right at all and a Sisyphean stone fell on me. Again the bitterness of disaster and exile. Exactly like the others from the Jaslo cemetery, I had to start pushing it up.

Sisyphus was also the nickname of the oldest worker at the warping machine in the factory in Lwów. He was as thin as a rake, red-haired, and yellow. He had eyes the colour of pale amber. He died as early as December.

---

*'violets in my head': an allusion to a poem by the Polish poet Kazimierz Wierzynski (1894-1969), whose first published volume of poetry was entitled *Spring and Wine*.
[All notes are by the translator.]

3

Amber. The last time I had worn amber was that same year, winter 1945, immediately after Twelfth Night, at a ball in the Bellevue Hotel in Bern. The ball was in aid of the Red Cross. Like every gala of its sort, there had to be a higher moral justification in wartime; it would not do to enjoy ourselves without one. The end of the war was approaching, news was increasing, conversations assumed a power of their own. It was felt, without talking about it openly, that this was the last ball for the present staff of the diplomatic corps. The more initiated were already discreetly changing the length of their conversations with their partners, a little longer with so-and-so, a little shorter with such-and-such; the women shuffled in their memories other women who were not present because they belonged to the Axis. People remembered certain former connections with Italy and how pleasant it would be to visit that country again, so beautiful, the older women were particularly stirred by it. Everyone turned out to be bored with being here in Switzerland, cosmopolitan it's true, very useful in wartime, but nevertheless a bit parochial, *n'est-ce-pas*?

There were many people missing from this ball whom the eye had become accustomed to seeing at similar galas during the last few years, so each absence truly shone because it illuminated several problems *in statu nascendi*. Silent soils, loud borders, whispered suppositions and surmises led a subterranean life of their own, yet not so subterranean as not to break through, now here, now there, in an unexpected sentence and in mouths other than one would expect.

The cold, as always indefinable smile of the Polish delegate seemed even more mysterious than before and was now remarked on in a different way, but I could not really understand this, nor could any of the Poles in fact. Although the people from the Intelligence Department must have known a lot more, they were never among the people invited to official fêtes of this sort. Although...

"How beautiful they are," Madame de Juge from the French embassy smiled at me, "you're right to wear them today of all days. If I were Polish I'd do the same. *C'est un très beau bijou. Larmes de Baltic.*"

"Maybe *l'arme de Baltic* as well. In both cases it's bound to be a very Pacific Sea."

"I hope so very much for your sake. I hope so very much for the sake of the Baltic. Unfortunately, I don't know it personally, but perhaps in time - nothing can be foreseen, but as you know, I'm not indifferent to eagle feathers."

"I understand very well indeed that you prefer them to pheasant feathers."

Madame de Juge laughed, and I smiled. Anything more would have been unsuitable. Pheasant was served so often in our delegation during diplomatic luncheons that the spiteful told one another that it must be the Polish national bird. The malicious also added that the cook in the Polish delegation had some connections or means of getting pheasants supplied at a very advantageous price, and since the cook was Dutch, her practical sense endowed receptions at the First Ally with Rembrandtesque associations.

I liked Madame de Juge; I used to visit her over and above the first visit required by protocol. I also knew from her that her husband, the first secretary at the embassy, intended to resign his post to enter a well-earned retirement; in other words, personal ambition did not drive this couple. Perhaps he intended becoming an *eminence grise* in the new government, which he foresaw in France, and this seemed quite probable to me. But I was not in the least interested in these people's future, and, apart from a few, all my conversations carried the obligatory pretence.

I had held quite a singular position in this notorious diplomatic corps since I had come to this team of well-settled civilians in 1941. I was someone who had heard real bombs in her own city and country, had survived the Polish war in Poland and had tasted both the Soviet and the German occupations. Against these experiences I measured the actions and psychological meanderings of people who discussed it all, sometimes vehemently, but who were far from the personal reality of war. In particular the women from the diplomatic corps, intact in their elegance and behaviour, preoccupied with ceremonies and receptions as well as with their private lives, seemed to be made of different matter. The wonderfully beautiful young wives or daughters of Middle Eastern diplomats aroused genuine delight, but any sort of conversation extending beyond the worldly life of such extraordinary creatures would have been impossible. Besides, I felt real gratitude to them for such perfect embodiment of beauty, which they fulfilled with a sense of vocation. There must also have been women of great intelligence and influence; the Polish women in particular often had difficult missions to accomplish, as did some of the Allied wives, yet everything was veiled by a benign cloud of tranquillity in a neutral country. This cloud was soon to dissipate. But I did not suspect that when it did, a precipice would open before us, bristling with spikes of every sort and revealing something unknown but choking, like gas.

First of all - and this proved the most difficult of all - I had to control my anger. Everything around me was moving me to relentless anger: the sight of people, ordinary streets, stairs, windows, and objects in everyday use. And it seemed to me that a special essence, particularly venomous, had been lurking in them for ages, and was only now starting to emerge. Everything was becoming suspicious and as if unreal, unknown, from the moment when I stopped being myself and began turning into this new human creation, human but not normal, marked as a refugee or exile, prior to ripening to the full status of a political exile.

At that time I did not think that it would be the status of many thousands of people; going around in my head was the Nansen document,* which seemed the anointment for a pariah. There was no use pretending that I was fighting to retain my personal identity; each day of the new situation was pushing me into brackets, shutting me from the world of normal people and ordinary events.

Had those from the cemetery ever experienced anything similar? They must have had a greater trust than I in the victory of their just cause, which in itself was no mean capital. But they must also have absorbed God knows what humus, sources, or sewerage. Who knows what they had to squeeze out of themselves or what was squeezed out of them, how they coped with the organic chemistry of binding themselves to a strange world. Although it looked different in their time than in 1945, they still sniggered, raised their eyebrows and watched me ironically, importunately. I was treading in their footsteps; I had fallen into their situation if not their role.

In this unfortunate trap I found one ally most helpful: London itself. In those days it still held to its foggy tradition. The fog had the ability some days, particularly

---

*The Nansen document, introduced by Nansen when League of Nations Commissioner for Refugees, enabled refugees and stateless persons to travel without a passport.

in the evening, to tighten into a fabric, or rather a malleable tricot; all-present and unyielding, it isolated, snuggled and covered. Similarly, people can pull various monkey faces, go cross-eyed, poke their tongues out, assume the poses of a buffoon, distort themselves, and thereby, it would seem, protect themselves.

I was overcome with stamping. I would stop in the thickness of the fog in the middle of a sidewalk which I thought empty and start stamping my feet as though very cold. The regular, strong beats of my heels on the slab of pavement caused an increasingly deep satisfaction, a primitive, ritualistic pleasure. Best suited for this were high-heels, my last expensive shoes, which emitted a knock more like hammering than stamping, and thus more sonorous, more significant. It was the joy of a real *auto-da-fé*, since reason bade me look after this particular, lovely pair of shoes bought while still in Geneva. But malicious curiosity prevailed as to how long the heels would resist being hammered against the pavement. Wearing high heels seemed the duty of the moment. To descend to low heels would mean accepting my fate, now already minor. No, not yet.

Almost always the stamping summoned someone from the depths of the fog. In one of the side streets off Cromwell Road, quite empty and convenient for this purpose, I heard someone's voice next to me: "Yes, madam?" And I guessed rather than saw the shape of a policeman in the fog. "Yes, madam." The voice sounded expectant and solicitous, so I quickly explained that I was stamping like this out of irritation because I had lost my way and there was nobody to ask. I gave my address; I lived in Harrington Gardens at the time. My foreign accent gave credibility to my situation, and the proverbial good-hearted policeman escorted me towards my underground station at Gloucester Road.

Walking under his care, I measured the novelty of

associating with the authorities of this country, which - if I stayed here - would become my authorities. I would deal with my affairs in their language. And if they attended to me, I would always belong under the heading 'foreigner'. I would be the object of their social philanthropy or private charity. The same sort that I knew so well from the consulate of the Republic of Poland in Bern, whose waiting rooms were filled with anxious and harassed supplicants, uncertain whether the Republic would extend its protection over them and whether issuing them passports would define their nationality, legal status and fate. It was such a short time ago. Then I was one of the privileged, one of the people from the Delegation, and coming into contact with this crowd, disowned because stateless, disturbed me with the complex feeling which overcomes us when we face too many problems at once.

I went to the consulate extremely rarely; I was embarrassed in front of these people, as I was neither an official nor a supplicant. I courteously greeted everyone who was waiting, as if a smile and courtesy could awaken their hopes for a good outcome to their cases. Sometimes I tossed them a few words which did not require a reply, until I discovered that it was the worst thing for them and what they most feared. These people did not speak Polish. They threw themselves into the care of the Republic which was their sheet anchor, and the Republic embraced them, these people who did not know the language, were unable to refer clearly and intelligibly to any significant links with it but who needed it so badly. The Republic issued them passports, recognised them as its citizens, came to their assistance, delivered them from oppression. In those days legal nationality was the most important gain of all.

It was such a short time ago. The faces of those people waiting have faded, of course, but some of them have remained in my mind, *pars pro toto*, like a scar I was not aware of.

I have retained a small memory of a certain winter evening when I said to the consul, Konstanty Rokicki, who was accompanying me: "It's an awful thing not to have a country," but we started talking about something else. Then we met Jerzy Stempowski in the Bern café Zur Munz, and passing The Casino on the Aare, I could hear a song popular at that time: "*Je suis seule ce soir ... avec mes rèèèèves*" and Stempowski was telling us the real reasons why the ancient Greeks regarded the Persians as barbarians: because the Persians wore robes with sleeves. The Greeks allowed only the draping of the material; cuts and seams were considered the height of bad taste.

Later, in London, I remembered those sleeves, since I had the impression that a strait-jacket had enveloped us: the Yalta agreements had immobilised us for an unforeseen duration. And maybe that was the reason for this passion of mine for walking. In order to pretend that I was a free person. As I had formerly done in September and October of 1939 in Lwów, then already under Soviet occupation.

As then, so now in London in this terrible year 1945, words and names were ceasing to exist. I did not regret that I was not seeing any of my friends, the majority of whom were still in Switzerland. Better not to have company and witnesses, and nobody could know about this kind-hearted policeman and my 'stampations' on the London pavement. The policeman was funny, like a film gag, but there was not even a shadow of real comedy in all of this. Suddenly everything was starting to amuse me. The location of the next bout of stamping could never be foreseen; it came upon me suddenly like inspiration. Various other shapes appeared out of the fog: the anonymous silhouettes of chance and unexpected passers-by, like figures from a fairy tale.

Today I am astonished at my complete lack of an instinct for self-preservation or any sort of fear that I might meet with an unwelcome adventure. The Greater Evil must have numbed me, shielded me against lesser wrongs. I was losing my country. I was becoming an incomplete being, somehow imprecise, different from others and because of it not subject to the course of ordinary or possible events. With the courage of a sleepwalker I would penetrate deep into small streets, dark and secretive, avoiding streets with shops since I was afraid of my own reflection in the glass, as if I had stood opposite my own apparition. Which they, the people from the Jaslo cemetery, could rightly mock; after all, I had served my apprenticeship with them, I was sharing their fate of a century ago.

Sometimes I would happen to sit down on someone's garden wall. These low walls delighted me with their good-heartedness: they demarcated yet did not enclose.

Walking in the evenings along the streets of the city became a habit, almost an addiction. I absorbed London. I told myself that London was being so good as to absorb me. I felt gratitude for this merciful fog, as if to a living person. It was the only city where I could lose myself. The brightness of Paris or Swiss cities seemed at the time a lack of mercy bordering on cruelty. The saying *on peut se passer de bonheur* referred to Paris, but in fact - I discovered it then - only London deserves it. Maybe I clutched the city all the more because I knew hardly anyone. In England I was a new person, known to nobody, having arrived from Switzerland in the last days of the legal existence of the Republic. Two weeks later the government of King George recognised the new authorities of People's Poland.

So I guessed rather than knew what moral and administrative vicissitudes the Poles who had lived here during the war had undergone. There must, I told myself, be various committees already coming into being. All national misfortunes condense into committees of one sort or another, then various wider unions will probably arise, associations, circles or other 'Aid and Care Bureaux', more or less as in the times of my exiled grandfather and his fellow soldiers, who had also formed themselves into self-help associations. Our sudden political stirrings would probably soon turn to the vinegar of grudges and accusations, after which the locals at official level would have to deal with us on an international scale, and as the former wife of an official of the Ministry of Foreign Affairs, I guessed in advance what a lengthy inconvenience it would be for our former allies.

I thought about it without the least curiosity, as if the fate of people so completely unsaddled could not fit into any legal framework. From that time we were like the wax melted on Saint Andrew's Eve and poured into cold water where it forms incidental shapes. The wax hisses and swells for a moment, thickens into small craters and clots, overflows in a last unexpected ooze before it is lifted out of the water and turned over onto all sides, its shadow cast onto the wall to find what can be divined from it. They will do the same to us exiles, once set solid and fished out; they will turn us over, touch us, bring us close to a surface, measure and examine us until something takes shape.

Politically? Do they foresee some political role for us, unknown at present? Are we to be a force in reserve, or trash without significance?

The Poles who settled here must know something about it. Somewhere in the depths of Polish London something must be happening already, a rescue service being organised for the shipwrecked. They are throwing us a lifebelt that we must grab hold of; arrivals like myself should wait until they include us. So I should wait. I must stop stamping too; stamping leads to nothing but ridicule.

I must organise myself somehow, organise myself.

I had to, but it surpassed my strength. The first step towards people already signified organisation: a refugee body, and me with the status of an exile. Crossing with open eyes a river already crossed in the dark.

No. Not yet.

4

There were five people, the last summer guests in Worochta, in the last days of August 1939. Apart from my mother and myself, professor Hugo Steinhaus and his wife and daughter Lidka, the wife of Jan Kott, were also staying in this lovely corner of the world. We were sitting at table in the late afternoon, not commenting on the situation at all, rather the opposite - pleased that all the summer visitors had already left, the guest-houses and villas had already emptied, and the immobile, corporeal yet soulful charm of this land lay on the roads and paths. Conscious too of its own beauty. The greens of the trees and shrubs were rich and abundant in variety, and although tended, they were not overly so, just enough for this to be a holiday spot without detracting from its natural beauty in any way. The greenery concealed and opened views on lower lying fields and something almost theatrical appeared before our eyes in this mutability of settings, each more beautiful than the next. Railings of thick rolls of branches over the bridges, bridges above the fields, and the fields extensive, already fading but turning gold, juicily, not drily. Hills small and medium, valleys mild as in poetry, roads white or there again black, clumps of trees settled as if deliberately here and not somewhere else, and all this extolled for years on many colourful postcards and therefore known to the newcomer. It was a kind of snobbery not to delight in Worochta, everything had already been said about it, everything painted in watercolours, gouache, oils, and even embroideries. Worochta was like a well-known model become over-famous. And now when everyone had left the place, when our small circle was looking at it, we experienced, each of us separately, feelings of bestowal and intimacy.

Then my mother said with that half-serious smile of hers which was her charm: " 'Because the purpose of beauty is to delight...' The poet Norwid was right. At least in this instance. And the most banal views are precisely the ones that are the most beautiful. Such a shame..."

Professor Steinhaus laughed. "Of course it's a shame. Man would like to be a discoverer, it's hard for him to bear the fact that he is himself a banality."

"Well, professor, you can't know anything about that. You belong to the very few people who are the least banal of all. What you told my husband about the mathematical impossibility of calculating some bubble or other on the surface of the water - maybe I'm repeating the problem imprecisely - already raises you above normal people, above all the bubbles that people can feel themselves to be."

"But don't feel in the least," laughed Steinhaus. He had a characteristic way of holding his head slightly bent back, which made his profile impose itself upon the eye of the beholder, and when he was talking he usually looked straight in front of himself.

"You hold your head like a coin. A precious one. Though facing front you're just as interesting and worthy of admiration as in profile."

"Ah, but I want to appear half as young," replied the professor in an excellent humour. We all laughed.

He was renowned for his wit, fine, sparkling and deep as well. Best known and most repeated was his epigram that "the world is a ball chained to mankind's foot." Looking at the beauty of this spot which invoked delight, one of us said with quiet, faithful wonder: "That ball of yours doesn't weigh on a man here."

"But it rotates."

And we laughed again. We had reason to be concerned at least about the immediate future, but we were laughing. I don't know if it was making light of the general atmosphere of war, or bravery, or the feeling that what will be will be. The calm and cheer of the conversation were not false or pretentious, otherwise we would have left Worochta by then, like the others. Perhaps we just felt a premonition that we would not easily be able to spend similar moments together in such pleasant mood and company. The shadows were already starting to lengthen; one of them was stretching onto the meadow, becoming a spike with a knob.

"Look, there's your bubble," smiled my mother.

A shadow really was growing out of the shadow of a bubble, now in the shape of a flattened and unnaturally large oval. It was the spire of the Orthodox church, invisible from where we were.

"There you are," continued my mother, "in fact the most comfortable thing in life is to be a real believer despite everything."

"As opposed to everything," corrected Steinhaus.

"As opposed? As opposed?" She repeated it and after a while she said quietly and as if just to herself, "But what about parallel fifths? Oh, those musical fifths."

We returned by the last bus from Worochta to Mikuliczyn, where we were staying in a guest-house. As we were getting off, a new sight struck us at this almost evening hour at this fork of the road. Directly opposite we could see a mobilisation poster stuck on the wall. So it was war.

Surely it didn't have to be. I looked at it, I read it attentively. Many of the people who had come on the bus were getting off at the same stop. The word 'mobilisation' was repeated; nobody shouted. I read the figures, the years, the dates. But someone behind me said loudly: "So it's war."

I did not believe it. This notice must be, I judged, a further step in the war of nerves. It was Poland's political reply and a rightful reply. The Germans will now start negotiating of course.

All the same we had to pack as quickly as possible and return to Lwów. For me there was no doubt about it; we had to get our things together.

My mother behaved strangely. She left the poster in silence, as if it did not concern her son too, my brother, and on the way home she said nothing.

I ran up the stairs first, to the porch at the back where the morning's wash was drying. On the porch stockings greeted me, wafted towards me with a sort of theatrical flourish, veritable comediennes, shrunken like the skeletons of legs and ethereal like ghosts. I tore them down, furious for some reason, then some skirts, a blouse, everything warm from the weather, smelling like a bouquet of herbs. I was still struggling with a white delicate shawl - be careful with it - when I heard the first chords of the piano downstairs.

I came downstairs very slowly and quietly. My mother was playing. From above I could see her dark head above the light line of her shoulders, her figure cut in two by the keyboard, her hands running over the rows of white and black keys, as over a row of printed words. As always - and because it suited this moment best - she was playing Chopin.

I remember my feeling of delight and shame so entwined as not to be disentangled. A laudable shame.

How can shame be laudable? How can one not be ashamed of shame? And the delight. But will this playing not attract evil here? Is something evil not already happening, becoming, being born there downstairs, in that huge room, under my mother's fingers? Does she not understand?

It was I who did not understand. Other people did. In a few minutes it was swarming in front of the windows, the windows became dark with people standing thick and fast; they were also standing in the open door. In complete silence, an ideal silence. Mostly men. A few women too.

I did not return to this memory during the whole of the war, nor later. In part I really had forgotten, but usually there was no time to retreat into thought, events were growing from day to day into a whole mound, and what happened yesterday already seemed almost as if it had not happened. And rather amusing. And less and less probable.

I remembered that moment in Mikuliczyn only in London, in that wonderful world-famous botanical garden at Kew where almost every exotic thing that grows and blossoms had been gathered, described, named and numbered. And I thought, I remembered, that we had lived opposite the botanical garden in Lwów as well. It belonged to the old university on Saint Nicholas Street, and nobody was allowed to enter that garden apart from students, as it was not a public park - to the general dissatisfaction of the people who lived in the area. It started to swarm only on the second day of the war. Light field guns and anti-aircraft artillery were spread out there, but fortunately not a single tree was felled.

5

The tighter space of my new room concentrated my thoughts and uplifted me. Putting my things and books away, I discovered a note from the first days after my arrival in London. It came from Józef Retinger,* with whom I had become acquainted here when giving him letters and papers I had brought from Switzerland. The visit had been interesting. So this was the Retinger who was talked about so much in the delegation in Bern, sometimes in a friendly way, sometimes not. He was discussed with admiration and with dislike, often with a slightly mysterious comment. 'London's man', as he was called in Switzerland, was said to know everything, and it may have been true.

He questioned me about many people in Switzerland and France whom I knew or might have known, but in my conversation with him I received the impression that I did not really know anyone or anything, as he had so much information and so many opinions and conjectures about everything. He was a man behind the scenes in all matters, a specialist in insignificant history, ancient and contemporary; interested in people with a curiosity that was habitual and disinterested, even mechanical. A genius of pragmatism. From him I learnt many things that 'might come in useful', as he assured me, and he would probably be right if not for my conviction that generally I have no idea what to do with things that other people find useful, but I can often make use of what other people do not

* Jozef Retinger (1888-1962): Polish diplomat, *eminence grise* and close associate of General Sikorski's wartime government in London.

find useful.

But I had to pretend. After all I could not admit that I was tormented by fear of being attacked by memories, and that I was afraid of my grandfather, that I was also afraid of figures in our history who might suddenly turn up for no reason whatsoever and distort the ordinary current of my thoughts.

The cataclysm named exile closed me in a circle with the force of an oath. It was as if I would never rise to the surface again. But to my astonishment, and also admiration, nobody fell into any irresponsible attacks or blinding anger - from what Retinger said it appeared that people were bravely starting to dig in their heels in England, for the time being at least. And afterwards: "Various other perspectives are sure to turn up. Of course, it's a hard test of life, exile always is. Stempowski's doing the right thing not moving from Bern. Of course he foresaw a long time ago what was lying in wait for us."

Stempowski had foreseen it. Yes, I thought to myself, listening to Retinger, he had foreseen it. Besides, for Jerzy Stempowski there was never anything new under the sun - but exile is experienced differently at his age than if one is not yet thirty. My generation could not have such a stoic philosophy right from the start nor comfort itself with redemptive scepticism. Stempowski had told me that it had come to him in time, "which people never want to believe," he would add, laughing in his own way.

And suddenly, during this conversation in London I realised that Stempowski was almost a born exile, and from the time he had left his beloved Ukraine when he was young, he felt 'somewhere else' everywhere, so he was hardened to the loss of familiarity. He replaced it, he knew how to replace it: by combining boundless erudition and imagination - odd bedfellows - but the world belongs to people who know how to dominate it by using their memory for magnanimity or revenge.

And I remembered that Stempowski always said of himself, to his close friends and others: "I am an East European," and it often infuriated zealous believers in the opposite theorem, that Poland was a part of Western Europe. But he said it with the unequalled lordliness and dignity of his intellectual authority and charm that made him such a unique example of humanity. The persistent refrain returned to me again - it was such a short time ago. I had not even managed to write him a proper letter then, apart from a greeting card showing . . . Tower Bridge! A bridge! How extremely amusing it seemed to me now when the slogan about the Polish bridge had finally crashed down.

Retinger was still limping after his parachute jump into Poland. We must, as it turned out, all possess courage and cold blood whatever our age. So that his generation seemed to me, not for the first time, stronger, more ready for everything, and I was ashamed at the thought of my internal furies and battles. This man of medium height, with an ugly and original face, Picasso-like eyes and endowed with hands of exceptional beauty, seemed the owner of many magic tricks and stunts in whose efficacy one should perhaps believe. Before time swallows everything one day, it is better and more comfortable to believe in something, to jump down from vain angers, head-first if necessary and hang on hooks and ropes of convictions or hopes. Or at least pretend, in order to gain time. In case time, skinning us of our erstwhile moral state of possession, offers something else, an illusion perhaps but useful and life-giving. Life without the oxygen of one's homeland is a false course of treatment, but hundreds and thousands of people undertake it. I must go among people, talk, bow, smile, invite, ask, thank, ask about close and distant friends and the relatives of strangers, say goodbye, greet, exist.

And so I decided to make use of Retinger's advice to present myself at the address he gave me. He praised this 'establishment' highly. It was located in my area and I knew the street, so I set off there early one afternoon, after returning from Kew Gardens. But this first attempt at approaching people ended unexpectedly before it had even started.

On the No. 30 bus as I was returning to my neighbourhood, I heard a conversation between two fellow Poles, a middle-aged man and a slightly younger one. The younger one was talking with concentration and enthusiasm, quite loud. He was convinced that nobody could understand them: "And at the very end, when the anthem reached 'Poland has not perished yet', blood started to flow from the huge eagle that took up almost the whole wall above the platform. Drop after drop, drop after drop, until it became a whole stream. I don't know how they did it, but the effect was incredible, I tell you, people were overcome with emotion and sang with tears in their eyes."

The older man nodded his head gravely and then started to say something. I did not listen further but immediately ran down the stairs. I was seized by anger, rage almost, and simultaneously by a realisation that now I was suddenly touching the very bottom. So this is what we had come to now? So something like this is possible and so close, the distance of an outstretched hand away, a row of seats in front. Of course, war immediately unleashes many types of kitsch, in word, thought and deed. I had defended it once myself, considering that the right to kitsch is one of man's deepest needs, but I had not foreseen an eagle bleeding above a platform.

I had to recover from the sensation. I got off before my stop. A quick step is exalting; the click of my heels accompanied me like a drumbeat, halt, forward, halt, forward. I entered a telephone kiosk, unlit and 'out of order', and I spent quite a long while there. All the eagles that I had come across or designed myself during my stay in Switzerland came flying at me, various white birds on active service. White or silver, small or large, the most frequent was the one from the emblem of the Republic, round but squared-off, our veritable squaring of the circle. It faced right, its wings shaped in a circle almost up to the neck, where they were fastened with a five-pointed star. The feathers below were long and vertical, similar to bared swords, between them thick feet and very powerful claws that held symbols of learning or art or a banner with an inscription, as the occasion required. The eagle often assumed a military guise as well: a quadruple row of short feathers - it must have been a young bird - in tight ranks like scales, a heavy cap-like crown, with a small cross. Small feet similar to an acanthus leaf held a semicircular cartouche, into which were driven thirteen nails.

A private, favourite eagle also flew into my mind, the one from the year 1733, from the first page of the reforming king Stanislaw Leszczynski's *A Free Voice Insuring Freedom*: a bird in flight bearing the inscription *elementum meum libertas*. I reproduced that eagle wherever I could, I favoured it in our little theatre's tours or decorations for national ceremonies, extending its tail somewhat and sharpening its beak more bellicosely as the need of the moment required.

Sketching charcoal on paper, cutting out cardboard, folding the required shapes, I acquired the hands of a midwife; and the birds created as symbols enfolded something personal, my own loyalty. I remembered that I had brought two and a half eagles from Switzerland in the bottom of a suitcase, two ready and one unfinished. I had brought them with no special purpose in mind, probably feeling that they might come in useful. When I returned to my room in Harrington Gardens, I opened that suitcase.

There they were, laid out flat, not crushed, and I was overcome by haste, an unpleasant haste, to put them as quickly as possible into a place where they would not fall easily into my hands or sight. I rolled them up, wound them tightly in paper like a mummy, tied them up with string and placed them in the farthest corner of the wall cupboard. I was flushed from impatience, irritation, even anger, that such strange feelings were invading me. I rushed out of the room to immerse myself in the streets of the city. But in the corridor the quiet clatter of someone's typewriter reached me from one of the neighbouring rooms. I realised then that I was not hearing it for the first time.

6

The establishment Jozef Retinger had told me about was located at number 63 in a mews off Old Brompton Road. There was a large dark green door and above it the inscription 'Decorative Arts Studio'. It was opened by an immensely tall young man, Jozef Natanson, who was in charge of this whole new world. He led me inside and acquainted me with the studio. It was spread out, with a landing and extensive wings containing elaborate rooms well supplied with everything the artists needed for their work. Natanson, endowed with great personal charm and social ease, explained the organisational work, plans for the future, the legal problems of the association, both technical and purely artistic ones, and he appeared not to be afraid of any of them. He wrestled with all these matters simultaneously, losing neither his good humour nor his patience. An astonishing person - I thought to myself, listening to everything he said, hardly believing that a disposition like his could exist these days.

As it turned out, there were others. Jozef Natanson introduced me to the other members of the studio, and I met Krystyna Hennenberg, a screen printer, and Rozanski and Witold Mars. Others bustled through the workshop, everyone full of energy, holding tight to the present day in the ceaseless battle to organise work in new conditions. Nothing of catastrophe or tragic deliberations. They simply did not allow themselves to be swept off the surface of life, and they were right. I admired this rightness and vigour and was ashamed of my battle with ghosts.

I learnt concrete and practical things here. The studio originally belonged to the former Ministry of Information and Documentation. It had been transferred to eminent Polish artists in order to give them a base for their work. I learnt here what the Interim Treasury Committee and the British Council were, what 'utility' meant, and the limitations and norms in the free production of art. This volume of information somewhat cleared the chaos of the world around me, where people are meant to clear a path and find a *modus vivendi*. Or at least try.

The studio was lovely. Stairs led to the landing, a kind of wide platform with tables pushed together for work, and Jozef Natanson designated a place for me there. He worked downstairs, dealing with all sorts of matters, and when he had time he painted upstairs. The back wall of the workshop was taken up by a glass door, and behind it lay a small stone-paved garden, one of the tiny and fortuitous intermurals whose charm is London's secret. So on this side it was quiet, intimate, almost homely, and conditions for working on the top floor were ideal.

I spread my things out on the landing and painted

porcelain. Nothing could be further from my state of destruction, nothing more contrary to the catastrophe, than the calm and precise painting of fragile objects. Occupying myself with them signified an act of perversity, as if the world had not crashed down and it was possible to concentrate on creating lovely objects. So I started imitating Jozef Natanson. The calm and concentration with which he gilded a cup with a small fish-scale pattern seemed to me almost superhuman and worthy of admiration.

As for me, unexpectedly, I occupied myself with recreating from memory the motifs on some old plates that had come to light in a trunk in Lwów in the winter of 1940, and which were bought by a Soviet commissar quartered in our house. He had guarded them so that they would not disappear. These plates had no particular value. They came from 'Vienner'; nobody really remembered who had acquired them, on what occasion, or who in the family had been given them. They represented the four seasons of the year surrounded by complicated swirls and flourishes. We sold them with no great sorrow, while the buyer paid the exorbitant asking price, with a smile of the greatest satisfaction, and wrapped them in a thick scarf and a copy of *The Red Banner.*

And that is how they always remained in my memory, season after season, Spring, Summer, Autumn, Winter, disappearing for ever. But suddenly valuable. I started painting them now, seeking in my memory the details of colour and composition, knowing that I would not be able to rediscover them exactly. Yet the very act of imitation and reconstruction was important; everything old, distant and transient brought me at least the semblance of healing.

However, work in the Decorative Studio did not solve my fundamental problem of earning a living. Selling lovely objects, particularly at the beginning, could not ensure a constant and sufficient income. My bank account became more slender with each passing week. In my local bank I would write a cheque which was always a pang of conscience. It was nearly always cashed by the same cashier, an older man in glasses who looked at me with good-natured and discreet concern. I sensed mute disapproval and the unasked question, "What will happen next?" He was the only person in England at that time who was concerned at my fate, and I was ashamed of this treatment for withdrawing money, in other words, my own inability to earn.

So I started putting off visits to the bank until later and later, right to the edge of my finances. The man in glasses exchanged a few sentences with me every time with an encouraging smile; he asked if I had any Polish friends, if I was well, until one day to my own consternation, I revealed that yes, I was working: "I paint, you know." I went on to explain that I was painting porcelain for a certain shop but it had only just been set up and could pay very little for the time being until it could gain a market for its products and a clientele of its own. "Oh, I see," replied the beaming cashier; he wished me much luck and most probably believed in the shop.

I left the bank covered in sweat from shame. It was not a lie of the sort usual in the diplomatic corps and to which I had been so accustomed. Lies like that could even be amusing sometimes. This one pierced me right through; it uncovered my fear about how I would manage in the immediate future. My divorce formalities, which were being dealt with in England by the Polish Catholic Mission, were keeping me in England, and it was only in this country that I had the guaranteed right to stay without restrictions. Besides, people should undertake battle wherever they are, 'for the brave all places are equal', as the poet says.

Sudden revelation: the theatre. Perhaps I could now

earn some money for what I did free of charge in Bern
with such enthusiasm? 'For the brave all places are equal'
- I must only nerve myself to courage. My men, REJ
Mikolaj, KOCHANOWSKI Jan, MORSZTYN Hieronim,
PASEK Jan and the others, might they be able to help
me now? That was how they came to mind, in the style of
an official form, surname first then the given name, which
worked comically on me, almost merrily. I examined my
idea more closely and started to be optimistic. I must try.
Other cadences clambered into my mind: 'The stars have
hidden, night's dark shades approach', sung on our tiny
stage by the worthy gentleman Vespasian, who returned
to me now like an affectionate comforter.

I embarked on a retrospective look at the whole of my
work there. I considered what could be changed or left,
what could still be developed and supported musically.
Even on the street, I could hear a distant stream
murmuring 'sycamores above the stream', and 'sweet
evenings with Justyna' appeared. In the sky of those
sweet evenings I had placed a herd of sheep made out of
curled paper in order to express the metaphor of clouds
literally, which Stempowski had liked so much, but now I
started to fear confusion. The sheep motif referred more
to the eighteenth century, so maybe the sky of evenings
with Justyna should not carry them? I must avoid
anachronism.

Walking along London's streets, I was studying no
longer relevant problems of staging. My return to these
matters stirred with such life and vitality that, filled with
self-confidence, I telephoned the Polish YMCA and
asked for the name of the manager or director in order
to know whom I should address. "Concerning what?"
asked a languid and very Polish voice in the tone of an
enquiries window, and I allowed myself a very crass joke:
"Concerning Mr Kochanowski."

I learnt the name of the director - it was Mr

Majchrzak. Armed with this specific information, and feeling behind me a whole detachment of Excellent Writers whose worth was not open to question, I was already changed inside. There is nothing like the classics.

But next day the classics let me down. I did not find Majchrzak in the YMCA; I was advised to present myself the following week. But the following week suddenly seemed light years away and the whole idea good for nothing. Who wants to bother now with the poetry of independent Poland, Poland still great and unquestioned? The only poetry that counts these days must be the second sort, the post-partitions one, romantic, post-insurrectionist, suffering, bleeding. An epoch of seeking shelter in 'eagles' nests red with thunder' will again arise. What use is there now for pre-partition verses? My whole cycle of the history of literature produced for the stage and entitled 'The Path of the Polish Muse' had arisen in time of war, storm and hope, but was probably unsuitable for the aims of exile. There was no point in my going to the YMCA.

I was sitting on a bench in Hyde Park and thinking again. Yes, the decision to present Kochanowski's *Epigrams* and Rej's *Pranks* had been the right one earlier; the soldiers' rich and rousing laughter made them favourably disposed to the whole of our theatrical undertaking, and I was happy when they laughed. But now, it was impossible to penetrate to Kochanowski through the ironic smiles of the old exiles, who were not at rest in the cemetery at all, as it turned out. They had leaned out of their graves, and it was they, the dead of yore, who were now becoming our allies. We were starting to measure up to them, compare ourselves with them, and they must have been giggling; they knew that history was repeating itself even though analogies are deceptive.

What we had in common, however, was of vital

importance, and it was precisely Kochanowski who expressed it best: 'For the brave all places are equal, but sweet freedom must be fought for with our last strength'.* The thing is, this 'last strength' was already slipping out of our hands, for who summons up quotations unless already feeling defeated? All past generations had fed themselves on words; they bulged and burgeoned with them, and now it was my turn too. A terrible circle, the 'unchanging circle' from the Psalms of David, snatched me up and carried me away. I again felt that I was hanging and twisting, like a gallows bird.

I returned to the studio near Old Brompton Road like a prodigal daughter. There followed whole days as if in brackets, filled with work and the semblances of normality. *Etre c'est paraître*, I told myself and went regularly to the Decorative Arts Studio. I would sit upstairs at my painted four seasons of the year, while downstairs people appeared and disappeared, artists, clients, friends and acquaintances of the studio, and even its opponents.

One day the artist Tadeusz Potworowski came, severe and furious at the existence of 'this work', saying that everything which came from the former Polish authorities should "be transferred to the present representatives of People's Poland, now the only Poland, and we must not throw sand in her eyes." He spoke hard and at length. Natanson replied uncompromisingly and would not let himself lose his temper, no easy matter in the face of his guest's aggressive tone. I listened from my landing, busy painting Spring's smile. This incident with Potworowski stayed in my mind as the first altercation of its kind

*'For the brave all places are equal': quotation from the Polish Renaissance poet, translator and dramatist Jan Kochanowski (1530-84). The title of Koscialkowska's book comes from Kochanowski's invocation to a beech boat in his verse drama *The Dismissal of the Greek Envoys*.

revealing the most difficult of problems - the question of revindication. What was Caesar's, what was God's? What was now due to the Polish people and how could it be seen, how could it be verified, at a time when the nation was becoming only 'a stage of revolution on the march'? Poland was changing into a double-headed vampire, divided into opposing concepts of government and society. Yet this vampire had a common bloodstream, and on Polish soil the separation of nation from system was starting to become a tragedy, while for exiles it was their *raison d'être*, their passion and pivot for all activity. I did not share their hopes; I felt that time was working against us. We, abroad, were truly a 'nation like lava', similarly shapeless, forming on furrows of chance terrain.

Downstairs the studio behaved as if it would fix itself for good to the present day, for itself and its contemporaries. It was organising itself, acquiring cohesion, accepting some things, rejecting others. Natanson was constructing an ingenious screen, installing a ceramic kiln in the cellar and above all worrying about the health of his friend Adam Kossowski. He was awaiting him in the studio from day to day; he talked about him frequently and joked that Adam's ghost was hovering in the studio. At last one day he appeared in person, and a beaming Natanson introduced an extremely slim man in a brown corduroy suit. Kossowski's very lively movements pleased Natanson. He considered them as evidence that his friend, who had returned from wartime misfortune, was healthy and fully active. He was right because very shortly afterwards Kossowski's first ceramic sketches on a religious theme started to appear.

In the darkish cellar I saw them for the first time in their initial form, barely delineated in clay with a touch of the fingers, a hasty compositional note. This shape, still hesitant and uncertain, nevertheless sketched a clear subject - the apostles gathered in a circle during the

Descent of the Holy Ghost. I looked at them for a long time, took into my hand and put back these smallish rectangles of fired clay; I had always been interested in the very first sketch of anything, the very beginning of the beginning, and unexpectedly these sketches were an exact record of the Dispersal.

The fiery tongues flickering above the apostles' heads were the most valuable gift of all, the conquest of the Tower of Babel. Reason, understanding, agreement. The most important human words, the greatest commandments. As if completely forgotten now, or buried rather, nailed down with a hoof. In my dictionary of emotions only the word anger remained. Every day was a *Dies irae*, and if I could pray for anything, it would be for proficiency in battle. Nothing was more inaccessible to me than appeasement through humble mission. The Descent of the Holy Ghost, evangelical wanderings. I moved my fingers over the ceramic notebook of somebody else's imagination, but what unexpectedly penetrated me most strongly was the stain of the white tablecloth between the figures. Something was standing on the table, barely delineated, but all the same I was able to decipher it as fish, bread, a jug perhaps. Food.

Eat, I must eat. I must not save to such an extent, I had overdone it with saving on food. *Primum edere*. I will feed myself up, and then perhaps I shall 'not be afraid for the terror by night, nor for the arrow that flieth by day', as the Psalms say. Yes, the Psalms are a text for today, vehement, vengeful but still panting with paradise lost. Surely, I thought, someone has already sculpted or painted it long ago. There was a Polish church in London, so perhaps biblical plants were growing over its walls and 'a sky like a tent' was unfolding above them.

7

I was embarrassed to go to the bank for money, I had none left. I remembered what Stempowski had told me: "Every sensible person who arrives in a strange town should find out first of all where the nearest pawnshop is." He said it, of course, with his characteristic smile hovering between mockery and sincerity, but it might come in useful for me now. A pawnshop is a difficult thing to find; besides, it sounds like something out of a Balzac novel. Maybe institutions of that sort did not exist after the war any more, and how was I to ask?

A pawnshop for a woman, like a brothel for a man, was, I thought, a relic of the nineteenth century. Resorting to its services seemed to me to reveal my want of resourcefulness. But the small watchmaker and jeweller's shop where I had a new watch-glass fitted might be able to advise.

It was. The shop was tiny, almost completely filled by its enormous owner. The tiny counter bore some boxes and bundles; about a dozen clocks hung on the wall, and underneath were cupboards with narrow drawers. This huge man agreed to buy my bracelet with a naturalness which gave me relief and pleasure, and at a certain point during the transaction he asked me whether I came from Poland. "I have a good ear," he boasted, and we started talking. He was from Lwów; he lived with his son and daughter-in-law somewhere near Hammersmith, and he immediately subjected me to a detailed interrogation: who, where, when.

"On Dlugosz Street, you say? That's not far from

professor Romer's."

"Yes, professor Romer lived at the top of Dlugosz Street. We lived at the other end; our windows looked out over the botanical garden of the old university. My father was a lawyer and for many years legal adviser to the Co-Operative Department. Then he was deputy manager of the Hipoteczny Bank on Maria Square. Dr Jan Wegrzynski."

The Hipoteczny Bank aroused his most lively memories, a veritable open sesame of reminiscences. The tiny shop became a magic booth full of wonders.

"That's the bank where we got a loan for our business in Brody. The manager at the time was Mochnacki."

"No, Mochnacki was manager of the Galician Savings Bank. We lived in his house at No. 4 Grodziecki Street for a while."

"Yes, Galician. How could I forget! The lawyer Longchamps worked there too. The Germans killed him, didn't they?"

"No, not him, but his brother, the university professor, Roman Longchamps. With his sons. On the Walecki Heights. Together with other professors."

"And his son died too? The one who married the Wysoczanska girl? What a match! The whole Mikolasch Arcade in her dowry. A pretty girl too, and lively. And he perished so miserably, you say? The cinemas alone in that arcade were worth a fortune."

But I preferred this fat stranger not to talk about cinemas, although he was suddenly not a stranger. There had been two cinemas in the Arcade, which had its own 'coat-of-arms', as the joke went. At the *Delight*, it was said, before the lights were turned on, the audience was warned with bells. That was gossip; I had been in the cinema once, not for a film, but for an interesting partner whom it was the greatest of pleasures to hug and cuddle, and both of us retained grateful memories of those cinemas meant 'for the rabble'. And of my then-fashionable angora pullover, a favoured article of clothing for the cinema.

That means, I thought at this point of our conversation, that my former world and city had disappeared because now they seemed unreal. Settled memories arose in such a specific way that there was an air of irretrievability. Mikolasch Arcade and Mikolasch Pharmacy where the inventor Ignacy Lukasiewicz once worked were probably worth a fortune, but this fat old man was not thinking of money alone. His hands turned the bracelet, but not to assess its value; I sensed that for him the bracelet was rather like a lifebelt. From one question to the next, from one sentence to another, he was touching those names and places with words, so I dared not finish the conversation and leave. The verification of details which we carried out gave us a sense of bliss. Later this sense became a habit, as is usual among exiles when they talk about their country, but for me it was the first time.

The owner of the shop was called David Baum. He wrote down his address in my notebook and explained how to get there. "Do come, I'll find something for you. Finding work in London's not hard. Even something not too heavy."

We both knew that I would come and one afternoon I did. The Baums lived on the ground floor of a small non-descript house, but they already had the inside furnished like people who are settled. Baum the son, as I learnt, had left Poland before the war; he married an English girl and had some business or other, timber I think. They lived in average English sufficiency and seemed fairly happy. But old Baum astonished me.

He confessed that, no more no less, all he wanted was to return to Lwów. He had his own connections there, as he put it; everything was thought out and taken care of.

He knew everything, he had made enquiries about everything, he would not be short of any papers.

"So what if the Soviets are there now? The city's there. What sort of a life is it here? Over there, somehow or other, you can sort something out. I've got people of my own there, and I'll manage with the new ones as well. I've already planned things through and through. Wouldn't you go with me?"

I was speechless. "Mr Baum," I said, "but you know it all. I told you..."

I had told him, not in detail it is true, about my work in the factory. More and more people who had nothing in common with industry or trade unions were in hiding among the workers; the factory was becoming a temporary shelter for anyone hiding from arrest or deportation. They were not necessarily local people, but I instinctively recognised the danger they were in. Sometimes I managed to say a few quiet words or slip a note into the appropriate pocket to warn when the next local meeting was going to take place, which might be bad for them. I was sometimes well placed to act as go-between in this factory, frequenting the canteen, to see who entered and to try to head off trouble.

Unfortunately I was not the only one who could recognise 'enemies of the people' disguised as proletarians. The registration of new arrivals was taken over by Chaja Unger and she could have been dangerous. Before entering the proffered surname she would often stop her pen in the air, place her elbow on the table, and examine the new 'worker' standing in front of her with a meaningful little smile, or ostentatiously look at the unsullied hands of someone from the intelligentsia, mute witnesses of his class origins. Just once there was a dare-devil. Chaja asked his name and he almost shouted: "My name is Sapiecha!"

And when Chaja Unger lifted up her eyes suspecting

something, he roared: "Sapiecha, it's allowed, isn't it?*
Except before the letter 'h' I have the letter 'c', 'c' like
'c...' "

The whole room roared with laughter and he still
managed to add: "And my name is Lew. Meaning lion.
Grr, grr. But I won't devour you because for me you're
not kosher."

And before everyone had pulled themselves together
from laughing, he went out briskly, pressing his hat on,
then in the door he turned round and shouted: "Cha,
cha, cha or ha, ha, ha," and people discussed it in groups,
smaller now, but still quite loudly.

8

The following day I was not working until the afternoon,
so at about 11 o'clock I walked through the city to a
cobbler I knew who might still agree to make me some
new shoes. Soviet vehicles with soldiers lying flat, their
bayonets aimed horizontally at passers-by, kept passing
along Akademicka Street. The fast nervous movement in
the street accentuated the long immobile queue of people
in front of the Communal Savings Bank who were there
to redeem pawned articles. Generally people were silent
or they whispered a few words, usually hiding their faces
behind their collars. Standing in front of the bank

---

*Sapiecha: the pronunciation of both surnames, Sapiecha and
Sapieha, is the same in Polish. The Sapiehas were one of Poland's
oldest and noblest families. Cardinal Prince Adam Stefan Sapieha
(1867-1951) was among the most powerful Polish churchmen of the
day. During World War II, while Cardinal of Krakow, he is said to
have served the German Governor of the city, Hans Frank, with a
plate of cold porridge.

branded them as bourgeois and propertied. There was a rumour that the authorities allowed the pledges to be redeemed in order to photograph their owners, and although it was not believed completely, people turned their heads away at every approaching car. High above their heads enormous canvas sheets with portraits of Stalin, Lenin and Mickiewicz billowed majestically in the wind; they looked as if they were experiencing the accomplishment and fulfilment of their greatness and history, each in his own way.

My glance caught a familiar face which disappeared almost immediately. To my astonishment it was one of the workmen, named Ginsberg, in a cap pulled over his ears and a dirty scarf up to his eyes. He was a newcomer from Lódz, alien to everything local, and particularly to something so specific to the city as a pawnshop. This pawnshop had the intimacy of a settled society, a good-natured familiarity tying people to the city like the squeeze of a helpful hand, beneficent yet rebuking, a familiarity almost domestic; the repository and sanctuary of objects of value which, in the face of temporary separation, acquired the warmth of a close friend departing on a journey. So what could this Ginsberg be doing here?

He realised that I must have recognised him in the crowd and decided to run after me. He caught up with me after the turning onto Sienkiewicz Street; he was perturbed, almost trembling.

"It's good to see you, comrade. Where are you going? I stood in the queue because lots of people are standing there, so I can't be seen. I'm afraid to go to the factory. You know what's happened?"

I did not know about anything.

Afraid, he finally removed the wet scarf from his mouth and babbled: "The whole merchandise for scrap.

What holes! Birds' nests and guts, *richtig*, for scrap. In the evening they unwound it and *kein meter gut*, to the very bottom. From the top you couldn't see anything, but in the middle *durch und durch*, through and through."

Then I too felt afraid, although I worked in the spinning shop, not the weaving shed. It flashed through my mind that perhaps this was provocation. But no, Ginsberg was not an *agent provocateur*. He was a bundle of anxiety. He did not want to return to the factory, but in the daytime he cannot have had anywhere to go, so he hid in the crowd. He gabbled about something else to which I was no longer listening. I wanted to be in the factory as quickly as possible.

The factory shops were not working. People stood in silence; even oaths fell into a void and were hardly heard. I pretended that I knew nothing and asked what was happening, but the person I asked only shrugged his shoulders. Besides, he was not a skilled workman and did not work in the weaving shed; he could not really know anything, and preferred to say nothing, just in case.

Only from Zylbersztajn's gesture hidden behind someone's back did I get an inkling: he put up three fingers to indicate the Trizub, the sign of the Ukrainian workshop which had been requisitioned and its workforce merged with ours. None of the Ukrainians were present. The accusation of sabotage had fallen on them as well, but that took place behind closed doors, in the union management's office. Nobody knew exactly what investigations went on there. Well, I thought to myself, the Trizub people have skipped out, please God they won't catch them now. Not that lot, although others may well pay dearly for them. Sabotage was obvious. Discussions in the office had apparently been going on since yesterday evening. Some of the members, even the fervent Communists, will be thrown out of work. There'll be changes, and the Congress of Trade Unions will start reorganising.

But I was not anxious about myself. I was more surprised than fearful when I saw Mieczyslaw Buch leaving the office. He said something to someone, touched someone else with a reassuring gesture, and then quickly approached me. "It's good that you're here just now, comrade," he said, "I thought you'd come earlier. There's a very important matter."

Really important. Inside the management office was the same Russian I had seen during the row about the minutes, as well as two other men I did not know and a middle-aged woman. Buch pulled a chair up for me, offered me a cigarette, and broached the subject himself; no one else said a single word. After the usual generalities about the difficult beginnings of the factory and fundamental changes in the system which had at last ushered in the longed-for socialism, he arrived at the core of the matter. The factory brigade bulletin, published every Friday, did not have the necessary personnel. The people who produced the bulletin had left; difficulties were growing; what was needed was someone talented and local who could take over the editing. At my astonished look he explained with a good-natured smile: "In Polish, in Polish, naturally in Polish. The bulletin will come out, for the time being at least, in both languages. Of course you would have the Polish section, comrade."

What surprised me most of all was my own composure, a veritable Descent of the Holy Ghost.

I listened to everything he said, let him have his say, and then, almost without raising my voice: "Have you gone mad? What do you mean? Am I to work in the propaganda office? Mr Buch, I have to work somewhere, so I earn my bread here, because whoever doesn't work doesn't eat, does he? Does he?"

I was speaking in a different tone, and Buch was confused; the others became agitated. Then something came over me: "I've never had anything to do with any organisation of the Party and you dare to propose that I..."

With the word 'dare' I said too much. Buch shouted that I was an idiot and a harmful one at that. He was shaking all over with rage, and probably with having been compromised in front of the others. My hand was already on the door handle, but I turned round at the last minute: "I'll give you a present, Mr Buch. The moment the atom was split materialism ended. Think it over, the Jews are an intelligent nation."

I slammed the door for good measure and left quickly, going on foot in order to recover, if only a little. Dusk was falling, pinching with frost. I walked through the city like one of the painter Grottger's patriotic martyrs. Lorries in front of houses again, shouts, the same sight as yesterday and the day before on a different street. Only, the streets had not changed. History had not changed. While I was walking, I gradually started to comprehend the danger facing me. It is not very far from Janowska Street to Dlugosz Street, yet before I arrived home, almost an hour had elapsed. Someone very visible in the dusk was strolling in front of the entrance to our house, and a bike stood under the wall. With astonishment I recognised Zylbersztajn, who was obviously waiting for me. On an important matter, as it turned out.

"Don't come back to the factory. The best thing for you is to disappear from Lwów, comrade. Even tonight, believe me. And just in case, you haven't seen me, remember."

And he grabbed his bike as quickly as possible before I had time to say a word.

I was scared of being deported by the invading Red

Army.* Next day I immediately put myself down for the evacuation of refugees, which the new authorities were organising in order to alleviate the city of wartime arrivals fleeing towards the eastern borders of the Republic. I had no difficulty in getting on the list, for I had various papers from Jaslo. My grandmother's house could serve me as a landing stage; it was still standing whole and normal, unaware of its fate.

Nobody knew that the train carrying this migrant population to German-occupied territory would not stop on Polish soil, but would set them down in the Reich if they were suitable for skilled work. And in this way I was assigned as far away as Weimar to work at a printer's.

But I did not tell old Baum this. What I did tell him was no argument for him. He nodded his head, not as a sign of understanding, but ritually, as if reading the Bible.

He reminded me of another old man, the owner of a small cosmetics workshop nestled in a house next to the factory. He was dispossessed for being a private capitalist, and the old machines were transferred to the factory. Deep in a corner sat a very old Jew in front of an open book, rocking in prayer. He took turns with his grandson, perhaps nine years old. Both of them rocked, enveloped with a mysterious insensitivity to what was happening around them. I do not know what became of them later. I remembered them in the act of summoning extraordinary forces from within themselves. Themselves and the Book.

But now I was angry with Baum for generating this memory. To regress with memory again. To lose everything once more, lose every moment, thicken with the

*After the Red Army attacked eastern Poland on 17 September 1939, the Soviets deported approximately 1,500,000 Poles from the occupied territory to labour camps or penal exile throughout the Soviet Union. They were deported in four vast railway convoys in February, April and June 1940, and June 1941. They had all been processed by the Soviet NKVD, and the vast majority were convicted for no known offence. They were simply Polish.

past, dilute into the present. My aversion to memories bordered on superstition, and I knew that I would always succumb. Always with the same unnecessary resistance.

At the same time I understood old Baum. He already had his whole life behind him; he wanted to return to Lwów to live there until the end of his days. So he was demanding a great deal from life. The right to one's own death seemed a rare privilege in those days. He believed that he would succeed. He staved off reason and persuasion. He had already prepared everything for this journey. He believed.

Young Baum was worried about his father. As he walked me to the underground station, he said that his father was only imagining all this: "These 'connections' of his, and those 'people of mine' are illusions. Father believes in the power of money. He's got money. He doesn't want to help us at all; he needs the money for this journey. But money can't buy everything. Here yes, there no. Maybe you know how to explain it to him; he doesn't believe us."

But I could not explain anything to old Baum any more. Next time I went to see him, he was dead. He had died three days earlier of a heart attack, suddenly, with no suffering, and it seems, not knowing he was dying. So he never returned to Lwów with the help of those people of his, unless he knew of some connections in the other world who had taken him there. Young Baum thought that it was the best thing, that his father had already been *myszygene* for a long time.

Then fear overcame me - was I unable to distinguish crazy people from normal ones? What could be called normal at that time in Polish life? But I did not take up such theoretical considerations, leading nowhere. At least old Baum had his vision and his guiding principle. He did not feel that he was a castaway. He did not want to be an exile.

9

Of course I never saw the glorious republic *Serenissima* face to face. Even when I thought I had in childhood. But nobody had really seen the republic after all, although its trace, its presence, might be perceived in very rare and ceremonial moments, in the chamber of parliament, in chancelleries, in Wawel Cathedral or in archives. It also appeared in complete privacy, in circumstances and moods unforeseen. Serenissima had an unreal life, an ideal existence, so did not lend herself to being scrutinised at close quarters; in exchange, everything could and had to be done for her. She was excellently adapted to giving people their *raison d'être.*

She differed from Poland in that Poland became accustomed to ill fortune rather than good, knew how to endure everything, was an unhappy homeland, the object of eternal concern, and only with great effort could be identified with happiness. Whereas Poland was always associated solely with difficult virtues, Serenissima demanded reverence but bestowed happiness, allowed one to hide inside her, contained something which stopped one's breath. And although unable to perform miracles, she acted on me like the Universal Mother of God. Not the Tarnowiecka Mother of God, neither the Tucholska one, not even the one from Wilno - they all required a devout heart and repentance.

Serenissima appealed to needs of a different order. She alone had the gift and authority to fill words and slogans with real gravity. And so she aroused gratitude. Her very name came from the depths of centuries. At one time it was synonymous with the monarchy; she led a double life that gave her an elaborate form. To this very day it gives me pleasure to explain to foreigners the nature of the Polish Republic of the Two Nations,* the nobility's republican monarchy on which we spilled so many grievances and accusations, with much justification. But it can still render us many services as the model and origin of the ability to create and endure paradoxes. The fact that in the end our faults prevailed and eclipsed Serenissima was another matter - they did not have to prevail. It was not Serenissima that was guilty. She could satisfy us all, feed us with everything good, content and comfort us all, and as a child I had no doubts about that. Obviously I have a eulogistic heart.

Of course in my childhood she assumed the likeness of people known to me, and I bestowed on her various faces in turn. When I was eight, she looked more or less like Mother Karnkowska, the mother superior at the Sacre Coeur convent in Lwów, where I received my first Holy Communion. Mother Karnkowska was quite impressive, very beautiful, quick and energetic. Her frequent smiles were full of friendliness, though distant. She gave audiences standing up, attentive, but always as if preoccupied with something more important; the notched white rim tightly encircling her face prevented anyone from kissing her. By contrast, Serenissima's head should be bared to all winds and directions, and her dress composed so that one could snuggle inside it openly or secretly.

Shortly afterwards other personages arrived, in illustrated books or old weeklies of fashion for ladies which my grandmother once subscribed to and allowed me to colour with coloured pencils. The best models were the

---

*Republic of the Two Nations: the Republic of Poland and Lithuania from the time of the union of both kingdoms in 1569 to the third partition of Poland in 1795.

women in the album of the Viennese or Munich painter Makart. It lay on a small table in the drawing room together with Matejko's nineteenth-century *Series of Polish Kings*. These figures usually represented various allegories. The firm and ample bodies, partly naked, partly shrouded in abundant draperies, showed a seductive pathos. I drew my finger over them in wonder at the beauty of these bodies and the gravity of their faces, awakening respect and delight. One of them in particular attracted me by her strength, sweetness and secrecy. That is what the real Serenissima must have looked like and I kissed her. It was not a kiss of reverence but of pleasure, and therefore grave. When grandmother received visitors in the drawing room, I was pleased to be present in that other company which I had discovered in the album and which was invisible to the visitors.

Serenissima appeared in that picture as an allegory of Night. Her uplifted hands were slipping on a coat of dusk. Borne by the evening breeze, she was floating earthward with her hair outspread above her like a sail. Her mantle, all of softness, was unwinding upwards. She was a blessing of protection. Small stars could be seen in the sky, and barely visible homesteads down below.

Today I think that all the likenesses into which Serenissima was personified revealed a basic need for security. She would guard me and I her. A childish need for certainty, order and trust, a cosmogony for children. Undoubtedly, this feeling of delight and harmony, almost pride, at the revolution of day and night, the fact that this is exactly how the world rolls along, rising and setting behind other worlds, as if we were personally the authors of creation - this feeling comes closest to man's longed-for bliss. The album did not survive the war.

Nor did our garden. On fine summer nights my father used to set up the telescope in the garden and tell us about the sky, my brother, sister and me - and Michas

Kunderka, the child of a very poor family, who went to school with indescribable joy. One evening Michas was standing in the strawberry bed, and pointing at the sky with a hand in an oversized sleeve, he explained that in school he had seen 'an empty ball that teaches with little rods'. As if peeling himself of his rind, he took his coat off to look through the telescope so that the sleeves would not get in his way. While he was looking, he covered his ears with his hands. His gesture astonished and amused me - was he afraid that the magnified sky would blow his head off or that he would go deaf? He survived the war; we wrote to each other for a while, then he fell silent.

Evenings like this were the most majestic celebrations, not only of the present but also the past. I returned to the magnifying glass in order to delight in the Romantics' mistake. Never mind the fact that I adored the genius of Mickiewicz; my grudge against him for so slightingly dividing the whole world into 'feeling' and 'the scholar's magnifying glass' was that much the greater.* He divided it once and for all, and by so doing he determined the division for long generations, and we made Romanticism our mark of national identity. In my youthful ardour I vowed that as far as my strength allowed, I would fight the antinomy of magnifying glass and feeling. That the Romantics' mistake would gradually be amended. Gradually. For what do we really know about Matter? And what will we do without love of the magnifying glass?

This is precisely how I was to serve Serenissima. Was I expecting something from her? Yes, definitely. I wished to serve her and she to recognise that service. To this day my vows and voiceless monologues surprise me with their

*'Feeling' and 'the scholar's magnifying glass': the references are from the poem *Romantycznosc* by Adam Mickiewicz: "Feeling and faith speak to me more strongly than the scholar's eye and his magnifying glass."

naturalness, as simple as an ordinary breath. There was everything to be done in Independent Poland and so it was simply enough to work, one person with the glass, the next with feeling. When I would die - an indecent thing but human - Serenissima would bend over me and kiss me. Or she would simply hold my hand.

It was not I who died, but Serenissima. And it took her a very long time. In the year of her death I had already known all her faults, sins or illnesses for a long time. I knew her history; it can bring as much shame as joy, but adjectives have a secret power of transforming themselves into nouns, and Serenissima stayed through force of habit. It was also easier, more comfortable, to shape or polish than simply to throw her out. When the war threw us out, a great reckoning with everyone and everything began, a real harvest of blame and illusions, and then in the year 1945 whose terrible face I saw in London, I unknowingly started my escape. I did not belong to the generation that 'had brought Poland to ruin', but I saw dangerous opponents in my own generation as well, capable of dispossessing the Republic of its dignity, and eclipsing it. But wounds hastily scored seemed shameful in the face of the enormity of this, our largest catastrophe. Some people had still not emerged from their utter dismay at the disaster we had suffered, although since then nearly a year had elapsed. But we all started to fumble - in Poland among the ruins of Warsaw, in exile among the ruins of history. Corpses were pulled out both here and over there. The ones from the old Jaslo cemetery who deserved such respect for their toil and suffering on behalf of Poland, patriots who had returned to their native soil and were buried in it, had now lost their lauded superiority. Some of them had literally turned over in their graves when their cemetery became a battlefield. Those inhabitants of old coffins could not contend with my generation any longer, with the new throng of martyrs; at most they caused a shrug of the shoulders.

Every time I heard about someone's awful fate or terrifying death, my heart would stop; fear and shame would run through my veins. One day, towards the end of my stay in Bern and towards the ultimate end of the war, they started showing films from the concentration camps on the territories occupied by the Germans. I saw one of these documents of the war.

Not to the end. At a certain point I left, fled rather. But it was not me any longer. I did not feel my own identity any longer; I did not want it. I did not want to be a human or an animal, nor a plant, nothing sentient. Not even a stone or light, or anything else inorganic. Nothing in the past, in that moment or in the future. Nothing...

Young Baum took in his fingers the necklace I was wearing on the day of my visit, examined it, asked if I had made it myself, and I nodded my head. Then he nodded. From this mutual nodding it turned out that "Things like that can be sold very well, I'll give you an address." He did so and the address did not disappoint me.

A woman no longer young lived there. She did not look English and was grave and taciturn. And there, in a well-furnished room half-filled with all sorts of boxes and parcels, an unwritten contract was agreed. I was to deliver necklaces like this at eight shillings each. I did not know if this price was low or high. I could sell six necklaces a day and earn forty-eight shillings daily, nearly two and a half pounds. If they sold well I would get more. I was overjoyed and proud of myself; I had won an important battle, not a national one it was true, but universal - to earn money. I would not have to go to the bank and be ashamed, an incompetent foreigner. In addition I could do it in my own place, although from now on I could no longer pretend that I did not belong to the new generation of losers.

66

I am already harnessing myself, already counting.
Those from the cemetery have caught up with me,
broken me, taught me a lesson, and so in my hands I am
rolling the mass known as papier mâché into regular
balls, larger and smaller, which will later be coated with
gold paint and strung onto a leather thread. I arrange
them still warm into small pyramids, six pyramids in front
of me, myself behind them, behind my first line of
defence, they my first ammunition. I have to defend
myself. Against those from the cemetery, against the alien
world, against the living and the dead. Every day I
acquire more skill in rolling these balls, smoother and
smoother, and to my naive eyes, it seems, increasingly
well-aimed, as if they were not to serve as decoration but
to defend an important position 'for so long as starry
night follows the light of day in an immutable circle'.

Kochanowski had responded again.

10

The new Poland surfaced for me unexpectedly one day in a manner that could be called anthropomorphic. Antoni Slonimski was going to Poland the following day.

In the White Eagle club, halfway through our conversation, Wlodzimierz Solowij said to me: "I'll introduce you to Slonimski. It'll be a souvenir of me." So I became one of the infinite number of people who had once been introduced to Slonimski, which he of course could neither remember nor notice. The three of us sat at a table in the midst of a swarming lunchtime crowd. For me the small square of the table became a boundary between Poland's yesterday and today. Maybe a drawbridge. Maybe a commemorative stone as well.

For me it was a privately historic moment. My faith, hitherto so watertight, in the resistance to the poison of memories, wavered. The very fact that I was seeing for the first and last time the 'heretic in the pulpit' who was even more important in Poland B than in the capital,* seemed not an irony of fate but an elegant farewell. Elegant, my God. Probably the least suitable word to describe that moment, but the only one that could relieve the tension. Here was Poland splitting into two in a tangible way.

Slonimski was wearing a grey jacket with large checks; he was sitting slightly sideways, taking in with a glance everyone in the room, maybe looking for closer

---

* Poland B: Before World War Two the territory of Poland included part of the present-day western Ukraine and western Byelorus. These regions formed the heart of Poland's most backward region, the so-called 'Polska-B' (Second Class Poland).

acquaintances as well. To Wlodzimierz Solowij's question he replied in the affirmative: "That's right, I'm leaving for Poland tomorrow." He raised his shoulders slightly, suddenly plaited the slender fingers of both hands together and added: "Well, I'll see what can be done. I'll do everything humanly possible." That is how he stays in my mind, with those decisive words and movement and a darting glint on the lenses of his glasses.

I envied him. He was excellently well born, and he had managed to be born in time. He sat astride two Polands, the pre-war one which made him and which he helped to shape, and the new one. To be able to return to the new Poland, you had to be someone. Slonimski was not returning as an anonymous, defenceless repatriate; he was armed with the significance of his person. Various difficult moments and problems might be awaiting him, but he was not faced with the unconditional surrender that threatened little-known authors or beginners. Nevertheless, I looked at him as at a warrior setting forth to hard battle and unforeseen adventures which would, as in antiquity, become the subject of common knowledge rather than simply the written word.

We were all returning to a word-of-mouth era, when the printed word was crumbling from above. In my heart I wished that everything would work out well for him, with an utter confidence and zeal that completely overcame me; but being only some woman or other, I could not tell him this.

At that moment in the White Eagle, crowded and noisy, I briefly saw a quiet green armchair which no longer belonged to this world. During childhood holidays in my grandmother's house in Jaslo, a huge green armchair, plush, with wide armrests was where I used to sink for hours of reading. This solid, old-fashioned armchair was always associated for me with the authors in *Wiadomosci Literackie* and its characteristic rustle, and there I listened to the 'heretic's' Thursday sermons.*

My great-uncle did not believe in the efficacy of the 'heretic's' battle against priggery, declaring that it was incurable, that "being an enlightened prig won't make anyone an enlightened unprig." But Great-uncle was utterly gnawed by pessimism, probably for the very pleasure of being a pessimist.

Slonimski's weekly chronicles radiated optimism and vigour. I would get up from the green plush armchair with a sure strength and the conviction that the world could be changed, and that change must succeed.

But in the White Eagle, it scared and almost offended me that my memory had made itself heard. Fear rose from the green armchair and from all the unrepeatable atmosphere of the countryside and grandmother's house. So had it already started, was it full about-face already, towards what used to be? Was the siege of memories already in progress? No, not yet. Not yet. I was pushing aside the former Poland which had created a new layer of intelligentsia, a pink one, as if the red and white colours of our national flag had run. It had fallen on me to live in this washed-out, progressive-cum-traditional-cum-evolutionary colour, unable to imagine that we would not have time, or that history would break us on its wheel. In London, when it was all over, certain questions would so frequently return - if I had known that we had only twenty years of independence, who would I have become? What would I have believed in?

---

* *Wiadomosci Literackie*: eminent literary , cultural and intellectual periodical published in Warsaw between 1924-39. During World War Two the periodical was published in Paris for a brief period and was then transferred to London, where it appeared regularly until 1981 under the name *Wiadomosci*. Antoni Slonimski (1895-1976), Polish poet and columnist, author of a collection of articles entitled 'The Heretic in the Pulpit', was a regular contributor to both *Wiadomosci Literackie* and *Wiadomosci*, as were many very distinguished Polish writers.

Would I have shared the radicalism of the extremist socialists, or else Great-uncle's political catastrophism and melancholia?

These questions persecuted me constantly, all the more because I was in a crisis of not believing in the power of literature and the written word in general. This is one of the worst crises that can happen to a person, removing their past, present and future.

I was wrong. Removing the past was precisely what it did not do, but it was so irritating. I could not fail to remember how my great-aunt, on the day the war broke out, was secretly triumphant. Already very old, she was experiencing the last joys from her reviving memories: the cold of 1939 reminded her of Zeromski's novel *The Faithful River*, about the January Rising in 1863. The subject returned as her favourite, well nursed and richer each time. Aunt, as she was called instead of 'Auntie' for no known reason, acquired a remarkable liveliness. A spring stirred in her; all through the war she drove the house in her own war. War was Aunt's natural ally. The children still remembered the one in '14; we, the grandchildren, had no idea about anything that long ago. And history does not like that. Grandchildren should also get a lick of cold, hunger and exhaustion, but only enough for them to find a common language with the past, with their elders, with tradition. 'Apples should not fall too far from the apple tree.'

We loathed this tragic Polish apple tree but fell, despite ourselves, right next to it; its shadow entwined with branches had caught up with us.

Well then, we should remove the conceit of youth from our hearts and recognise the undoubted truth, that Aunt possessed the technique of war, as we called it.

It started with the question of appropriate dress. Whatever was to happen and whatever our feelings were to be, we had to think about practical and suitable clothes, the sort that would give ease of movement though warm and comfortable. All our things seemed unequal to the task, in other words, to the historic moment.

We had the material, and the dressmaker, Miss Antonina, was always at hand. The question was, which style? Both my sister and I chose a wide skirt of thick wool, a thick pullover and a jacket with a belt. The belt seemed an important detail, classic, arch-Polish and out of a Grottger painting, something patriotic that we could not manage without. But the discussion was quickly extinguished in the face of Aunt's shrugged shoulders and her ironic smile. "A wide skirt was a good thing when they were worn long to the ankles," she declared curtly, "but in a wide short one you'll look like cones. Especially as you'll probably want to have low-heeled shoes, sports shoes, as you call them. A short skirt must be narrow. Have a deep pleat made at the back, and it'll be just as comfortable for walking in. And a plain classic suit. In a well-cut suit you can face the firing squad more easily than in a badly cut one. This Miss Antonina can make the skirt, but the jacket must be sewn by the tailor. I'll pay the tailor."

We thanked her reticently but very gravely.

Of course, when she talked about the tailor, it was understood that she meant Mr di Vecco. Never mind that his workshop was in Lyczaków and not in the city centre as in Aunt's time; he did not stop being a master of his craft because of that. In addition he had inherited the gift of good taste and a liking for excellent detail from his father and grandfather, both of whom were master builders of Italian descent, settled in Lwów for ages.

Aunt really was right. Jackets like this made us feel we had a suit of armour against the bombs flying from the sky. And as early as September, between serving in the canteen for refugees and the Piarist hospital, I would run to the master in stolen moments for fittings. Excellent jackets were being made there, perhaps the last ones in Lwów. When I was collecting them, still knowing nothing of what was going to happen in an hour's time, it gave me pleasure to place the new and beautiful banknotes on the plush cover of the table in the workshop. Face after face of Emilia Plater, partisan of the 1830 November Rising, with her windswept hair rising above her head like a banner - there were many of them, these identical Emilias, all with wide open, huge, romantic eyes.

Of course I could hardly go wearing a costume like that to the factory where I started working later, but which Aunt pretended that she could not see. She was pleased with the supplies of tobacco I was guaranteed by Ginsberg, my colleague in the factory, the weaver from Lódz, in exchange for clothes, worn but still good. He did not believe that anybody local who had lived with their family in this city for ages could not possess stocks of everything. He did not believe it because hardly anybody would. But he did believe Aunt when she told him: "Because, you know, Mr Ginsberg, it wasn't decent to lay in supplies. Only wealthy people could do it, so what were the poor to do? But there are thirteen refugees in our house, you understand, thirteen! Any supplies we may have had could have been used up, couldn't they? It's now December. So that's it."

Handing him the clothes, she added emphatically, although without irritation: "Don't look at me like an idiot. You don't understand that it takes all sorts, because you, Mr Ginsberg, are Communist. What on earth can you understand? It makes me want to laugh and cry when I talk to you. But let me tell you that I know your city. When I was young, I used to go there from time to time." It was probably untrue, at least no one in the family had ever heard about it. It was an actor's speech for the occasion. Aunt in Lódz?

11

In London I heard something quite unexpected one day, extremely strange, like a miracle.

It took place in an apartment in South Kensington where the Polish landlady received paying guests for lunch. I had been eating there for a few days because it was near and inexpensive. On that memorable Tuesday when I arrived at one o'clock as usual, I found a middle-aged man on his own finishing his lunch in the adjoining sitting room. Obviously he enjoyed the land-lady's special favours, for there was a table laid in there solely for him. The stranger was drinking his after-lunch tea, all the while perusing some document, holding it so that it did not roll up. He was marking or noting something or other and kept consulting a green note-book.

Someone slightly younger entered the room and clapped him on the shoulder with a cheerful gesture. "Well, how're things, what's new?" At this the first man, not moving from his place, tapped the paper gravely and thoughtfully with his finger. "Everything's here," he replied slowly, "look, see for yourself, the rest of the details will come later. The most important thing is that they let themselves be persuaded. Why the devil should we be buffeted without a place of our own? The money's still available, a lot of money, what's the point of waiting? The Polish government could do nothing better than buy the island. A good size, the climate more or less like here, and quite near. Everything needs doing from scratch there, but that's all for the best. Your own country's your own, after all."

I pricked up my ears. Really staggering news. The Polish government had bought an island? And I hadn't read anything about it so far in the émigré journals or papers? It can't be any state secret after all; perhaps I had misheard something. My table was just next to the door of the neighbouring room, their table right behind the door which was wide open. I took a closer look at the two men. The first stranger was inhaling cigarette smoke and again writing something on the edge of the paper which, as I was able to glimpse, was a map.

I could not see the face of the seated man very clearly, only his profile: he was neatly dressed, but did not attract special attention in any way. He frequently drew his fingers through his thick combed-back hair, and he moved his cup to the edge of the table so it would not get in his way, pushed away the salt cellar, a bud vase and flower, and straightened the document out better. He drew lines on it with his finger pointing in various directions. His calm, factual voice was reaching me less clearly now. I think that he was mentioning some figures and showing his companion various places on the map. Yet his neighbour, sitting opposite him, was not looking at the paper, but at his face. He was not saying anything; he only asked if he wanted something to drink. "Have you got cigarettes?" He must have been a good friend because at a certain moment he stretched his arm out across the table and touched the other man's elbow with a delicate, jerky movement.

The first man opened his notebook to another place and handed it to his companion pointing to a passage to read. His companion looked for a while, or pretended he was looking, and said warmly: "You already showed me that yesterday, don't you remember?" and started talking for a long time in a whisper and with an animation which he clearly wanted to impart to the other man. Then he got up quickly. The seated man let himself be persuaded, rolled up his paper very carefully, put on his coat, and they went out.

Almost at the same time the landlady stood in the door and gave me a sign that my usual table nearer the window was free. I started talking to her about this stranger who said such peculiar things. The landlady, a rather straightforward and very sensible woman, was laconic. "Him?" she said and nodded her head, "Yes, he's an unfortunate man. There are all sorts of misfortunes following people about after this war. One person loses a hand, another a leg, and someone else his head because it's become all mixed up although he lives and looks like other folk."

I learnt that this good friend of his was looking after him and even wanted to take him along to Scotland, where he was setting himself up. She did not mention the first or the second man's names and I did not ask her, respecting her discretion. Besides, there was no need for me to know any further details.

I had caught sight suddenly of this further rock bottom. So it does exist. So my conviction that my rubbish heap of history was the last word in baseness was mistaken. It was possible that straying into a snare, one could become insane. And insane in such a particular way which sank strangely into my soul. My rubbish heap suddenly seemed quite simply safe, and I felt ashamed. It was only a chimeric creation; I might manage to crawl out of its trap.

That stranger seemed not to experience any unpleasant associations or obsessions; he had a calm self-confidence and something like a restrained satisfaction in what he said. He believed in the island. Uninhabited of course, it was said they still existed. We will set ourselves up on this island, "We'll start everything from scratch."

A vision appeared to him. Because of this vision he aroused sympathy and obvious pity in people. He had to be looked after, no one could treat him seriously, he was beyond the pale of normal people. Yet there was something splendid in him. People nodded their heads over him, tapped their foreheads perhaps, but he alone had arrived at the ultimate consequences, had wrenched himself beyond the borders of our situation. He saved himself through Utopia. An eternal prototype made itself felt in him, the myth of Renewal. To start everything from scratch. To build a new state, not depend on anyone. Maybe he had even found a specific island for us to settle on and was drawing up plans and technical documentation, or maybe it was only an island in his imagination.

I will never know, but to this day I remember the emotion I experienced then as if that stranger had remained faithful to the oldest and most important commandments. "Start everything from scratch." In this could be heard a turn of my accursed national wheel and the repetitive fate of exiles, but something more as well, the huge impetus of the human condition. The stranger could already sense this eternal motion raising us up in order to start everything differently.

Had he become like this after a violent shock, perhaps after an accident caused by the war, or had our mutual fate turned into redemptive absurdity in him? What happens then with people, how does it happen? My atavistic respect for utopia attempted to raise something, balance something. For our sake, for people in Poland and beyond it, condemned one and the other to endure all turns inside ourselves and outside, all temperatures and pressures. New Poland was arising from post-war chaos like a true mysterious isle, a land of dread.

We lose when we are unable to change quality into quantity. Or were we made of insufficiently good material? Even if we'd had enough time, would we have known how to repair the Republic, introduce changes upon which everything could have depended? Everything? Meaning what?

Different people had seen this 'repair' in different ways. Seeking comfort in time lost and stolen from us by the war was an empty and terrible occupation. In exile the whole twenty years of Independent Poland suddenly exploded with the flame of a vehement battle over what it was really like. What was it like? What would it be like...?

I was scared of the press. I did not know how to find the ordinary landscape and history of my country. What country had I really lived in? Which was true, some people's accusations or other people's defence? The opinions of some or the arguments of others? What pedigree of arguments? How to examine the proof? From what position to see most clearly? Everything suddenly revealed previously unknown snares and precipitous drops, dark, ever-changing, full of ambushes.

Ambushes. Strange, for me the word summons up the most paradoxical associations. The dim and deep interior of the chapel of Saint Kazimierz in Wilno Cathedral. The huge chandelier and the wan, mean light of the candles. Beneath it a small group of kneeling figures, barely visible in the huge and empty expanse of the church. They were all young people and immersed in great concentration in this darkness and silence from which one voice suddenly echoed, light and distinct: "Let us pray for those who have greatest need of it at this time." The gathered students took up the prayer in an undertone, "Our Father," barely audible a few steps away.

Ambushes. Next door to me lived an Englishman. A young man who lectured in one of the London colleges and wore the same suit winter or summer, ignoring all changes in the weather with truly British stoicism. He was working on something at home; the tapping of his typewriter reached my room quite late at night, soothing, beneficent. Angus Dean was a quiet and polite neighbour, obliging even. One day he suggested that he would leave me a glass of milk. Seeing as he did not need all of his daily portion, it would do him no harm.

He could not have aimed worse. With this glass of milk I measured the situation which had befallen me and all of us. Milk. A liquid for babies, a basic requirement which brings no honour or pleasure to anyone. In addition my good neighbour was offering this fluid as an act of philanthropy, having probably noticed that I never ordered milk. Perhaps he thought that I could not afford it. I explained to him that I always drank tea without milk, that it was generally drunk like that in Poland, and that personally I could not stand milk in any form. As I told him this, I remembered seeing, by chance, a place for Poles, perhaps located in Eaton Place, near the seat of the Polish government-in-exile, where milk, and milk alone, was given to our people. Many similar rescue stations were appearing at that time, devised and run by Polish or English authorities of some sort, or the two jointly. We had to admit that we had fallen to the level of the most basic requirement of all. This milk suitably expressed the mystery of the bus stop along history's route where we had been set down.

Now I could observe this bus stop objectively, through someone else's eyes. It became my neighbour's habit to wait for me until I returned home in the evening from Lyons in Gloucester Road, and we would sit down on one of the stairs in the corridor and talk. The stairs were comfortable, covered in red carpet; no one used them just there, and both of us believed in an *esprit d'escalier*.

Angus was an educated and catholic individual, the latter a virtue which brings to mind a cudgel or a halberd that bludgeons and impales. Our conversations concerned the state of the world which, he said, was improving. It was seriously beginning to do so only now; national states had formerly obstructed this change. Hiroshima and Nagasaki had marked off a stage in the history of mankind. One should know how to look at the new world which was just starting to form from a supranational perspective, like it or not, because that was the only correct point of view. So in this perspective Poland was the most important experimental shooting range for the new social science - the word 'politics' should stop existing altogether. Grafted onto new ground which had been ploughed over by the war, Poland would bear fruit successfully. A lot of time was needed, of course; the first collision with a new current was always difficult.

I realised that for my neighbour everything was happening in a correct, foreseen and appropriate course of history. Poland was an experimental testing ground and should be observed with the greatest attention for the benefit of other nations and the whole world. A demonstration in the anatomy of system. Documentation, laboratory tests. The beginning of the new era, the new science or knowledge. Important things.

And I realised that for my neighbour, pre-war Poland was divided into two zones - dictators, and nationalists wanting to take their places, again as dictators. He did not call them fascists, probably out of politeness towards me. Besides, he spoke calmly and slowly, in the slightly hesitant tone of a well brought up Englishman and was inclined to repeat and clarify every expression so as not to allow his opinion to be deformed and become ambiguous. It was an infectious way of speaking and his patience was likewise infectious. It seemed to impart itself to me unnoticed, and with heroic composure I explained something to him which was important to me: that there had been yet another Poland, neither the governing one nor the nationalist one either, that socialists and a legal parliamentary opposition had existed, that agricultural reform was already a *fait*, not *accompli* but *commencé*, and that even household servants had possessed an institution called the National Health Service which was ahead of other countries in its concern to care for working people in case of sickness.

To this day I do not know how the National Health Service came into my mouth; it had not received due recognition in Poland, after all. The servants did not believe in it, employers were unfavourably disposed towards it, and a peculiar snobbery linked the lady with her servant in their critical attitude to this social achievement. I saw in my memory a small man visiting my grandmother's kitchen twice a year, and when he asked questions and wrote down details concerning the servants, they always said to him with a slightly ironic smile: "Eh? It's not worth it because if need be, they'll pay the doctor for me." The man licked his indelible pencil and instructed them that "the law has taken the people's part, and it's a great pity that they still don't want to understand."

That little man whose name I never knew now pierced the jungle of time and events to my thrilled astonishment. He assisted me. So I waded further, explaining to my Englishman about the existence of a Poland different from his simplified vision. All the intellectuals and humanists, who were not yet called progressives, but were exactly that, arose in order to testify to my words. Various men and women from the liberal professions and the law who believed in social reconstruction in their own country reappeared. I quoted my own world, the one which had not had time to weigh with the right scales and change anything, although it was the one meant to change everything. That world had deceived itself, as I had known for a long time, but I did not tell Angus this.

Great and grave were the sins of the Republic, but we had counted on the so-called long run. At our table it had been required that politics should be 'person-oriented', without closer definition, as if it were a term clear in itself and comprehensible to all. So the national democrats' line was not person-oriented, neither was the Sanacja movement,* as favouring its own too much, and all that really remained were the trenches of socialism in the Christian spirit or only the laity, and in particular the liberal democrats, that is, an unassociated élite that lived more in the rights of its élitism than in organised action. As if the very existence of people who were educated and incapable of any fanaticism, like the biblical ten just men, could impart the correct tone to the country and ensure a better future for it. There were not enough of them; they were badly organised. They probably regarded themselves as the salt of the earth, Attic of course. Maybe there was a certain rightness in this, but being in the right has never led to anything.

The truth looked brutal, and I remembered always the words of my great-uncle during a conversation with my father, words breathing venomous scepticism: "Poland can only stand by practising the politics of the muzzle - either white or red, no third way." And the words of my father: "You can't stand up for long being muzzled; you always end up lying down." "Yes, and we're almost lying down already," concluded Great-uncle and tapped his cigarette rolling machine against the lid of his cigarette case as if cutting off the question once and for all. He was already very old, so we acknowledged his pessimism as the bitterness of old age.

Yet it was hard to deny that we with our views were a minority and that in Poland 'the political horizon', as it was called, was darkening. Great-uncle did not even want to hear about liberals, 'soloists' he called them. He did not prophesy the socialists a good future either, and to

---

*Sanacja: Popular name, which may be translated as 'Return to Health', given to Pilsudski's government after the May Coup in 1926 until the collapse of the Republic in 1939.

the argument that they were a numerous and serious organisation he would reply: "Pilsudski is serious as well, but what has he permitted to take place?" Maybe personal grudges lay concealed behind these words. We comforted ourselves by thinking this was probably the case. Great-uncle was a doctor and a colonel; his only son was an officer too. So maybe we should ignore what he said. In any case we did not understand all the complaints of older people.

Apart from the 'soloists' another category of 'sleep-walkers' existed for Great-uncle, which word from his political dictionary described everything that other people branded with vehement fury as 'Jew-Communism'. Why he considered them sleepwalkers remains a mystery to me; reality contradicted him in the near future, as he lived to see. Yet for us, the rising generation of his closest family, there was no redemption. He pitied us, which irritated and offended us. Aunt and Great-uncle's traditional Easter visits poisoned the holiday for us. In addition we were angered by the fact that despite ourselves, our eyes were drawn to his face and could tear themselves away only with difficulty - he was exceptionally and uncommonly handsome, and by a strange whim time had respected and seemed to have immortalised that face.

I did not mention a word of my great-uncle's catastrophism to my English neighbour.

In the late autumn of 1945 the first trade mission of the Polish People's Republic arrived in London. I found out about it in a letter from my family in Krakow, who asked me to see a Mrs M. whom I did not know. I surmised that I was to send my family something by this means. Strange, it was only the name trade mission that impressed on me so deeply the thought that history had been dissected into past and present, bestowing three-dimensionality on the new authorities of Poland. No articles or communiqués had possessed this plasticity until now. After all, the new government's embassy already existed in London, so there was no cause for special surprise. Foreign trade is a serious matter: it is a real confirmation of the state of affairs; the to-be-or-not-to-be of every country depends on trade. It would be a Poland dragging itself from the ruins towards life, and I immediately wished this mission the greatest success, the best contracts and conditions. Trade now signified the living body of Poland, fatally emaciated, and needing to be rescued as quickly as possible. From hunger, cold and death.

12

I was to meet the representative from the trade mission in a small tearoom. I arrived punctually and waited a good quarter of an hour before a middle-aged woman came up to me and addressed me by name. She introduced herself and apologised for not being the Mrs M. I was waiting for. She immediately explained that she had come in her place, and she added in a lightly confidential tone: "You'll understand, of course." Her words imparted a foul air of conspiracy and anonymity. I instantly felt myself returned to the furtive atmosphere of the Khrushchev factory in Lwów.*

The woman was dressed in the English style, a pullover with a string of pearls and a costume adorned with a fur clip in the lapel. She spoke with a pleasant, quiet voice. She had attractive, intelligent eyes, and she immediately

*Nikita Khrushchev was primarily concerned with Ukrainian affairs from 1938-47, and Lwów was annexed into the Ukrainian SSR in 1940.

pulled a packet addressed in my mother's writing out of her bag and handed it to me. She explained that she had lived in London since the war and that Mrs M. was her close friend from before the war. "We spent the last holiday together in Jastarnia," she added somewhat privately, as utter exaltation burst over me. Republic-on-Sea.

She continued in a calm and almost colourless tone, although she was talking about what was most important for her: "I'll probably return to Poland. I've no close friends and relatives here, and I'm not anyone important or particularly talented. I can be of more use there than here."

I wanted to reply that I was not anyone important either, but the very posing of the matter stopped my mouth. It seemed the edge of a precipice. In it lived the demon of weights and measures, another demon I did not know until now. Weights and measures. How can people possibly foresee where they will be more useful? You can remain faithful to your opinions and ideals and be fit for nothing, advance or improve nothing. Remaining faithful was barely zero on the scale, the mere start. Usefulness is a game of hazardous forces and nothing is more deceptive than most people's conviction of how useful they are. But a hazard which can decide about everything. So my very own grandfather, when he returned to Poland from exile after the January Rising in 1863, was said to pronounce: "Hazard can exist only in your own country, in exile it hasn't the right." A strange sentence, heard from Grandmother so many times and never understood, not even arousing interest.

"Every day I throw a half-crown on the pillow," I heard the voice of the woman sitting opposite, "I told myself that if it falls face down for nine consecutive days, then I won't hesitate any longer and I'll leave."

"Does it fall face down?"

"So far, every time," she replied and smiled at this game of hers. As if she did not sense that she had said something uncanny. The hateful wheel and some smaller wheels turned in me again, and I saw the torture of her indecision.

Undoubtedly my grandfather would have declared that this stranger friend of mine was not in exile any longer since she was seeking refuge in the doings of chance. But I was aware that still another wheel existed, a further wheel downwards, and I was meeting it now, perhaps no less tantalising than a rubbish dump of history or than landing on an imaginary island in order to found a new homeland. I did not reply.

There was a lull in our conversation, and evidently it was interpreted as my disapproval of her returning to Poland because suddenly my companion started to talk volubly and more quickly, to explain herself; she probably thought I was engaged in some political activity or group. She appeared to endow me with rank, virtues and roles that were totally untrue. I started to try them on. *Etre c'est paraître*. They did not suit me. Nothing suited me at that time. But perhaps in cases like this one should create appearances, should not admit to one's own friability, to a basically pointless state of ceaseless anger, although only that seemed a support and aid. *Etre c'est paraître*.

So I sat quietly like a concealed wrongdoer, masking my own impotence, indefensibility and nonentity. From opposite me I heard: "We've got to have a lot of patience. It's Poland's cornerstone now, and we've got to arm ourselves with it for a long time. Except it's quite hard for people to find comfort in it."

A revelation. An almost new word had been uttered, pushed so deeply aside that it had even been forgotten and dropped from private use. Patience. A word for old people - losers, devout, meek, resigned, enslaved - a loathsome word. Hard to comfort people with, needless to say. But all of a sudden it seemed a secret, enumerated cipher. There was no way of evading it; it was combat kit, heavy to drag, overwhelming, simply terrible - yet indispensable. The discovery that patience can be the eye of the needle which has to be squeezed through was stunning. From within I heard an unexpected "aha"; today it seems like a comic reaction, but then, in the tearoom, I sensed it as my own summons.

The new rulers of Poland also intended to rely on it. Everything was for future development, in Poland and here on the rubbish dump. Which the new government in Poland feared since it had banned the members of its mission from meeting their fellow Poles here in the most private matters. Mrs M., replaced by someone else at the meeting with me, fell victim to that prohibition. She was sent back to Poland as soon as it came out that she had a husband who had been in General Anders' army,* was currently in England, and had decided to return to Poland after seeing his wife. This incredible instruction was the naked truth, but at that time we were still not used to those practices. So it came to my mind that for them, our countrymen in Poland, we had become lepers.

Yet another small wheel turned in me, this time a more gracious wheel, the first to touch my paralysed sense of humour. The fact that in somebody's eyes I could be considered a dangerous person, that someone could be afraid of me. Perhaps consider me unworthy. Even more ridiculous, the fact that I was 'stigmatised by my class' and incapable because of it of accepting the 'new reality', as it was called. More and more ridiculous! What an unexpected gift this tide of humour was. The landscape

---

*Anders' army: after the Nazis attacked the Soviet Union in June 1941, a Polish army was formed in the Soviet Union under the leadership of General Wladyslaw Anders. Its members were Polish citizens who had been deported to the Soviet Union following the Soviet invasion of Poland in September 1939.

was changing, the rubbish dump had become a smooth hill, and on it were people standing calmly, expectant and self-confident, exactly like the pictures of the just men in books for the very young. A tonic-like naivety, invigorating. The weight of the combat kit decreased, then disappeared. For quite a while it seemed that nothing was rubbing me, that Justice was going to be done with the assistance of patience and that this unattractive virtue must be the shared possession of Poles on this side and that, as also a virtue of our ancestors. But since we did not know how to be better than they were, since we had a similar fate...

Could a better word be found than patience, less catechismal - maybe, for example, moratorium. It sounded like the term of a loan to be repaid later, and accorded with the obvious fact that we were, as exiles, a part of the nation lent out and destined to defend its interests. The word moratorium smelt of deadly gravity, which was also correct. In the performance of our duties we would die far from our native land, and in the majority of cases we would never see the fruits of our endeavours.

It does happen. There is no need to barter with fate about it or take pity on it. I was overcome by a feeling of greater and greater ridicule, above all at my own person so very engaged in patriotic deliberations of a general nature. My moratorium I imagined as a period of twenty years, which at the time seemed to me longer than a century. After twenty years, I told myself, we will see whether we are 'with a shield or on a shield', as my professor of Latin liked to say. If the woman from our meeting is still alive, I think about her with gratitude. She did me a good turn unawares by talking about patience as if it were natural and necessary, and in that way she opened a valve vital for me to live.

I gave her a silk scarf from Harrods. It had been

intended for Mrs M. from the trade mission and depicted
- the irony of it - Magellan's voyages, and a box of Black
Magic. When I left the tearoom with the packet of letters
and photographs from my family home, I again tramped
over a huge expanse of London to the limits of my
endurance, got lost in a jungle of streets, and by chance
came across the No.30 bus which I knew served my area,
and got off near Battersea Park. I had to re-examine the
situation.

Above all patience meant reconciling myself to the
written word, believing it again, to some extent restoring
the conviction that beyond it there is no redemption. Yes,
the language of figures was already reigning over the
world, a true talmud of economics and cybernetics, but
not everything could yet be expressed in this language.
Intermediate territory obedient to a form inaccessible to
machines did still exist, and I had tried to talk to this new
friend of mine in this language. But who was she really?
Everything she said could have been accidental or
imagined *ad hoc*; it was really all about establishing
contact with me. The real reason could have lain
elsewhere, and for the first time it occurred to me that
for various reasons I could become the object of possible
propositions.

But I discarded that suspicion. My most important
anxiety was fear for the language. For it not to start
drying up after a few or a dozen years, and crumble or
wither. It might become simplified to helping verbs. My
God, what a providential expression, helping, when each
one will now have to be treated both as a meal and as
sustenance. If only it did not petrify into the Polish jargon
I knew so well from Switzerland.

That I was afraid of. A long and crowded stretch of the
Thames can be seen from Battersea Bridge. In the
approaching dusk, boats lay on the black river. Various
were their shapes, colours and purposes. Some of them

must have been cargo ships and might sail to Szczecin or Gdansk as a result of the trade mission. On the side of one small boat close to the shore I could see part of a wing painted white and part of its name, but only the last letters, 'ngs', were visible. The boat must have been called 'Wings', a name unsuitable for a sea creature, very inappropriate, but for me a connection, a sudden reminder, and the words from Kochanowski's verse drama *The Dismissal of the Greek Envoys* whispered in my memory:

> O white-winged voyager
> Pupil of lofty Ida
> Boat crafted of beech!

But this time the new picture did not anger me in the same way as previous ones had done. Quite the reverse, something abruptly stopped in me, became silent. I understood that I was struggling over a feverish, baroque and hallucinatory landscape – the face of Janus, Magellan's voyages, the beech boat – grasping all connections, comparisons, imaginations, chaotic and accidental, flimsy, random, without rhyme or reason, with a manic tenacity, in order to fashion something, build my own private boat and not let myself be drowned. The beech boat I remembered most deeply, for on Battersea Bridge I was starting to measure patience, to begin preliminary bargaining with it.

13

The end of December was drawing near, and I was more scared each day. Then unexpectedly one afternoon my cousin Kostek arrived. I hadn't seen him since the end of the war; I knew only that he was living in Scotland and that he had decided to return to Poland. We had talked only once over the phone since my arrival in England, and we greeted each other warmly.

"I've come now specially to see you. I couldn't very well come before, although I know I should have. It'd take too long to explain."

"Don't explain, don't apologise. Who's got time these days for things like that?"

"Exactly. Except that for me, and for you too, certain things haven't stopped being important all the same. I mean this year's Christmas. I don't know what your plans are, but I do know that whatever one does, the first Christmas abroad - if you really are abiding by your decision - is very hard."

"I don't deny it. Thank you for thinking of it. You really don't know how very grateful I am."

Kostek was in civilian clothes, very slim, quite pale, and he did not try to crack jokes as he used to, nor to put a brave face on things. He was right.

"This Christmas is going be very hard for me too. In a different way than for you, but all the same it won't be easy. I almost regret that the war's over, but it's out of the question even to think like that. Not as if I've become attached to England, although naturally all of us airmen are, even when we're grousing about this country. What we did here can't be forgotten. Besides, it's a country which has got many good points, without a doubt. But to spend all your life abroad - well, let's not talk about it, these are exactly the sorts of things that can't be talked about, I realise that. And you do too. But I do know that whatever happens, I'm the one with the prospect of every Christmas in my own country in front of me, and you're not, so I'm the winner. But this year's Christmas won't be merry for me, you can probably guess why."

"Yes. You're parting from someone, aren't you? Your

last Christmas."

Kostek suddenly thrust both hands into his pockets as if he could pull out a weapon. But situations like his leave nothing to defend oneself with. I was sorry for him.

"At first," he said after a while, "there was even talk of marriage. That is, not me, I give you my word of honour, so you can believe me. Not me but her. She talked about it, she didn't see anything impossible in it, and you know, English girls are different from Polish ones, they're able to feel at home anywhere, and anyway what's simpler than travelling? From time to time to see her parents and family. Because she has still got parents."

"Yes, I know, I've heard that Polish airmen had the chance to make very good matches."

"Yes and no. Many of us could have married much better. I can see that you're not aware that unfortunately many colleagues married very much beneath themselves. Both from their own and from the social point of view. And it did a lot of harm to all of us Poles. The English paid a lot of attention to who married who, and even to who your girlfriend was. We had the highest standard of flights, but on the ground... Sometimes it was simply difficult to understand people. And the fact that they chose 'mediocre' partners who couldn't stand a chance with the native English, and not even with some mere British, that settled the question."

It was not news to me, I already knew that 'our boys were falling victim' to the least suitable type of women, but I did not take up the subject. Besides, I really did not attach so much importance to these various personal dramas which in the face of the political disaster seemed to me to be of secondary importance. But I was wrong. Kostek seemed to sense it.

"Some situations can't be imagined. They're so complicated, sometimes so incredible, that you don't know if it's a tragedy or a grotesque."

"Yours, I think, isn't a grotesque."

"No, it isn't. That's the whole problem. So, as I told you, Betty was thinking completely seriously about getting married."

"And you?"

"Me? Well, yes. Me too, although naturally I foresaw all sorts of problems in our life in Poland where everything will have to be rebuilt. But English girls are passionately fond of the prospect of problems. Something fascinates them in overcoming difficulties. Something like the missionary or colonial spirit, I don't know, a kind of Samaritan attitude, especially as everyone knows what Warsaw looks like after the Uprising.* All that stimulated her rather than put her off. It was only this political split that changed a lot of things. Not as if she told me directly. Her father told me. I had a long and serious conversation with him; in fact it was me who'd asked if I could speak to him. I want you to know. They haven't deserted me. At precisely the time when England was recognising the new government of Poland, some English people felt terrible because of it."

"But they'll come to terms with it. They've already got used..."

"I'm well aware that people can say that and think like that; it really does look that way. What's happened has unfortunately happened, and neither you nor me nor Betty and her family will change it."

"Unfortunately."

"Unfortunately. But precisely in this situation, since I've decided to return to Poland, then it has an additional aspect, but I don't think anyone will understand if he's not in the same boat himself. Namely, that it might look

---

*The Warsaw Uprising started on August 1, 1944, when the victorious Red Army was approaching the city and the German army was retreating. The Polish insurgents fought for 63 days, and Warsaw was almost completely destroyed.

like a pretext for breaking off on my part. Under the pretence of patriotism as it were, or national feelings, or whatever you care to call it. And it's not a pleasant part to play."

"Yes, I can imagine it."

"What?" Kostek bridled.

"That it can be very unpleasant."

He was pacing the room. His raised eyebrows changed the expression on his face. He was quite similar to his former self, but at the same time something was starting to change his face, perhaps the vertical wrinkle on his forehead, but also a habit of quickly opening his eyes which he did not have before the war. Poor Kostek.

"These aren't our last moments," he said sitting down. "I want to go back to Poland together with Adas and as you know he's with Anders' army. It might take until the spring. But this is definitely the last Christmas. Betty is insisting that we spend it together, although I'd prefer to live in London from now until we leave. It's better to cut everything off at a stroke."

"But what's this Betty afraid of? Communism? Shortages? Of not belonging?"

"It's me who's scared of that, for her sake. I've no idea what I'll be doing and how everything will turn out for me. With a foreign wife there might be all sorts of unforeseen problems. Of course her family might want to help us, but that's not to my liking since I'm not staying here. No, it's not possible. After all even I don't know..."

Exactly. That was the key to the situation. He was returning to a country which no longer seemed familiar to him. It was different. It was difficult to explain this to an outsider; perhaps Kostek was not very good at it. But I understood him very well.

"I've brought you some spruce branches. They're in front of the door in the corridor. I thought perhaps you'd prefer them to a whole Christmas tree. Yes? You see, I guessed. See how subtle I've become because of the war; I know how to feel my way into what other people are feeling. And also, if you don't have to do it, I advise you not to go into town. London's raving of course. They always celebrate Christmas in a big way here, and this year in particular, the first Christmas after the war. So you can imagine. I find it unreal to look at all this, the lights, the lamps, the garlands, the Father Christmases. What's more, we come. from Malopolska; this Father Christmas annoys us. Remember back at home it was Saint Nicholas on the fifth of December or the sixth at dawn, presents under your pillow - they of course have no idea about all that. Well, never mind. It's enough that all this fun is unbearable for us, and these crowds. If you can, don't go out, don't look at all this. It's not a sight for us."

I did not reply. He was right.

"By the way, where are you going for Christmas Eve? If it weren't for this position I'm in, so extraordinary, I'd invite you to me, to us."

"Marian Koscialkowski has invited me, but I won't go there. Too far and you know, kind of terrible. The Solowijes have also invited me for Christmas Eve. I'll go there."

"So she managed to leave at last. That's good. Besides," Kostek laughed, "they're letting older ladies out of Poland now, as you know. They're doing it on purpose. To annoy the various Polish generals or colonels for whom their wives' return really isn't something they've been longing for. And the wives revel in telling awful stories, completely as if we didn't know what the war was like here, hadn't fought personally, but had only sat in the corner by the fireplace and sipped tea or whisky. You know, a few days ago I was invited together with a friend to our colonel, whose wife had just come here. In fact he really did try hard to get her over here although he had a first-rate English woman. Well, this wife of his will simply ruin him utterly. She was talking about such awful things all the time; really it's better not to talk about them. A complete lack of tact, or even of decency. We, my friend and I that is, felt terribly embarrassed. We felt sorry for the old man, who was ashamed of his wife. The colonel's a very decent fellow, an excellent commander. And now, I've heard say, he wants to hire a garage and start working there so as not to be at home. Brrr."

"He should make sure she's financially secure and leave her."

"It's easy to say."

So that was it. Everything is returning to how it used to be. The war has finished, and so old habits and so-called principles regain the upper hand. Really, what's the point of wars, what's the point of evolution, what's the point of any axioms or experiences, since everything has always got to be 'like it was before'. There are also wives who are waiting for their husbands, to learn who they have become and who they themselves have become after such a war, and they have no intention or desire to poison their lives. Some men also waited with dignity and decency to join their wives, even idealising them in their minds. But until now I had spent too little time thinking about the individual private dramas being played out among people. Maybe out of the conviction that life is always richer than the imagination and catches us unawares so much, as if we did not believe in the rules of the game but in the absurd. How to manage life for it not to seem absurd? Because it is more comfortable, more decent that it should not. I was thinking in the old way as well, only to rest, to shake off the first darkening, to feel tradition under my feet and catch my balance.

"So I'll be with the Solowijes for Christmas Eve. I'm really extremely grateful for these branches and for the fact that you thought about such a change for me. I don't think I'll have to go to town; I can get everything right next door. There are stars, candles and garlands in that shop as well."

All the same I had to pass through town. I took a taxi in order to have the least contact with it. You can shut your eyes in a taxi and traverse the necessary distance blindly, not brushing against the external world with a glance. Like all London taxis, it could deprive you of your gravity somewhat and also admonish you that it is not the form that matters, but the destination.

When I arrived at my destination, I paid with nervous zeal and gave too high a tip, then almost ran the few steps to the front door. I closed it behind me with the feeling that I was saving myself from a flood on a scrap of land. I leaned against the wall for a moment and rested just as if I had overcome an extraordinary obstacle which required a huge effort. Nothing, just lean like this and be lulled, rest, recover my breath, reel the present moment onto something invisible, hide it in my bag, slam it inside and wait again.

There was no one, fortunately, on the staircase just then nor leaving the elevator. I finally entered it and pressed the button.

The Solowijes lived in a small apartment in the well-known Chelsea Cloisters. Not too high up, which I regretted. I would most willingly have risen into infinity in this elevator, not leaving it at all. A slight tugging beneath the floor pulled the ground from under my feet, quietly and treacherously.

The Solowij apartment, arranged like all flats of this sort, bore the hallmark of its tenants' personalities. It was homely and pleasant here. Yet it was already another world, a detached one, equally distant as unreal.

Maria and Wlodzimierz Solowij loved each other with a long-standing love, maybe even first love, and they had been happy together for many years. The magnet of their successful union in the turmoils of our wartime events acted on me even more strongly. It contained the genuine authority of something exceptional. Love has the power to assuage absurdities, invest them with defined meaning and importance, and check deliberations about ultimate matters.

"I think that you couldn't have made a better choice," I was saying to them, "it's probably most pleasant here. I like Chelsea. You couldn't have chosen a Christmas Eve guest better either."

"I know," said Wlodzimierz and his wife at the same time, so all three of us laughed.

I sat down into rather than on the armchair, and the wisest thing to do was to admit to what had happened to me just before I arrived.

"I came by taxi although it's so near from South Kensington, but I didn't want to look at the city or anything belonging to it. That doesn't mean I don't appreciate English Christmas customs. They're lovely."

"They don't have cribs," said Maria.

"Cribs? Ah, you haven't had time to look yet. No end of cribs. You forget how many Poles there are in England, and the English have been 'cribbified' for ages."

Many maps hung on the walls, elegantly framed. Every now and then they would disappear, darkened by the reflection of the lamp and furniture, depending on the eye's angle of vision. Entire continents, huge buff and green expanses vanished into thin air, blurred by the glitter of the glass, then reappeared, as if lifted onto the surface of the earth by a wave. The maps were old and in good condition; the descriptions were in Latin, less often in Cyrillic, and the tracts so colossal that if these maps told the truth or foresaw it, then the whole base of Eurasia would stretch to fantastic, mythological limits. Wlodzimierz Solowij must have been aware of the fairy tale nature of these pictures of the world, which were less a document - maybe some were - than a dream or a paranoia. But since they concerned his nation and unborn country, it was not surprising that he collected everything he could find. And it was not right for me to ignore them.

"You've an excellent collection. It's becoming more and more difficult to get authentic old maps now. The Poles are said to have had the time during these past few years to buy everything the bookshops and antique shops had."

"The Poles, and us, of course. Us even more, although maps like this are only decorative. It's hard to win anything with them. Please don't think I'm so naive, Nina dear."

"I've stopped believing in the difference between naivety and cunning. I sometimes don't know whether I'm dealing with the one or the other. This isn't a political point; I can see the dissociation everywhere. Besides, what would the philosophers and sages of all kinds do if all causes produced the right effects, if the one resulted clearly from the other? I'm suffering from scepticism to an inflamed degree."

Wlodzimierz Solowij was not such a pessimist. He considered that despite everything, much could be achieved, or at least done. He believed in many responsibilities.

But I had seen certain scenes and I could not help seeing them again and again. They took place on stations large and small, beautiful places in the East Carpathians. Kamien Dobosza or Dora or Delatyn, places we were passing through while returning from Mikuliczyn to Lwów with my mother.

It was already teeming with people in Mikuliczyn. Our train was for conscripts as well. Steam was pouring from under the engine. I shall remember for ever the face of the train driver, a Pole; I fell in love with that face. From the crowd burst violent cries in Ukrainian, individual and then universal, "Poles back to the San, Poles go home, we won't fight for Poland, down with the Polish state", and I am not repeating these shouts verbatim so as to strip them of the venom with which they were swollen. The shouts did not spring from the misfortune of call-up into the army, call-up to war. They stemmed from deep layers of old hatred. It seemed as if it was material, that you could touch it with your hand, like a hard object. Centuries stood behind this shouting.

The women were shouting and sobbing very loudly, reaching a real lament which sounded like the verdict on the Republic. This sob was like the coffin nails of our country.

I saw how the men's hands embraced the women's bodies, how they grasped their breasts with whole handfuls as if they wanted to hold onto the earthly globe for just a moment longer. I saw the heads of men strangely shapeless, falling as if in random movements to kiss now a face, now an arm, now a hand, now a mouth, any which way; they were like the blind, like a pecking bird. All of a sudden they froze, grasping the women to themselves; the world stopped for a moment, as clenched fists were raised into the air next to them, threatening, menacing, vengeful.

The peasant women had dressed in their festive clothes; young or old they all wore their best bodices, some embroideries shining with beads, peacock and gold light. New and festive were the skirts and scarves, the necklaces old, newly washed the blouses, stiff and deadly white. The shouts were increasing; it was harder and harder for the men to tear themselves away. Some of them were throwing themselves with a desperate leap onto the steps of the wagon, so as to finish with this torment quicker, so that the train should move off quicker, so that everything should end quicker. The women clutched their heads, hid them in their arms, their hands pressed to their faces. *Praklata Polska* - cursed Poland.

It is said that people who have experienced an earthquake never free themselves of the feeling. I was never freed from this earthquake in the East Carpathians.

Solowij was talking about someone who had just written and published, privately, something new on the subject of a Federation of Central Europe, about someone else who had discussed the matter in one of the émigré papers, I did not remember the name, then someone else had taken up the same question in another journal, names were being mentioned, but yes, certainly, an excellent idea, not new of course, so much has already been said and written about it, why yes, even before the war, why yes, it's the simplest thing possible to join together, our situation will never change without it, names mentioned again, the address of a club, what could be more natural, so many obstacles, why were there so many, so very many obstacles. A Federation of Central Europe is a power after all, so many countries and nations, of course, I will belong, however could I not belong, the only correct way, well, whatever else could be more successful, one day, in time, people themselves will come to understand.

Yes, of course.

14

A few days after Christmas Marian Czarnecki, editor of *The Polish Daily and Soldiers' Daily*, phoned me suggesting that I write a book. A novel. He knew my short stories which had been published in *Wiadomosci* since 1941 and he was giving me a free hand, although he would like it to be about 'Polish reality'. Did this mean that already there were people who could find a place for themselves beyond that reality? Now, so soon? They must have been Titans whose existence I had never suspected.

I agreed. I already knew what the book would be about. It would be about the shame of fear and fear of shame. The sequence into which man fits. Sometimes the sequence changes and is unforeseeable. It was not a strictly Polish subject although it inflicted itself on us more frequently and with greater force, or at least that is how it seemed to me at the time.

I was most afraid now for the language. All emigrations are said to silicify, to lock themselves into the vocabulary of their epoch, not subject to changes, even afraid of them. Great care was now being taken over unimpeachable Polish, the only treasure and possession that we could not be deprived of. But it could be spoilt. Yet this very spoiling can turn out diverse and interesting.

In Poland another language was also coming into being, had already done so. Rockets of new words were shooting up there, in particular new invective and curses, truly obscene yet creative. We were beginning to lose contact with this new language, with all its slanginess. Curses fascinated me, and I was becoming increasingly aware that they are the reserve and acknowledgement of the principle *cuius regio* and that a certain ungraspable but vital intimacy exists between your native land and the insolence of the language.*

We exiles could not afford to be insolent. We had the same rights and reasons, if not more, to curse and execrate our fate, but somehow we did not do it. Because it was not done. The linguistic root stopped at the level of dictionary words, while faddish words circulating in Poland, one-off words, did not include us; they slid down as from a glass mountain. It's probably for the good, I told myself and tried to believe it; the qualities of classical language are important, like enforced virtue. We'll sin with words borrowed from the languages of the countries we've settled in. We'll fall, we're already gradually starting to fall, into a Polish-English barbarism, but that's not the point. I was afraid of drying up inside, a thing not yet named but undeniably present and growing in the future. Lengthening like a shadow-cum-companion-cum-traitor.

Well then, I persuaded myself, too bad. So we will speak to Serenissima, to her and for her, in our own words, meaning the language we removed from Poland in the year of the war, and later, one day, one day... 'A rose for you, a guelder-rose for me.' Man lives by the word, but the word is like a sword, it can be double-edged. What are we to say to them, the people remaining in Poland? What? That we wake, warrant, watch and wait, we withdraw from the national treasury that has just crumbled in our hands both there and here? Should we simply bewitch? Resort to age-old sequences and steps on the subject of 'ours' and 'yours' within the same

---

*The Latin tag refers to the political settlements made in Europe after the Reformation. The full quotation is *cuius regio, eius religio*, meaning whoever controls the territory dictates the religion.

nation, since a division into 'these' and 'those' has been made and only the same skull is jointly cited? With a crowned eagle on this side, uncrowned on that.* A skull?

All the survivors had a head on their shoulders; now the future was dividing us, rather than the past. There was no use counting on the past any longer. All the more since we were not a nation like others, we were 'conjunctural and facultative', as I had once read somewhere, and the reason for it was that we were divisible. The third partition of Poland is the Original Sin of the contemporary Pole. Our political absence in the nineteenth century was now of double, treble, importance, despite the expectations and victorious battles of the war just ended. Except that becoming a civilian European was turning out to be a difficult step, something particular and special, similar to quarantine. Whatever had we not become resistant to after so many experiences? Answer: to the commonplace.

Every time I returned home in the evening there was a stranger standing on the other side of the street looking in the direction of my window although I now lived on the ground floor, in a different room from before. It surprised me only now. Who was he? What did he want from me? I had no doubt that it concerned me and not another resident because after a few minutes when I had already had time to settle in, the phone would ring. I would lift the receiver but no voice replied. My 'hello' repeated a few times remained unanswered in a dull hum; then I would hear the receiver being replaced. Some days when there was no one on the street, the phone rang all the same, more or less at the same time. Someone was observing me, although perhaps making a mistake about my identity. In a certain paradoxical way

---

*The crowned eagle was the emblem of the Polish monarchy and the Polish republics prior to World War Two. After the war the emblem of the Polish People's Republic was an uncrowned eagle.

he was doing me a favour - I preferred to be someone different.

I did not want to write my book in my room, where I would feel domesticated. I returned to Battersea Bridge a couple of times and looked at the boats, at the one that carried the name 'Wings'. One day I made a decision. Someone was there, among the old motor boats. He might be able to inform me. He found the owner of the boat for me, an ageless person who spoke an incomprehensible language which must have been a true English not suitable for foreigners. On my part I had to think of a pretext and present it in the most natural way possible. My words told of a large family at home and how I needed peace and quiet to study, how I did not fancy staying in the park or any public place, but if I could spend two to three hours on the boat every day...

I do not know how much this person understood of my reasons. I added that I did have somewhere to live and gave the address. Basically I understood nothing of the owner's reply; I think that he preferred me not to stay on the boat at night. At night? I quickly repudiated the notion - most amusing - and after this the short inarticulate words of the stranger seemed at a certain moment to be an assent. He nodded his head slightly. Now it was my turn and I had to suggest a price, but this was a problem. How much could a two- to three-hour stay on a motor boat, which looked unused anyway, cost? One shilling or two? Just to be on the safe side I suggested two shillings per afternoon on the days when I would use the boat. There was a metal tobacco tin in the bottom of an oilcloth bag, worn and shapeless like a galosh. The person nodded his head again.

"Stranger," he said, neither as a question nor a statement, and without looking at me. Then I nodded and he did not ask any questions about where I came from and I was most grateful to him for it. I offered him a cigarette and then left the Senior Service packet on a board next to us, not knowing clearly if it was a kind of tip or mere absent-mindedness.

So that was how the strangest conversation and transaction in my life took place. Strange and bizarre. What was the reason for my attraction to this neglected, indifferent place belonging to someone else and where it was hard to find any particular charm? Instead of writing in my room, which was warm and comfortable, though banal? Did living officially at a legal address bestow refugee status on me irrevocably? On the water, on the lightly rocking bottom of the motor boat I continued to be borne by the deception of not being fastened to dry land, of living in real extra-territoriality, fluid and inviolable.

I did not believe in political changes in the near future; the present shape of the world seemed the beginning of a long epoch. So I ought, treating the matter logically, to unpack my trunks right down to the bottom, get organised in my new surroundings, sort things out a bit, seeing as I did not trust that fate would change. Meanwhile getting organised surpassed my strength; it still seemed indecent. So I should hide myself away furtively in a peripheral place, throw myself outside the brackets, and the old motor boat, 'Wings', suited this purpose wonderfully. At least for two to three hours, maybe longer, I would be in no man's land. The sight of the Thames with its distant view contained something beneficent. To this day I am grateful to it. It endowed me with a feeling of anonymity different from that in a crowd, which was irritating and unpleasant. Anonymity often serves as redemptive provocation: lose yourself, but find yourself also, let yourself be buried by the sand of nothingness, but be unearthed as well. To be and not to be at one and the same time.

Maybe I will get some relief, will unearth myself or dig

down to something that will be important to me.

There was a bench on the old motor boat, a table fixed to the floor and very narrow, a shelf rather than a table, and a rough chair, a kind of stool. Everything I needed. So I bought a writing book of the worst quality possible and started to write on a hard piece of cardboard.

Writing on paper of the worst quality was not in the least the result of poverty. It was an old habit, from when I imagined in childhood that I was going to be a writer. The habit probably started with writing novels on the margins of newspapers, or on wrapping paper, or on the blank pages of books, and I filled these pages with illegible scrawls even before I was taught to write. These zigzag scrawls, veritable runes, signified words for me alone, and only I knew what they were meant to express. Later and for a long time, when I could already write, followed the pleasure of writing on unused forms or receipts, on the reverse side of various printed sheets and accounts, while the most wonderful find of all was discovering in the attic of my grandmother's house huge country registers which dated from the time when my grandparents lived in the country, in Jasiony. These registers, sturdily bound with thick covers and tied with tape, had huge stiff pages of a yellowish colour with columns that ran lengthways from the edge; three quarters of the page was an open field. The rustle of the pages, their solidity and dignity delighted but also somewhat intimidated me. That's for some later day, I thought to myself and transferred the registers to another part of the attic so that they should remain at my disposal.

The paper in my writing book had a shoddiness of quality which I liked and which was usually to be found in the provinces before the war. But also in Lwów. I once found a writing book of similar quality in a small stationery shop on Akademicki Square. Despite being so well located, it was one of the oldest and most provincial shops I knew. It was below street level. Two steps led down to it, while the interior, not very big and quite dark, was filled with the characteristic aroma of stationery, so condensed as if the souls of all the papers of the world had assigned themselves a rendezvous here. Behind the counter the owner, an oldish woman with jet-black hair, always wearing a dark scarf on her shoulders, sold her wares in an old-fashioned way, with a friendly goodwill towards the customer whom she greeted with a smile more sociable than commercial. She also entered easily into conversation, and once I heard her saying something about herself to an older fellow while rolling up sheets of foolscap paper for him: "I never saw the likes of those flowers and greenery again outside of Siberia; it was like the garden of paradise there. My father had been exiled there. We were repatriated when I was sixteen, but I spoke Polish from childhood."

A smile of departed memories. I listened in complete astonishment, hearing and seeing for the first time someone who viewed Siberia differently from Siberia the menacing, the location of the martyrology of the Polish nation. Siberia in flower like the garden of paradise was absolutely unimaginable, and from then, every time I went to buy something from the insurrectionist's daughter, I always felt a perverse satisfaction that there are no unshakeable certainties.

If there are not, then perhaps my conviction that exile is an honorable disaster, similar to suicide, could in time also turn out to be mistaken. If such beautiful flowers can grow in Siberia...

And so, at the thought of that shop, I located the first chapter of the novel in close quarters, clearly feeling that if I approached them while on a boat, then I would be able to escape reality which, like a hound, would lose the scent in water and not catch up with me. Yes, that was precisely what was important, not to feel attached anywhere, not to be on dry land, not settled, but on the sidelines, almost non-existent.

I also noticed something peculiar. Whatever I wrote before had been written in ordinary script, natural, the same as in private letters. Starting this book in Battersea I was covering the pages with minute handwriting, tight and dense, without the slightest margin on either side, although there was no question whatsoever of having to save paper. Rather of a cipher which was to remain secret, and the smaller it was, the easier it could be concealed.

The feeling of a cipher surprised me. Literature is generally the denial of such secrets and is born out of the need for open communication. At least that is what I had thought until then. Now it was ceasing to be so obvious. Communicativeness had become extensive, too large even. Everyone had been through the history of the last years in a group or team, deliberate or accidental. Hardly anyone was a wild horse. The communality of experience was tying unforgettable knots between people. No one needed to introduce himself to anyone, and no one was surprised at anyone. People had already started preserving their experiences in the most varied forms of writing, as if only this preservation guaranteed personal authenticity. Were they thinking about a testament for posterity, about the so-called transfer of history? They probably were, although it might have been secondary. The fundamental impulse of writing is repetition, in that we have no summary sense capable of registering the entirety and the simultaneity of an event. The one outside and the one inside us.

Repetition of an experience does not ensure depiction of the objective course of events, yet it soothes the desire for conscious survival, and possibly gives it meaning. I had always thought that literature contains one line of division, something like the division of waters, which can almost always be detected, but which separates two kinds of realities, the inventory and the magical manipulation. *Pan Tadeusz* always seemed to me an inventory of Polish ideas of happiness, in the same way as *Forefathers' Eve* presented an arsenal of ways and means, joint and personal, for warding off evil.* I could never admire the originality of Mickiewicz highly enough. He had the ability to be landlord and magician in one person and in the same way as he was the first to start the Romantics' quarrel with the classics (he too), by writing a national epic, so he also resolved the quarrel within himself.

The drawing up of inventories, literarily good or bad, became the first requirement of every writer. Memoirs took stock of the past, which should be recorded as accurately as possible so that nothing should belittle our condition. Every record was tolerated, often even a scribble, so long as the substance of our property and identity was preserved.

Magical means were being taken over by poetry, as exorcist and quack for sicknesses of the soul. Forgotten verses from once upon a time emerged. The repertoire of the aching and painful past was renewed, promising and uplifting 'the soul in the nation' that we had so amusingly travestied before the war. Certain that it would never happen again. I, for one, had not belonged to the gloom-and-doom tendency; I had not believed in war.

Like poetry, the novel can also assume the role of exorcist. The creation of characters from nothingness or half-existence, entrusting them with various tasks in the plot or narrative, relies in its deepest assumption on the same technique of doubling as sticking pins into a wax doll or other superstitious practices. They avenge the inventory of losses or dreams. The very act of writing is

*Pan Tadeusz (*Master Thaddeus*) and *Forefathers' Eve* : major works by the Polish national poet, Adam Mickiewicz (1798-1855).

perhaps the last vestige of old curses and rites, a way of translating life so that it should not terrify us with its incomprehensibility. Whenever I happened to see someone's draft novel by accident, it always gave me the impression of a liturgy for the initiated, a master or journeyman.

Sensitivity to this kind of literature might also have arisen from my feeling of impotence and disaster. The poet Norwid taught us that 'the word is our ultimate weapon' and this seemed terrible to me now. We had obviously lost because we did not know how, or did not want to have recourse soon enough to the words which really continued to be weapons. We were not the only ones. Although I still felt only rage, resentment and contempt for all forms of the written word, it was impossible to escape to any other means, or to replace the written word with anything else. I could only punish it with minute lettering, as if it were something shameful.

I really was ashamed of what I was writing. In it I returned to my own point of departure, that is, I participated in what was happening to me and around me in Lwów at the beginning of the Soviet occupation. That seemed like the very beginning of the world, posing fundamental questions. People who had come into contact with that reality, even without labour camps and prisons, learnt and saw with their own eyes how the heaven of noble illusions turned into a hell of mistakes. But something had to exist between one extreme and the other, a line or transitional zone, something that I was still unable to name. When in the year 1939 we were flooded with pathetic words from the highest register, we described it in short as 'tankant'. It really was the tanks that were canting, not ideas. The whole effort and art of the new arrivals depended on transforming the quantity of tanks into the quality of convictions.

I took another look at it, this time from the depths of

the old motor boat on the Thames, writing the first chapter of my book. Knowing in advance that I would never use it, that I was writing in the same way as one shakes the first drops off a glass.

I called the main character Jerzy Plawicki. His surname came from an already withered branch of my family. I made arrangements with him about what he was to be like; the fundamental points of his story loomed in my imagination.

You'll be a young man, still at university, a law student and rather grave. Your father will be important to you. Before the events that will dig a ditch between fathers and sons take place, I'd like you to understand as most important the way one generation passes into the next. You won't avoid conflict, but drawbridges have existed for ages, inherited from history, and they'll help you succeed or be useful. As for women, you'll know how to 'mount' them of course, but not to possess them. In general, possessing anything won't be a passion of yours, but you will want to understand a lot and know how to find your bearings in complicated situations, and also to observe scholars, as much as you're able without being a specialist. But you'll suspect that they're helpless too. Yet your moments of nihilism will only be short.

15

Concerning Hania. She turned up suddenly and accidentally, when I was not looking for her or for anyone at all. But when I was crossing Brompton Road, I unexpectedly noticed her coming out of Harrods. Both of us hesitated whether to approach each other or to slide away with an unrecognising glance. We had different reasons for doing so. Her reasons I understood all too well; she did not know mine. But she stopped and maintained the smile of recognition on her face. I was pleased. We greeted each other as if we were friends, though we had been only colleagues at the Institute of Fine Arts in Lwów.

"In the past they used to say 'mountain never meets with mountain', in cases like this, didn't they?" she said with her pleasant, matt voice. "But now it's more appropriate to say 'low never meets with low', isn't it? After what's happened to all of us."

It was good that she had said so. In this way she joined into the general and universal course of events, identified herself with others, as if crossing out her private past.

Hania's past was extraordinary. Her story had a Shakespearian dimension, and in those days was an unextinguished source of scandal because 'a thing like that has never happened as long as Poland has been Poland'.

Yet it did happen in the R. family, wealthy landowners from Podole, where, it was said, they were in the neighbours' bad books, which was ascribed to their unspoken, but swaggering manner. Hania did not inherit this trait. She was quiet but direct, she did not swagger, she was not distinguished by anything in particular apart from the colour of her hair. Golden like a wedding ring, it was cut short like a tomboy's, and with every movement of her head a glistening wave flowed sideways across her forehead. Underneath it sat a pair of blue, typically Polish eyes and a fair face. She had the attractive looks of women from the Polish gentry, made even more pleasant by an even disposition, which foretold a happy marriage and quiet family life. She was engaged but continued to study because, it seemed, it was the done thing to have a degree. Apart from that, she intended setting up a workshop in the country to make hand-woven and embroidered linen. She was sure to be good at running it. But it did not come to that.

When I returned from my summer holiday the year before the war, I learnt that Hania had attempted suicide. She shot herself with her father's gun, in his room, but the bullet had passed near her heart as it was contracting. Hers was an exceptional case; the operation was long and difficult, but after a while Hania returned to health. She did not return to our art school.

There were endless remarks on her action, but no one could add anything to the bare facts. It was said that three days before marrying her fiancé, with whom she was deeply in love, Hania chanced to find his letters. How that happened was not known for sure. The letters had been written by her future husband to her mother, and two obvious facts emerged: their passionate two-year love affair, and then his decision to marry Hania in order to be able to remain in the family and stay under the same roof as often as possible. The letters were said to be very beautiful, but no one thought about that, and anyway where could anyone possibly know from, apart from Hania? The force of this illicit and insidious love was said to have been stunning. And so no one was surprised that Hania's first reaction, or maybe not the first at all - that was conjecture as well - was to lay violent hands on herself.

It was also said that when it became known she had survived, flowers sent from various quarters arrived at her clinic, but hardly anyone wrote wishing her to get well, as if not wanting to touch her drama in any way. All the more, since it brought in its wake fundamental changes in the family. Hania's parents separated. Her mother went abroad to Normandy. Not on her own, as was generally imagined, but with her lover from whom she never parted. Maybe that ending shocked people in Poland even more than the beginning of the relationship.

Even Mr R's estate when it was put up for sale - he was moving to Malopolska - did not find a buyer for a long time, as if the presence of people like this and their tragic events had a repulsive power. Apparently the parish priest himself went there after Mrs R's departure and - it is not known whether invited or on his own initiative - stayed for two days with the master of the deserted manor house. He also grafted - it was in late autumn - some fruit trees in the orchard, which he had never done anywhere and which caused surprise. In this way the manor was given the aura of a legend, even while the protagonists remained alive. It was not known who ate the fruit because the next autumn something even worse happened. The Red Army occupied the whole of Podole, and the new republic of the Western Ukrainian Union of Soviets unfolded on those lands.

"I didn't know you were in London," I said. "Were you here during the war?"

"No, I came later. I'm waiting here for my husband; he's in Anders' army. They're due to arrive in England very soon."

"That's just like me. Except I'm waiting for my brother. He was deported as early as 1939, lived through Russia and survived Monte Cassino. I heard about it while I was still in Switzerland."

"Through the Red Cross?"

"No. I lived in Switzerland. The news came a very long way round, via Ankara."

"You lived in Switzerland during the war? You were lucky. I got out of Poland by a very complicated route shortly after the Warsaw Uprising. I was wounded but not too badly. I got better."

She smiled. So, thank God, she had married, and life had continued normally for her. Thank God.

She was little changed. She was slimmer and more attractive. She wore a neat little hat and a light grey coat with the collar standing to attention at her neck, giving a darker background to the light profile of her face.

"Mother's in London, you know," she said unexpectedly.

I nearly asked if they had come together, but I said only: "Oh, yes," which meant nothing, and Hania slipped her hands into her pockets, as if she had withdrawn inside herself for an instant. "If my husband returns from the war alive, I'll see Mother. I made a vow when the Italian campaign was under way. It was at Monte Cassino."

These words seemed so natural, just like Hania, that I did not reply, but she must have noticed how the emotion flashed through me. Also, I did not feel worthy of Hania. She had fought in the Uprising, she had been wounded, while I...

"I've got to find a certain shop here, it's somewhere nearby. Will you come with me?"

I went with her. There was a side street nearby, but the shop was not there at the address she had been given. "They must have moved elsewhere," said Hania, "this is probably the most expensive part of town."

She was right. A note fastened to the door gave another address, not too far away, in a courtyard surrounded by former stables turned into apartments. We found it with no difficulty. There were some lovely toys in the shop window, artistically made teddy bears, squirrels, billy-goats and cats. The interior comprised two medium-sized rooms almost completely filled by three huge tables covered with scraps of leather, material, papers, and all the equipment for tailoring. Along one wall ran shelves where the already finished creatures stood arranged in a row. When we entered, a sewing machine was humming at a side table. An older man got up from it; he seemed familiar to me, and I was not mistaken although I did not know him personally.

"Teddy bears? Here you are. Any size, any colour," he was saying jovially and with satisfaction. "We're doing best with the teddy bears and giraffes; they're going like hot cakes."

Another man with rolled up shirt sleeves came out of the second room, undoubtedly the fellow worker of the first man, and I suddenly remembered where I knew them from. They were the same serious men whom I had seen crossing my street carrying briefcases and the Polish paper. Not long ago I had thought that these men were engaged in important national and political affairs, concentrating exclusively on organising Important Matters in the heart of Polish London. Ah, so it was here, these toys.

I bought a bear and a billy-goat, and Hania bought two squirrels and ordered something from a piece of material she had brought. It was a bit of suede, probably cut from the inside of a chest for silver cutlery because I could see the still distinct gold lettering - Jan Jarzyna - Jeweller - Lwów.

"Hania," I asked suddenly, "if there's a scrap of that suede left over, do you think I could have it? I'd sew it into my purse."

"Yes, it'll be cut out so that a small scrap is left over," the older of the men assured me with a smile of understanding. "Well, they've cut us up so well that every scrap counts."

I was angry that he said it so loudly, so normally. The fact that 'they've cut us up so well' burnt me like a personal shame, like venereal disease. I had been running away from my fellow Poles as if I had been caught committing a crime. But here now, I felt it distinctly at that moment, I had crossed the final threshold. Souvenirs of time past were already playing for me, this small bear led me to a chain of memories and beat on brass plates an alarm for the Republic, an alarm for me.

As I was leaving I wished good luck to this little business which was doing so well. After we went out, Hania wondered aloud: "They've got so many orders, there's a lot of work there; if they needed someone to help or to work, I'd willingly agree. I always liked sewing."

But I, as I was leaving, accidentally caught sight of the inside of an open drawer and automatically stopped. Inside it I could see small cannons, tanks and airplanes, recreated in detail, miniatures of the real thing.

"Oh that, that's not for sale any more," the owner of the workshop hurried to explain. "They're models we make in our spare time. What you've got in your hands is a model of our anti-tank guns. Modelling is our hobby, my colleague's and mine."

But this hobby of theirs pierced right through me. So this is what anti-tank guns looked like, the famous light gun that was talked about so much before the war!

I had never seen it with my own eyes. Only now, here. It must have been not so much a hobby as an order from some Polish authorities or institution. It probably concerned an exhibition or reconstruction. No matter. This miniaturisation was a revelation, like seeing everything on the scale of Japanese gardens. Artificially shrunken trees and shrubs had always aroused my distaste and irritation. It seemed that I myself had suddenly become smaller and was getting smaller and smaller all the time.

16

One day the person I had seen watching my window from the street finally made his mind up. When I was close to the house, he came up to me quickly and stopped right in front of me, saying my name to assure me that he knew who I was.

"Yes, that's me." Then he gave me his name. Weissman. Józef Weissman.

"Is there something you want to discuss with me?"

It turned out that he was a friend of the Baums. He mentioned old Baum and the young one.

"They told me about you, but they didn't want to act as go-betweens themselves, not even to phone. They're people who are now completely on the sidelines."

"On the sidelines of what?"

"I'd say that they're on the sidelines of everything. They want to survive, to earn enough to live on, to raise their children and perhaps above all to forget. But they did say that you might be able to help me."

"Help in what?" I said impatiently. "I don't understand what you mean."

"It's hard for me to talk standing like this and detaining you. If we could sit down on a bench..."

There were some benches a few steps away. Old, wooden, of the sort you do not notice when walking past in the street, but there they were. I agreed to sit down on one of them. Weissman sat down next to me, put his hat on his knee and straightened his scarf.

"You've come from Switzerland. You were with the Polish legation..."

" 'With the Polish legation...' I was simply the wife of an official in the legation, so I don't know if you call it with, or alongside."

"Please don't be angry, I didn't express myself correctly. In any case, you knew a lot of people in Bern and also in Zurich and in Basel."

Probably in Basel least of all, I thought, mentally running through the people I had met there.

"I haven't taken the liberty of asking you about it all of

a sudden. I've often come here, but each time my courage failed me. I phoned and then at the last moment I didn't know what to say."

I believed him. It must have been something very important and he wanted to get used to me. With my voice perhaps, the way I spoke.

"Yes. I've had strange calls and there's been no one on the line."

Weissman sighed heavily and rubbed the nape of his neck.

"I'll tell you briefly what it's about, and the details later. You must have heard about this terrible business with our people. That is, I mean to say with the Jews. There was an entire organisation, not big of course, organisations like that never are big, and for huge amounts of money it undertook to get people out of Germany to Switzerland. You must have heard about it. It came out into the open before the war was officially over."

I was silent for a long time. So that's what it was about.

"Yes, I did hear about it. It was talked about, but as for the details..."

"Exactly. No one took any interest in the details because when you touch a detail, then various surprises come spilling out. Details are always the most dangerous of the lot."

It was said with particular bitterness, and rightly so.

"Perhaps you remember one name which was mentioned most of all at that time, precisely in connection with that affair."

He mentioned the name. I wondered what to say.

"Yes. I heard that name. He was Jewish too, so it was said. But you see, in this case an accusation or a suspicion is of such dimensions and of such weight that you'd have to have some proof before you mention that name."

He nodded.

"Exactly. If I showed you a photograph, maybe - maybe you happened to see him. He's said to have been seen frequently in the consulate. Except that we haven't got his photograph. Besides, what good would it do us? It's no proof, but it might come in useful in the future. You never know."

"No. I never saw him personally. Neither in the consulate nor in the legation. Unless he was using a different name. Except that I don't see what he'd have been doing in the legation or even in the consulate. I don't see any connection."

"I don't either. But there are people who like to squeeze in everywhere, on business as it were, and then they say that they know someone or other personally. And people believe them. Besides, in some situations there's nothing left but hope."

Or else quite the reverse, I thought, but I did not say it.

"And what of it? You're one of the people who are looking for him, is that it? He took the money and..."

"Not to investigate a thing like that? To let it be, as if it concerned the theft of a packet of cigarettes? Are you able to imagine what these people felt and what happened to them? Well then. And he's sunk without trace. But with time some stones do emerge from the water. Even entire rocks."

"And you imagined that I knew something about this subject, is that it?"

"You might have heard about someone who was looking for one of the people who didn't cross the border, someone we don't know about. People in misfortune talk a lot, particularly Jews. Just in case. And Jews did hang around the legation."

That's what my conversation with Weissman was like. I could not tell him that I sympathised with him because that word had almost stopped existing; it was, at any rate, going out of use. But suddenly another circle engulfed me. I was challenged by the former exiles from the Jaslo cemetery, as if surpassing them in something, subduing them in something. They did not know about genocide or Hiroshima or Katyn, although they did know terrible things from their penal servitude. But that was very long ago, and we had time to descend to ever lower circles of hell.

Weissman's story reminded me of something strangely familiar: our Weronka Perkuc, a housemaid, a young girl who wore a gold coin on a thick tape under her vest. It came from as far back as her great-grandfather, who had received it for apprehending Polish rebels and handing them over to the Russian gendarmes. I had no idea how many such coins he received for giving up insurgents, but he kept this rouble as a souvenir or a medal, bequeathed it to his son who also respected it and did not spend it, and in turn her own father gave it to Weronka before his death, when she was going into service in town, telling her to keep it well hidden and use it only for a rainy day. Weronka told us all this with reserved but conscious pride. Once she undid her blouse and I saw it with my own eyes. It hung quite low between large breasts drooping slightly downwards like money-bags made of the finest white silk. It lay there in the warmth of that young body like a third teat of gold. It had not been drilled for a cord but was instead wound into a cross with thin wire finishing with a small ring as a clasp. Our cook was always advising her that it would be better to sew the coin into something because "it's always safest when it's hidden."

The girl granted that she was right, but she had a different reason of her own: "I like it when I touch it, but only on the wires, so it won't wear thin. And when I give myself away in marriage, I won't give that away," she added with a smile, pleased with this saying, and left the money inside her vest and fastened her blouse. It was a checkered blouse, ah yes, I remembered it well, and if it were not for this Weissman, I would not have thought of it: small light pink and brown checks.

I was not much help to Weissman, but the very fact that I had heard about the case had seemed to hearten him a little. He was one of those people who were prepared to wait and search long and patiently, and investigate the traces and perpetrators of crimes. He left me his card, adding his telephone number 'just in case'. He had a cigarette in his mouth, and the smoke was shading his face as if annihilating it. I shuddered at this unavoidable association.

17

Kostek turned up again, pleasant and effusive as always, in a new suit and loden and new shoes. He started showing me all his acquisitions as if they were archaeological objects.

"I've fitted myself out for the future," he said with good humour, "because afterwards it won't be possible any more. But of course I won't wear all this for the journey. I don't want to be conspicuous or look like a Westerner.

"Do you remember that boy Mirek from our schooldays? His parents dressed him up in everything so new at the beginning of the school year that his friends ragged him mercilessly. And I think it was the second day of school, one of the boys, accidentally on purpose, spilled some liquid or other out of a cylinder in the physics lab and it burned holes in his socks and the hem of his brand-new trousers. Do you remember?"

"Yes, I remember."

Why did he remind me of it? Did he know that I had been friendly with this little culprit who knew the poverty of the very poorest and always fascinated me with his particular way of being, hard to define accurately, and his way of looking at the world. Meaning, the world of ordinary people of middling wealth, even very modest, but they were full of some rhyme and reason and their world could not be his. The son of a peasant, said in fact not to be his son but 'a neighbour's child', living literally in a corner at a crazy aunt's or some distant relative who was childless and solitary and with a life story equally sad as that of this boy Mirek.

Being friendly with him would be saying too much. The boy would never have been friendly with me on account of my social origin, although that concept was not yet defined in those days. I was the daughter of a so-called good home which was visibly good from the inside. Not many of my contemporaries were fortunate to have parents to love and respect and also feel good in their company. This privilege of fate was a gift for the whole of life, whatever its future course.

That same evening I eagerly opened the envelopes of photographs and souvenirs my mother had sent me through the woman I met in the café. I opened them quickly and nervously with a feeling of almost heroic courage, with the greatest sensitivity, with trembling fingers. And by a strange coincidence the first of the photographs showed not my closest family, but myself as a little girl of eight or nine, in school uniform, although at that age I did not yet go to school. I was taught privately. In fact uniform was not compulsory - only the sailor's collar and pleated skirt dubbed me as a future schoolgirl.

In contrast to other photographs of myself which generally I could not stand, I felt this one was successful, which means flattering. Above me grew a tree which I remember well. Too well even. Because just behind this tree was a path, little used and leading to just one house, if you do not count the sawmill and all its enormous cubes of cut beams and planks.

Someone moved into this house on the hill. It was called 'on the hill' although there was no hill in the least; the land barely rose above the rest of the town. From the back, however, a fairly extensive garden stopped short and fell steeply toward the river. The house could be approached only from the street side, from that path in fact, if anyone wanted to go there.

But no one did want to, and from when I remembered it in childhood, the house was always shut up, empty, seemingly distant among the greenery which had run riot. This greenery, abundant and unhindered, exploded high into the air and beyond the wooden fencing, giving the whole place its appearance of seclusion, neglect and intrigue. But no one talked about it. It was as if it did not exist, and I asked no questions.

I never saw the house in its entirety, just partially, from one perspective. Next to this tree in the photograph you could glimpse quite a high roof whose tiles had become green, a chimney and the top of the window of one of the first floor rooms. Nothing more. And wide silhouettes of trees, when the wind was blowing, bent over against the background of a completely empty sky which also seemed to be secluded here. They closed and opened, presenting a neutrally distant expanse of sky. Only huge thujas remained rooted to the spot on both sides of the iron gate, always immobile, like guards on watch. They looked particularly inhospitable.

But somebody did come to live there. One day it was the talk of the whole kitchen, that is, the house servants and Marysia the Fifth, hired to do the washing. She always knew everything and certainly more than the others about what was happening in town. She prided herself on her extensive contacts in 'better houses' and thanks to her, the washing became almost a social event. The house servants, Helcia and Marysia the Fifth, never complained about the growing mountains of linen. The hall would resound with various sounds of water, splashing, trickling, whistling and gurgling; a whole orchestra of vessels, wooden or metal, would reply at various intervals, at times drowning the women's ceaseless chatter. That was how I found out that some people were now living in the 'house on the hill', but as was my custom, I did not ask about anything more closely, not for a moment imagining that I would make an extraordinary discovery there.

The house, because it had become inhabited, lost its prestige of secrecy, turning out to be a house like other houses, serving people to live in. Yes, but - there are all sorts of people, as children know best from their youngest years, and so the people in this house could be different from the ones I knew. According to Marysia the Fifth, it was not the owners who were living there, only some relations of theirs whom no one in town knew. They were said to be young. It did not arouse my particular curiosity; washday always abounded in tales of human life whose shreds passed through to 'the rooms' later, brought by Helcia and served in a tightly corsetted version.

It was precisely this that irritated me most, the difference between the juicy and gushing kitchen tale, full of the joy of discovery, and the strained essence in its modest cover of calm sentences and restrained insinuations for the 'gentry'. So for this reason when we were children, we instinctively felt attracted to the living world of kitchen odysseys, and the kitchen was endowed with special authority. It was there that values were established, the visible world was ranked in hierarchies, while the presumed invisible world, the one 'not down here below', was acknowledged with a short sigh over its unattainable perfection, with mixed regret and secret pleasure.

But what was the reason for their sudden explosions of laughter or silent smiles - I did not know. The kitchen code was inaccessible to me. But one thing I did understand well and very early on: being able to tell the tale is more important than the events described, and only the telling really counts. Gossip is necessary, a natural defense against boredom and the flatness of the world. My grandmother understood this well. "If all gossip were true, how much more interesting life would be," she sighed sceptically, probably also wanting in a friendly way to shock Mr Makowski, director of the Bank Polski, a frequent guest of ours. For Mr Makowski believed in telling the truth, the unadulterated truth.

It was no gossip that there was someone in the house on the hill. In the evening and as early as dusk, a light could be seen in the one window through the trees. The slender October branches unveiled a larger expanse of wall as well; the surrounding area had become light as it were. The grass in front of the gate was mowed or cut, and a detail previously non-existent and even unthinkable was added: a letterbox. Hung outside the gate, made of tin and rather commonplace, it stood out sharply against the riotous growth of the garden, dispelling the former secretive atmosphere of this backwater.

But my astonishment bordered on enchantment when, next time, as I was walking along the road below, the tin letterbox which had shone from a long way off had disappeared. I stopped, looking carefully into the depth of the path swerving upwards. The letterbox had not disappeared; it had merely been replaced by a different one. Wooden, larger, not glaring, harmonising with its surroundings. In other words, it had been done deliberately. Because the other one was out of place. So they thought the same as I did. The unknown inhabitants and I, an eight-year-old child they did not know, had something in common, something shared but which would not be told to anyone else. Should I tell the grown-ups how pleased I was?

I made a few extremely hesitant, timid and unexpected steps along the path, then further still. I did not intend to direct myself towards the house, but I was nevertheless going towards it. Perhaps to test my own courage? As a child I took extreme pride in not looking through a gate into someone else's garden or into a stranger's window. But now this very gate drew me towards itself and I wanted to see at close range this secluded garden, strangely unlike itself because already transparent, as if inhabited by ghosts. Leaves blew sideways at me from the left as if someone were scattering them. A few still glistened on the hill; down below dusk was already thickening.

The gate was made of iron bars, once painted green. Beyond the gate led the carelessly maintained path; it probably wound towards the main entrance which was not visible. Trees right next to the fence, an indistinct flowerbed, tall shrubs. There was evidently no one in the house, for there was no light in any of the windows. Complete silence, intensified by the falling leaves.

In this silence, dusk and immobility, my eyes were drawn by a dark shape lying on the ground against a lighter background of leaves and grass. Rather similar to the form of a cross but it was not a cross. It was a person with his arms spread out wide, his face next to the ground. To his head adhered a large and longish stain, while the fingers of both hands were holding something light, like faint flames, barely visible. Only the cuff of his white shirt was distinctly separated and a glittering spot shone on it. A light wind blew and the black stain suddenly moved, seemed to raise itself slightly and dissipate around a head lying there. Hair, it was quite long human hair. And when I understood this, a shudder ran through my own hair, my skin. It was not one person lying there; there were two of them, killed dead.

At last I unfastened my hands from the gate and raced down on legs stiffening with terror. Home was a fair way off and the road stretched out pitilessly, endlessly. At last without breath to fill my lungs I fell into our hall, our kitchen, to life, to people.

"Murdered, killed," I kept repeating chaotically, "Helcia must go to the police at once, at once. Maybe they're poisoned. I couldn't see anyone. They killed themselves."

"They killed themselves?" Helcia suddenly seemed to turn it over in her mind, casting a glance at Marysia the Fifth, "You don't say!"

Marysia the Fifth shrugged her shoulders, added a few more coils to a long sheet wrung and rolled into a snake. And suddenly the silence burst, both women exploded together with quiet, then convulsive laughter. Helcia hid her face in her elbow and sobbed with laughter, the tears stood in her eyes, blue as paint, while Marysia the Fifth sat down on the bench next to her, the snake of the sheet wound on her knees in a double coil.

"Killed," I insisted, shocked and terrified by this laughter, "they weren't moving at all, they were lying on the ground."

"Eee. They must've been thrashing about good and proper earlier on, so they were taking a breather."

And again she was seized by laughter. A hairpin fell out of her hair and she did not bend down to get it, only clasped her hands on her stomach, afraid that her laughter would tear her insides. But hatred for both of them poured over me, blind and deaf, and like their laughter, swelling into eternity. Suddenly Marysia the Fifth stopped laughing and spoke in a human voice, the voice of a reprimand. "But why did Janisia go there? You shouldn't go to people you don't know. You shouldn't..., and that's that!"

But I was already through the door. I bounded across the hall and, beyond the kitchen's watchful eye, I lurked on the stairs to the attic in order to recover from my anger and shame. What did they mean? What were they cackling at so much? Those people were not dead, only pretending? Impossible. I had a good look at the immobile fingers, and those light flames were also fingers, entwined with the other ones. I had seen the immobility of the body; evidently one body had set on the other so that they seemed one. And the head, only one head. What about the second one? There had to be another one, the one with long hair which the wind had scattered as if sighing. While they seemed to penetrate each other, as if they were joined one on top of the other. In the dusk, softly lying on dry leaves which did not even give out a rustle. Discreet witnesses.

Naturally this story could not stay concealed within the confines of the kitchen, and to the amusement of the whole family it became famous as 'Janisia's dead bodies', which sounded like the name of a defeated tribe. When I was growing up I participated in this mocking game, but my initiation in that garden fell into the depths of my soul like something important to be remembered, and I never admitted it to anyone.

18

Stempowski had been right, in the Rosengarten in Bern, when he quipped that in Europe the calendar holds sway, while with us it was the hourglass. And then laughed in his particular way.

The Rosengarten is an eighteenth-century municipal park which had retained its character and even its atmosphere unchanged. The park was hardly frequented. Only a few people went there for walks; you never saw mothers with children or indeed any children at all. The very few passers-by considered it appropriate to nod in greeting although they did not know each other personally, and this exchange of discreet and old-fashioned courtesy contributed a charm of its own, as if it were a garden initiated into arcane rites.

It was my favourite place for meeting Jerzy Stempowski, whose silhouette, while not departing from the prevailing fashion, was well suited to this backdrop. His famous unhurried step* - it had not been called that yet - his way of wearing his hat, his pastel colours, and hands always holding a small volume or a scroll of paper created an image of aristocratic animation of which he was, of course, perfectly aware.

The empty paths ran in a perfectly symmetrical arrangement. Small neat fountains played as if for themselves; some rose high in a thin stream and then billowed out. Low shrubs surrounded towering beeches, and at sunset the views deepened. "This wouldn't be the Count's favourite landscape in *Pan Tadeusz*," laughed Stempowski at this panorama, which was the antithesis of the style preferred by Count Soplica in the poem. Then he usually started a discourse about botany, which in the Bern period was a frequent subject of Stempowski's deliberations.

But the conversation quickly turned to literary subjects, since at that time I was not yet sceptical about the written word, but believed enthusiastically in its value.

---

*'His famous unhurried step' alludes to the title of Stempowski's regular feature in the émigré periodical *Kultura*.

I admired Stempowski's serenity and his philosophical way of looking at all contemporary events as if he had concluded a non-intervention pact with someone. The price was interpretation.

The menacing face of the Republic which had so convulsed me in Mikuliczyn was not unknown to him. He also knew the feeling of disbelieving one's senses, which I had experienced on that first of September when I got off the train in Lwów, in the shattered rubble of the station I had known. It looked white, like bared bone. An immense and previously unknown perspective opened onto a strange city. The station had been bombed that very morning and dust still stood high above it, the last breath of the ruins, my first bated breath of war.

That might have been why Stempowski liked me. I was the only person in Bern who had spent the last day and night of the Republic in the East Carpathians, delighting in the beauty of the world that he also loved.

I saw more final reflections of the Republic, as if on the reverse side of a mirror, in Marian Zyndram-Koscialkowski's apartment in London's Acton Town. The former prime minister - I met him only then in London - was already paralysed, and he got about in a wheelchair among the people and objects near to him in this apartment which seemed to have been brought whole out of Poland. There was something in the greenish light of the rooms and the extensive view through the windows, the arrangement of the furniture and small bits and pieces that recalled Polish interiors, rural rather than from the capital. A few friends and family members circulated in this retrospective atmosphere: all mutual friends with the warm intimacy that was once the charm of Polish life.

Commonplace matters were talked about with frequent allusions to the past in a way that was as natural and unrestrained as if all these references were still topical.

One could imagine that these people held the key to an untouched expanse of time and that mechanisms still not fully unwound were at work in them. It was astonishing and enviable. Maybe that is what always happens to prominent personages, or perhaps it was the natural state of affairs, not previously comprehensible to me?

The light in some rooms was sunshine yellow; in the rooms opposite it was shady blue. All the faces on the edge of these hues were half in sharp relief and half faded. The sun set, the blue air thickened, the lamps were not lit - Poles like this grey hour - guests arrived, the tea table was drawn up, the room became imbued with the intangible breath of Poland's eastern borderland. Was it from the cousins with Lithuanian surnames, or from the taste and smell of home-made cheesecake?

There was talk about the Bialystok region, about Bialystok, about a local fish. They were right, the animals and plants had remained there, in the same place, and it was enough to touch them with their names for them to pass before the eyes. Through sound and smell, I could almost feel their presence.

I suddenly realised that I did not know or perhaps did not remember whether this Bialystok was still in the new Poland, or was it now the Soviet empire. Had it stayed with us or fallen to them? It is strange to wonder where we are located and what borders have divided us. Bialystok. Nothing linked me to that city and I had no friends there, but it appeared as a warning sign, a frontier between what is yours and someone else's, the attainable and the unattainable.

"Is it an attractive city?" I asked. The geography of our homeland was therefore becoming slippery ground. I would have to learn the new map of Poland by heart.

It was the first moment I had thought territorially: Poland. Until this time not once had I thought other than Republic, and my ceaseless anger referred to that

Republic's death. With this Bialystok a new concept was born, an image perhaps. Of course it was obvious but all the same unknown to me personally until now. Poland. With no addition, paled of its due title, disguised. A growth without a face but seeing with a thousand eyes, terrifyingly distanced by hundreds of miles once again just as it had been a century ago for the former exiles, as if a revolving stage had turned full circle.

Someone was saying something to me with a smile. Beside me I saw the beautiful face of Maria Balcerkiewicz, who was repeating something I had obviously not heard. It was Koscialkowski proposing that we drink together as a pledge of friendship. I was shortly to belong to the family, and I drank what I was given with an internal astonishment as if I were attending a wake uninvited. What on earth was I doing here among these people whom I had known before the war only from newspaper photographs and who had already fallen into the abyss of the September catastrophe?

The generation gap had its cruelest effect on my generation, 'Generation D', meaning the people who received their graduation diplomas in 1939, a few months before the war. The generation for which 'the horse had run'. They had mounted it, yes they had, but those who survived that ride had become somewhat humpbacked as a result.

What hellish forces are driving us into this corpse-like colour, into this props room of symbols and theatre from which there is no exit? At Acton Town, nearly an hour's train ride away from where I lived, for the first time I felt how far the Republic and Poland had parted. That is why I remember so well what the platform of that far-off station in suburban London looks like. Today it seems amusing, arch-eccentric, but then...

I was pleased to have my watery shelter on the Thames where I felt extra-territorial and where I could write my book. All writers have their own private and imaginary vehicle with which they visit the landscapes and expanses of their choice, discover unknown lands, promontories of hopes and dramas, unexpected havens of reflections, deep sea grottoes or eternal mountains. What could equal my boat at Battersea? Mickiewicz's Arabian horseman? Saint-Exupery's airplane? A flying carpet?

That was a bad association of ideas, a point of sensitivity unnecessarily pressed. My grandfather was said to have maliciously declared that every Pole should be equipped with a flying carpet because we liked travelling so much. That was my grandfather on my mother's side, Bogumil Szeligowski. He was also my godfather, as well as a councillor at the Viennese court, and was said to be a difficult man of inflexible convictions. He had the most intense distrust of the Poles' ability to govern, but despite that he did not in the least consider himself a bad Pole.

It is said that he viewed the outbreak of war in 1914 as the start of a general cataclysm which would give rise to nothing good, that he did not want to hear about Pilsudski or his government, and that he placed universality higher than all the ambitions of individual nations, arguing that national cultures could flourish in full only when they were not made degenerate by politics. Political sovereignty was in his eyes the source of ceaseless wars. Grandfather did not live to see independent Poland and died in Vienna convinced of the end of Christian and European Europe. He came to my mind at this train station, I know not why.

19

My small volume of poetry entitled *Stage-coach Poems* had just been published in London pseudonymously, and I wanted to take a copy to *Wiadomosci* for it to be mentioned there. The poems were written in 1943, at a time when exile had not entered our heads, and when I still believed in words. In 1946 I no longer believed. The word was perhaps faithful to me, but I had become unfaithful to it. All the same I fancied going to *Wiadomosci* to see with my own eyes what the editor, Mieczyslaw Grydzewski, looked like. I had already been in touch with him for a few years, writing for *Wiadomosci* from Switzerland under the name J. Wadwicz, but I had never met him.

The *Wiadomosci* office was in Rosary Gardens at this time, and the name seemed to me a slightly malicious stroke of fate because of the similarity to the Bern Rosengarten. Hardly anyone went to the park any longer, but the *Wiadomosci* office was visited by those who wrote for it, those who read it, those involved with 'culture in general', maybe even with politics, I cannot say. The editorial offices of those days were like state ante-rooms, between the past and the future, Poland and Polishness; and people were starting to believe in this exceptional demi-state as in something established. Maybe that is why I was so scared of crossing the threshold, since to honour the defeated seemed immoral, indecent and unendurable. Today it sounds merely eccentric, but then...

So I made a round of the street where the office was

situated, crossing from one pavement to the other. A quiet street, not long, but pleasant. The day was off-colour, one of those London days that does not divide the street and houses between sunshine and shade, allows you not to blink, not to wear dark glasses, and attracts no attention to itself.

At last, putting on my best social behaviour, I found myself in the office. I gathered to me all the attributes and virtues which a writer should possess when paying a first visit to a publisher or editor. Maybe for an instant, for a second, I regretted that it was not Poland 'A'. It was as if I had forgotten that Poland 'A' did not exist any longer, nor did the one nearer to me, Poland 'B'. Everything and everyone were from the past, that is, of little importance. How had Kostek who was returning to Poland put it? "At least I'll be real there, whatever happens." So it meant that I, that we...

Unexpectedly there was only one client or guest in the office, and he was just saying goodbye. I guessed that Mieczyslaw Grydzewski was the person opposite me in the depths of the room behind a desk. I recognised him by his dark, wide-open eyes with which, it seemed, he eagerly wanted to know everything about any newcomer, and of course he must have had long experience in this. He was very polite, not in an editorial or café fashion, but homely as it were, slightly lost, as if the servant had just left and what was he to do about coffee? In the way he talked, at once in general and in detail, fast and suggestive, he had a wonderful gift of immediacy. He could probably have established contact with everything and everyone without the least difficulty; within five minutes he knew my own complicated curriculum. When he heard that I was currently working at Decorative Arts near Brompton Road, he was alarmed that I might want to dedicate myself to illustrating books.

"Illustrating books?" I groaned, shocked. It soon

became clear that we would be friends: I cannot stand illustrated books, and neither could Grydzewski. I admitted that yes, there had been a time when I had done it, but only as an assignment for my professor of graphics. The subject irritated me, even though many of my colleagues adored it.

I told Grydzewski the amusing story of a colleague, Ignacy Witz, who had declared that he intended to specialise in illustrating the erotic scenes in Polish literature. So first of all a catalogue of such scenes had to be drawn up. Witz carried out a survey among his friends, and when my turn came, I replied that the scene that made the greatest impression on me was from Sienkiewicz's trilogy, when Kmicic kisses Olenka in the sleigh. Never mind the fact that it is so banal, I like it.

We exploded in discussion about whether this scene could be accepted as erotic. The discussion was long and vehement, but it was the unexpected result which startled me. Namely, as I found out a few days later, this selfsame colleague Witz had said that he thought I was sympathetic to the rightwing Polish Youth Organisation. It was an astonishing assumption but very characteristic of those times: from the strap to the stick, and if you took anything from Sienkiewicz, well then... In fact Sienkiewicz is not in the least one of my favourite writers. But the episode in the sleigh is one of my favourites.

Grydzewski liked the idea. "It'd be a good subject for a questionnaire in *Wiadomosci*," he said, "but the times are inappropriate."

Yes, they really were inappropriate. But during our conversation I realised that before the war Mieczyslaw Grydzewski had been the most fortunate man in Poland. An institution more than a man, he did what he loved doing and exerted control like a dictator, moving with everything that represented the social and artistic elite, and one day, one day he would be sure to have, if not a statue, then at least a street named after him. One day.

During my visit to the office, the very fact of talking about such insignificant matters seemed a miracle. The conversation led us into the pre-war world in the way a drawing is transferred on tracing paper to its proper place. The proper place was and always remained that soil over there, though we were hanging in the air as if we had become two-dimensional, flattened and deformed.

As I left, I became aware that I was indebted to Grydzewski, as if I had found a handrail in the dark. Maybe his office, and other offices like it, were not subject to the iron laws of pessimism, and despite everything they were a necessary road or path and there was no salvation apart from that path. I admired all the people, known and unknown, who, in surviving and in preserving what was most important, believed blindly and unwaveringly, without looking to success.

I tried to comfort myself: I am on this road as well... even by bringing the classics to the YMCA. No one would know what state of mind I was in while doing this, but the work would undoubtedly come in useful - for someone somewhere, some time, in the national route of exile. And it may even make its way to Poland. The obsessive need to touch those old texts was perhaps a help in spite of my unyielding disbelief in any hierarchy of values. Here was something tempting and convincing, presenting itself as obvious. The absurdity of the world. The absurdity of life and the increasing secrets of darkness. Both present and eternal. Understanding does not imply agreement. It flies from it instinctively, being, particularly for us Poles, something too difficult, demanding constant effort. The memory of Stempowski's words stirred again, "One cannot expect easy reason from the Poles because they become uneasy at the very word 'reason'." But then, when he was saying it - so recently after all - it was still a time for jokes.

20

And Kostek again, his departure was being deferred, waiting for a friend still in the Second Corps.* That day he ran up the stairs, excited by his news: "Do you know who I met?" he started as soon as he was on the threshold, "Mrs Grzesik! Her very self. Of course she's changed since then, but I recognised her at once, although in fact it was she who came up to me first and reminded me who she was. She didn't think I even remembered her. 'From Siedlicze', she said to make it easier for me to remember her. And do you know what she's doing here? She's set up a restaurant or canteen. She's got her own staff and there's such a crowd there, I tell you, a crowd."

The word 'crowd' suddenly tugged at him. I understood why. That other crowd, that different one, had probably come into his mind as well. "She's the last person I'd have thought would have stayed here in exile", I said, "and since, as you say, she's set up a restaurant, obviously she's got no intention of going back to Poland. Her, my God. Of course I remember everything."

Indeed, I remembered better and probably more than he did. Everyone in Siedlicze knew her. The whole Krosno district was starting to talk about her more and more.

"The only thing I don't remember is her name," added Kostek, as if it were important.

---

* In 1942 Anders' Polish army left Soviet territory for the Middle East and became the Second Polish Corps of the British Eighth Army. At the end of the war in Europe the Second Corps stood at Bologna.

"Kunegunda."

"Kunegunda! The name's just right for her. There were lots of Grzesiks in the area, but there was one and only one Kunegunda. You could say she was 'a providential woman'."

Providential for sure, although not in the traditional sense of that word. This energetic woman believed not in God's Providence, but in the value of work and the ability to organise, and especially in reason, which she considered obvious and which she sought among other people. She chaired the Country Housewives' Circle in Siedlicze and had been in charge for three years, maybe two, I did not know exactly. In Siedlicze that was like being inside the very jaws of the lion.

There were probably not many landowners left in Poland between the wars like the owners of this village. Staying with them, I was aware what an anachronism they were, and I observed this with astonishment, although from a different angle than Kunegunda Grzesik.

Siedlicze belonged to a close relative of my father, and we sometimes went there during our holidays. The old manor house, shoddy but authentic, long, narrow, whitewashed and with a porch which I remembered well, had been demolished and a new manor erected on the other side of the park, a new monster, as malicious neighbours used to say, something between a very large villa and a mansion, with no defined style. It no longer had the former traditional Polish entrance hall, only an enormous space with adjacent salons, there being several on the ground floor all furnished partly with pedigree furniture, but partly with some town-made imitations of antiques or completely modern pieces which paid homage to the fashion of colourful cushions and knick-knacks in china cabinets. Only the dining room all lined with wood retained something of the former soul of old country seats.

The administration of the house had always been in the hands of Aunt, the wife of Uncle Walerian S., a woman in love with her class of great landowners, believing unwaveringly in their role and historic mission, and having aristocratic inclinations which increased in strength as time went by. After Uncle had a riding accident and suffered something like mild confusion, Aunt's administration increased the incomes from the estates, and there were quite a few of them: apart from Siedlicze they owned Chlebna (which my father could also claim a right to), Chorkówka, famous because Ignacy Lukasiewicz, inventor of the paraffin lamp, had lived and worked there, Miastowice in the county of Poznan, and Uscie Ruskie, which was Aunt Zofia's dowry. Her uncommon self-confidence was probably equalled only by her deep dislike of peasants, and because of this, it seemed as if I was seeing the former historical Poland, and from its worst side at that. I accompanied Aunt unwillingly in some of her expeditions, but I did want to see Chorkówka, I wanted to write about it. Not knowing the place, I had imagined it differently.

What I saw startled me. The house was long and had a verandah without masonry reinforcement, glazed with tiny panes in wooden slats with the glass missing where bits had dropped off here and there, while the walls on one side had subsided and were distended on the other. But the roof, once beautiful and high, now in very bad condition, was straight. What irritated the eye of the beholder most intensely was the area in front of the house: a large stretch of gravel not intersected with any flowerbed or lawn, just the nakedness of the ground which rose lazily in one place and added a sense of being deaf and dumb, maybe also an expression all its own of sour and bitter wasteland; no one had lived in this house in living memory. That is, since Lukasiewicz's times. One of the rare manors in Malopolska which were said to be haunted. No effort was made to be original: it was said that Lukasiewicz walked through the rooms at night with a lighted lamp in his hand, and so the story was really too obvious. But it was true that the annual retreats which Aunt organised here during Lent always ended in failure. The peasants came unwillingly, the priests too. I decided that one day I would come here before Easter, next year perhaps.

The interior of the house consisted of a strange arrangement of rooms which adjoined in two rows not separated by a corridor, so that you passed from one room to the next and quickly lost your bearings. This was probably caused by the numerous rebuildings which the manor had undergone over the years. Yet the rooms were all large and almost completely empty. Kostek and I - he was accompanying us then - had run through the house calling out to each other as if we were instinctively searching for each other, and when I did not hear his voice, I quickly ran through the nearest door, then through the next two rooms and then stopped in the very middle of an extensive former dining room or salon. I had caught sight of a portrait hanging on the wall between the windows. It occupied the whole height of the wall, from floor to ceiling. I examined it.

It depicted a man in a black frock coat with a scarf round his neck, dressed in the style of the 1860s, except that his boots were high and thick-soled like a peasant's. He had a very severe but not old face, black hair and a black beard. The blackness of this picture gripped the eye; only the face and hand stood out against it. He was holding a roll of papers at chest height. A true pose for a portrait, suggesting an important public role. In the completely empty room this picture looked slightly eerie.

Probably an exile, flashed through my mind, someone who did something somewhere for the country, a friend of Ignacy Lukasiewicz maybe. He had friends like that.

I examined him for quite a long while although I wanted to run away. But to run away would mean that I was scared of history and that history was chasing me. Therefore no. I must look, then find out what sort of a man he was and maybe I should try to get his portrait hung in the museum in Krosno or some other place accessible to visitors. But classification removes the intimacy of discovery and of mystery. So I resolved not to ask about anything until evening; there were still a few hours before me.

I left the house as if passing from darkness into light, from one era into another. Yet the era of darkness was also in evidence outside the house, and I watched it in all its archaism, accompanied by Kostek's quiet giggle. Kostek was helping to carry some chairs and benches from the back of the house with the 'gardener' who was in fact a factotum. Ageless, but what mattered was that he was local and had been discovered at last, found by Staszek the chauffeur.

So they were carrying chairs out, but because it was windy they carried them back to the nearest room behind the verandah, where Aunt had something like an office, though unfurnished. She received people on business there, in particular the Mother Superior of the Felician sisters, brought and settled here years ago. They had founded a lace-making school here, and Aunt still entrusted the Mother Superior with running this group which was to contribute to keeping watch over the good behaviour of the local girls and in time create a national centre of professional schooling, which Lukasiewicz had dreamt of and fought for.

Two nuns led a herd of children to the front of the Chorkówka manor house and arranged them into a shapeless semicircle, the older girls behind the younger ones. One of the nuns ordered them to be silent by raising her hand and then, lifting up the front of her habit, she stepped onto the verandah and entered the room. Aunt gave the nun her hand graciously. Mother Superior pushed forward the small cross on the rosary hanging on her belt, then she entwined her fingers and sat down on the edge of a high-backed chair. Under her cornet was a pale face, faded, with a tense smile with which she tried to satisfy her guest. The forced humility in the nun's whole appearance, the false courtesy of this severe and cold woman before the expansive, smiling landowner made a dramatic, even theatrical, impact.

"We are privileged and overjoyed to greet our lady of the manor and patron, and present to her our group, unfortunately not very numerous this year."

"The worthy sisters' group is always the subject of our care and attention," replied Aunt. That word 'our' must have meant both her and Uncle, although it sounded like the royal 'We'. "And Mr Tysik always informs us about all the group's needs."

"Not all of them, definitely not all of them," interrupted the Mother Superior, removing two fingers from her clasped hands. "We are not sure if Mr Tysik has not neglected some of our requests, particularly concerning plastering the north wall of our establishment. The rain is coming in, and rot is rising from the floor."

"Well, that is Mr Tysik's business, he is responsible for all works concerning the establishment. The wall is wet, you say, Mother Superior? Aha, that will have to be seen to before autumn; of course it must be seen to."

"Damp is very harmful to the materials, particularly to silk," added Mother Superior quickly, clutching the best argument. "It's not far to autumn now."

After which, changing her tone to a more official one and rising from her place, she said, "The children would like to greet our lady of the manor and patron, with her permission." She turned towards the entrance and clapped her hands.

The ceremony of the correct greeting ensued. Another nun entered the room, young and lively, and behind her several girls of various ages, the youngest might be about nine, the eldest not more than sixteen. They arranged themselves fairly sluggishly, giving an air of awkward shyness; the young nun gave a sign, and they started a song. Then I quietly went out into the next room.

Kostek had taken himself off somewhere, so there was no one close by who could understand, with just a glance. Namely this: that it was 1938, but here everything was taking place in an almost feudal way, which had a comic whiff but also something more. Time seemed never to have moved here. As if I were inside a bracket, a huge bracket, pushed inside by antiquity, not knowing how to be equal to my tasks nor perhaps to anything at all, mute witness of matters outworn but still living in the present day, here and now, this one and no other. Here and now, but surely this was not the whole reality of the country, surely it was different too, different, different. Better was on its way...

My contemporaries in the Lwów 'Renaissance' student movement laboured in the villages during their university vacations, organising gardening and, above all, cooking courses, because apparently most Polish peasants had no idea about cooking. What these students described on their return gave a truer picture of the poor countryside of Poland, not the well-husbanded parts, but the land on the eastern edge of the Republic, rich in natural wealth and in almost supernatural stupidity. I came across something completely different in my own social work, no stupidity whatsoever, but my territory was not the countryside, only the suburban proletariat. I had spent the previous vacation helping the leader of children's summer camps in Borki Dominikanskie near Lwów, and the experience sunk into me as the basis for my attitude to social and moral education, and also to what was known as political awareness. Never afterwards would I be capable of loving my neighbour, only of helping. 'Other people's misfortune disturbs our own happiness, so we must combat it!' Both the evil we knew and the one we did not know personally but sensed from the time when our contemporaries were completely taken in by Chrobry's dagger.* It's good that they wore this badge; at least you could make no mistake about the identity of your opponent.

Chorkówka, where Lukasiewicz died, was a land flowing with oil. It surfaced in the form of a command to live, work and achieve success. The Chorkówka refinery was established in 1864 and brought relief during the depths of our historic disaster. The kerosene, produced in ever improved and enlarged refineries, found buyers in Berlin, Prague, and Vienna and then in France and Italy. It created a new type of local inhabitant. Foreign guests were brought here to visit the Paraffin Industry Museum and what was probably the largest collection of kerosene lamps in the world and from all countries of the world. After the war I wrote about Chorkówka in *Wiadomosci*, but I had left Chlebna in the shadow, a remote spot untouched by the word in the same way as one leaves a family souvenir undisturbed.

Chlebna really was a family souvenir. It was in Chlebna that the Glewskis were buried, a family that had died out but had been related to us on the distaff side. In the cemetery there I learnt various romantic details about them from Alfred Wysocki with whom we had gone for a ride in the neighbourhood. The Glewski grave was already sinking so deep into the ground that the top of

* Chrobry's dagger was a badge worn by members of the rightwing National Democratic Movement. King Boleslaw I the Brave (Chrobry) turned Poland into a powerful and internationally significant kingdom during a period of expansionism in the eleventh century.

the letters carved on the front wall was barely visible. We always said that we should arrange for the local stonemason to carry out a thorough overhaul, but this constituted a delicate problem on account of Aunt's attitude, as she disapproved of old family disputes from previous generations being revived in any way.

But someone placed candles there, probably on All Souls', as evidenced by the shoddy and rusted tin candlestick driven firmly into the ground. A hawthorn and a birch straggled wide and shapeless over the top of the grave, and they always made me think of the words from *Pan Tadeusz*, 'like a peasant weeping for her son'. The ground descended lower behind and beside the grave, and flat among the undergrowth loomed the traces of old graves, marked here and there with an iron or wooden cross.

The wooden ones were usually covered with a small narrow canopy, long ago cut into zigzags like lace, and these were the places where the Greek Orthodox were buried, although there were not many of them in the neighbourhood. One grave attracted my attention, all encircled as if by an extremely long rosary, transected every tenth bead - which was formed of cob nuts - with a red spot of shrunken hawthorn and finished with a knot made of string. A small piece of board had been tied to the knot and to that again an irregular strip of brown card which I examined close up. There was a sentence, scribbled very clumsily, half-blurred by damp, and I was able to make out only the first words, 'Jesus only Mercy', after which the rest, very short, formed a purplish-blue damp patch. I was cross with myself for having intruded on something so intimate. I placed the board with the card, writing side down, on a twig. For safety's sake, and to disguise my indiscretion.

Dusk was falling. We were returning from the cemetery in Chlebna almost by night. One of those Polish country evenings where everything seemed just right and just as it should be, where you felt good in the world because the world belonged to you, and all important questions remained suspended in a distant, invisible net. The angel of justice would transfer his sword from one hand to the other, and whatever needed to change would be changed... but this would take place tomorrow or the day after, or after the vacation.

In the meantime the house servants were smiling good-naturedly, perhaps even sincerely, for Aunt took good care of them. Besides, tasty titbits of news could be carried out of the dining room to be discussed later in the servants' quarters and the kitchen, moving down the hierarchy of those who 'had heard it with their own ears' to those who heard it only second-hand.

'This business' with Mrs Grzesik was one of the subjects at dinner that evening. People smiled, but a certain embarrassment was also perceptible among the gathering. The Country Housewives' Circle intended to organise this year's harvest festival in its own group and was said to be sending a delegation to the manor within the next few days with an invitation. Until now the harvest festival had been organised as always: in front of the entrance to the manor with all the usual ceremony of carrying wreaths and sheaths of corn, handing the traditional harvest festival round loaf to the lord of the manor, colours and ribbons playing in the wind, with the historical context of the occasion much in evidence, followed by dancing and a party on the lawn which on this day deserved to be described as green sward.

The manor certainly rose to the occasion. There was no shortage of beer, meat or cakes; attractive towns-women as well as house guests frolicked on the arms of the peasants. Folk dances ensued, it was colourful and merry, there were songs, musicians sat on chairs arranged at the foot of the 'chocolate box', the name given to the round and bulging part of the lower terrace, with Aunt on her armchair brought beyond the steps and Uncle circulating among the peasantry, the sun in the sky and then a white moon, and always someone holding a camera, that black spot fixing the present moment for eternity.

The eternity of this order seemed normal. Nothing threatened it in spite of Mr Poniatowski, Minister of Agriculture at the time, whom Aunt spoke about as if he were a sinister spectre of unfortunate future Poland. She felt personally threatened by the new agricultural reform which Juliusz Poniatowski had already introduced and demonstrated on his own estates. He now wanted to break up the big estates throughout Poland. This terrifying novelty was already approaching with the talk of a harvest festival, not at the manor, but at that Housewives' Circle of theirs. If it really comes to that, with a delegation being sent, then...

Exactly. Then what?

To her it seemed the second bad sign in a succession of unknown and dangerous changes which were not to be taken lightly. The first one in particular seemed cruelly unexpected. Or rather, its occurrence sank in a bit more each day, with an increasingly venomous effect. An affront. Public. Perhaps deliberate? An intrigue?

This affront was the omission of a visit to the Siedlicze manor by the newly appointed District Officer of Krosno. The man had been in his post for three weeks, had settled in and assumed the management of the chancellery and his accommodation, was already receiving people on business, had been to look at the plans for a statue in honour of the oil drillers, and attended the opening of an exhibition of folk industry; in a word, he was active and performing his duties fittingly. But still he failed to pay the traditional call on the owners of Siedlicze, unlike all his many predecessors.

One afternoon at tea, Aunt could no longer conceal her indignation and resentment, her fingers shaking from repressed irritation, as she at last complained out loud to her cousin, Alfred Wysocki, who had been in Siedlicze for a month. The fact that Wysocki was the Polish ambassador in Rome conferred additional plangency to her complaint.

"My dear," Wysocki was saying, calmly and as always very slowly, "you have to remember that Mr Kirchmayer is proceeding in accordance with new government orders and he cannot act differently. There's a new instruction for District Officers not to pay official visits to the landed gentry. In any event, not first and foremost, as used to be the case. My position changes nothing here. I'm staying with you privately on holiday and this does not create any obligation on our District Officer. It'd be different if he were organising an official reception. But after all he's not doing that, not now at any rate. The fact that I'm having a villa built for myself in Siedlicze shouldn't be any concern of his either."

Their long conversation uplifted Aunt's spirits, and from it I unexpectedly learnt something. When asked by Aunt which country could be regarded as the best organised, Wysocki replied, taking into his hand a porcelain figurine in order to read where it came from: "Lithuania, my dear. Lithuania."

He remains like that in my memory, his glasses pushed back from his forehead, the figurine in his hand, half turned towards the people behind him, three of them at that moment, from three different generations: Aunt, Pietrek the servant who was just entering the salon to announce a call 'to Mister Ambassador', and myself. No one had any inkling that within two years the Germans would be proposing to this same calm gentleman that he should enter a government created under the auspices of the Reich, nor that he would be nursing his very sick wife in difficult conditions in Warsaw. Nor that the Germans would be making themselves comfortable in the Siedlicze manor house, politely clicking their heels together in those very rooms and trawling in the neighbourhood for all traces of opposition, to be punished by summary execution. Nor that I would never see that part of the world or the Republic again.

Neither would Mrs Grzesik. But she got her own way, during that holiday at least.

21

She got her own way, but not as she had imagined. Aunt extricated herself in an extremely diplomatic fashion: she received the delegates, promised that the manor would participate in the ceremony, asked about the children, nodding her head with sympathy over how numerous these 'little ones' were, complained about the drought and the damage it was expected to do, demonstrating a real talent for talking about nothing.

In the evening of the same day she turned to me and said, "My child, it would be best if you represented our family at this 'harvest festival'." I could feel the inverted commas in her tone. "I also know that the District Officer is attending. Try to talk to him. You and Kostek will be very good at it. You should make sure that he is well aware of who you are, and you should mention something, so that he realises that former traditions have been overlooked."

I was game for this. I had fancied attending even without Aunt's suggestion, and I wanted to meet the District Officer about a completely different matter. I had in mind a design I had conceived for a cemetery gate for which I had received a prize at the Institute of Fine Arts in Lwów. Since the cemetery gate in Siedlicze as well as the ones in neighbouring villages were very old and needed replacement, I might have an opportunity to execute the design in these parts.

The design suited our neighbourhood best of all, as its fundamental motif represented flames. The flame of Prometheus suited the flames of oil wells. Prometheus had stolen fire from the gods on high; we, the local people, were extracting it from the earth. This light led no one astray, intended no destruction, and brought no dead souls to mind. Rather, it spoke about the concealed soul of matter transforming itself into gentle beauty like a halo. This halo would encircle the heads of all when they die and cross the cemetery threshold.

It was not an easy matter and I changed the design several times for fear that the flames might suggest hell fire. That is why they rose from the holy letters IHS which burn with love, and were also repeated in the motif of an oil lamp, symbol of wisdom and the providence of the pious. I do not know whether Lukasiewicz was a believer, but the oil lamp recalled and honoured his achievement.

I entered the Country Housewives' Circle harvest festival with a roll of paper in my hand (like the portrait of the stranger at Chorkówka), and Kunegunda Grzesik bustled about us, Kostek and me. With flushed cheeks and in regional costume, she greeted us warmly, knowing as well as Aunt how to conceal her true feelings, the disappointment that the manor had sent only its summer visitors. But no other young people had ever been here; Aunt and Uncle had no children. She did us the honours of the house, regretting that we had arrived after the District Officer's opening address and, "as you can hear, they've started on the folk dances, they're already stomping an *oberek*." They really were dancing. I was angry at Kostek for being late; I had wanted to hear the District Officer's speech.

Meanwhile there was chatter around us among the group, which still had the character of a small gathering. Perhaps because this was the first time and it would look better in future years. For the time being a pale yellow, almost white floor made of fresh boards glowed on the green grass, and on it the dancers were trying to cut a caper. But the caper was neither spontaneous nor suitably rehearsed and the dancing couples looked awkward. They were dancing with muffled spirits, maybe it was still too early for the full blooming of the occasion. It always starts sluggishly and only later does the soul let rip.

Everything was well organised. The orchestra sat by the wall of the manor house, somewhat over-pink for our landscape. The slightly projecting roof created some shade, and a long table had been set up on the other side of the door. On it three separate piles of plates, next to them a detachment of glasses turned upside down, beside the beer barrel a beautiful girl handing out glasses swelling with white foam, her smiling face a symbol of the harvest festival. I took my camera from round my neck. Immortalise her, hold her, nothing should ever detach her from the view beyond, flat and faint, neither fields nor courtyards. But far behind floated the line of the horizon transecting everything, a clump of trees and a fragment of a wooden house that people were continually coming out of, slowly and sedately. The slightly backward sway of her body and the way she carried her head brought to mind Renoir's waitress, who has beer glasses too.

This association summoned up others and experience was sieved through this foreign reference as if we really were infected by culture and could see nothing in a straightforward way. But there were people all around us, local and therefore homely, and very full of themselves, coming and going, arriving and passing, with a slow festive step, chatting among themselves, observing the new ritual which was taking place before their very eyes in the village for the first time and would be the subject of all sorts of gossip for a long time. They should have been grateful to Mrs Grzesik for that reason alone.

I was cutting off these heads, these faces in one instant of photographic fire, old people in hats lowered flat with a wide smile on their thin lips, a smile neither of pleasure nor of derision, full of a peasant's distance from what is happening, as if pleased that they were being relieved by the young. Young people were dancing, but not all of them; here and there they stood in small groups, or individually, with ribbons pinned to their lapels. The multitude of brightly painted wooden birds inserted into the lower branches of the nearest trees jarred and attracted attention. My camera was hunting. Fragments of earth, sky, trees, people and objects were flying across the view-finder in a motion shorter than a single second, in a twitch being thrown off balance from their established, ordinary existence. From time to time appeared from nowhere an uncanny revelation, something perversely disclosed, as if the world were taking the photographer as a witness that things can look different. At times my eye tore itself away from the lens involuntarily in order to make sure that everything was as it used to be, that it was only the lens deceiving me, after which the quiet photographic click gave reality a fillip and 'meted out justice to the visible world'.

At that exact moment I saw a dark spot suddenly disclosed by the movement of someone's back, the eye of the camera jumped left and across, was darkened by a branch fastened to the window latch, then it flew in an arch across the whole wide and swirling world. I lost myself again. All of a sudden and for no known reason, taking photographs seemed a barrier separating me from life. As if the part, the extract, the fragment, were laughing at the whole, above all at me, and mimicking me. Why? Perhaps reality segmented and dwarfed in the frame of the lens to miniature proportions was taking revenge for this very act of immobilisation. Time after time a picture severed by the instant of blackness seemed untrue, shielding something, hooded and unfriendly, and forced me to retreat, to look for a new point of view.

In this retreating and defining of a new position lurked an insidious game of hide and seek, duck and dodge, sudden revelations and revolutions, the sky was falling to the ground, the ground was seizing it, someone's ear was growing out of the ground, no, of course it's not an ear but a trampled crustacean, and this pink flame is paper torn from a garland, and down again, up, front, side, across, the sudden intrusion of another dimension, can we really have only three? Impossible. Discover the new one, the fourth and the fifth, and the tenth. Constant temptation, constant thirst for something which is beyond all this, beyond us, or between us and the nature of things. And what is the nature of things anyway?

I heard singing: 'Geese over water, ducks over water. Run away, lass, or they'll butt you'. Yes, yes. That was exactly what overcame me incomprehensibly and powerfully: the desire to escape. From what and why and where to? Where is there any escape to if you suspect reality, so-called reality, of being a false bottom, a game, disloyalty established once and for all like an unknown dogma. Taking photographs causes a lightning resistance against the visible state of things which does not want to be a state of things, but an explosion, a splash of unsettled matter or its denial, and revenge for the habit of daily commonplaceness was now reaching my most sensitive cell, my sight. It was my sight that had to pay the price for our tranquil existence in this daily ordinariness which did not scare us; we were it, with it, in it. Yet the eye discovered a hermaphroditism, hidden everywhere and by all manner of means. A change of distance, a millimetre of deflection imposed a veritable spinning galaxy in whose interior I lay alone, now abandoned, now attracted by the Thing or its Designation, Form or Appearance.

In this treacherous and flickering campaign was it best for me to defend myself or allow myself to be overpowered and consumed? 'Geese over water, ducks over water'. Disbelief, eternal disbelief, frequently affecting me for no reason at all. Disbelief. But what's the use? I disbelieve, but I still exist and feel. Except I do not think the same way as before any longer. I will defend and secure myself. The eye of the lens casts its lasso on the landscape, people and objects, trammels them, tramples the living and the dead and treats them in its own way, in a scholarly way, and the skill will fuse with a vehement repulsion of delusions, unhealthy whims and transformations. I will detain them, apprehend them, possess as much of heaven and earth as I need. No more, no less. I will arrange and pierce them. Aim, fire. The quiet release of the camera and suddenly, like a prize for restored confidence in my ordinary senses, I came across an unexpected figure in the glass of the view-finder. Oh yes. I know. It's definitely him, only his name has slipped my mind.

I had never seen him before. I knew that in the village lived a former inmate of the Holy Cross prison who had returned after serving his sentence. He had returned, to the general dissatisfaction of the inhabitants, his former neighbours or acquaintances. Perhaps he had once had relatives or friends here. He must have committed a grave crime, for the prison on Holy Cross Mountain had the evil reputation of being exceptionally severe. He had received a fifteen-year sentence. A long time. How old could he have been when he was locked into his cell? Twenty something?

Now I saw a silhouette sitting slightly behind the musicians' platform, immobile, somewhat hidden by a bush, with hunched shoulders and his hands hanging down as if made of wood. A narrow ribbon of cigarette smoke seeped from the depths of his palm. So he was not a cripple. Half his body gleamed in a terrifyingly white shirt. He had thrown his jacket over his shoulder and the sleeve dropped forwards, a third arm, as it were. His hair was not grey.

I watched him through my small, elegant opera glasses inlaid with mother-of-pearl. That this precious object was directed at him of all men was again loaded, I felt it well, with a whole mass of associations, complexes, and perhaps even allergies. But this time I did not give in to them, I held on tight, my eyes next to the mother-of-pearl. The man in the deathly white shirt had not changed his position. He was sitting on something low, holding his head stiffly, not turning it like the others to investigate what there was to see. Whether he was looking in front of him, I was unable to tell.

A woman ran up to him quickly from behind, flung the jacket round him and then straightened it, with an impatient and unkind movement. She probably felt that he was too conspicuous, that he was attracting people's eyes with the whiteness, that he had sat himself down too close. Perhaps he interpreted it like that as well because after a moment he got up and slowly walked a few steps away, sat down on some beams lying on the ground, pressed his knees closely together and parted his feet. Cut in half by this position, almost as if he were squatting, he now looked like a square block on which a human head had been placed. Immobile like before. Now! Aim, fire! I took his photograph, almost a portrait, the background surrounding him was empty apart from the gashes of the beams. At least that's what it seemed like to me.

Things always come out different in the darkroom from how they are seen in broad daylight. The black rectangle of the negative severed the chosen fragment evenly and detached it with all the cruelty of finality, from here to there. But why did it seem cruel, since that was exactly what I wanted, all incompleteness making me bristle with fear? Was it only the exaggerated number of subjects that seemed cruel? A harvest festival is a difficult subject, excessive choice, a dispersal of shapes. I had only twice felt that it would come out well, yet as the hunting proceeded, the quiet rattle of the camera was repeated again and again. I was assailing the world with the sheer quantity of photographs, like Saint Dominic with his sword, saying 'the Lord will recognise his own'.

Sometimes people arranged themselves of their own accord, with the natural stiffness of posing, knowing spontaneously that the larger should not hide the smaller and should not put their feet in front of them. They formed an instant group, they wanted to be shown, and then they thanked me, they raised their glasses to me and I did the same to them. They were bathed in the heat and the smell of sweat, I was too, the day was hot, shirts were already becoming soaked with smudges of sweat, dresses and skirts stuck to bodies, the sweat was streaming down the faces and necks of the musicians. They changed over with a group which stood on two school desks knocked together and scattered with millet and spruce branches, and these new people managed to be original, they all had their sleeves rolled up to their elbows and so it looked as if they had introduced additional instruments. They were not as colourful as the others, they all wore dark trousers and pale green shirts, a wide ribbon was waving from the double bass and someone's dark hand took hold of it and then a row of women holding hands appeared in front of them. Generally oldish or middle-aged. They separated into two sides, as three men joined them at the edge of the rows. It was clear that they formed a choir. Yet before any song rang out, a wreath the size of a cartwheel was brought out and placed in front of the singers on an ornately painted wheelbarrow.

In the foreground straight ahead something colourful and lazily mobile lay on the ground, and it was not without astonishment that I realised it was a peacock. Enclosed in a wide area of wire netting, it was making a few distinguished but unwilling steps. It must have been angry at being forcibly enclosed. It was winding its neck in all directions like a snake, and every so often its sharp and strangely unpleasant cry reached us through the music. Crest of feathers on a small head. It was pecking into space, and seemed to cast an eye at the people gathered round, an eye which for a moment stared into mine. The quiet whirr of the camera and its cry again. Was it a cry of anger or a mating cry? There was something wicked in this idea of enclosing a peacock with net. It jarred. Accidental? Intentional? Symbolic?

The only peacocks in the village were in the presbytery; none of the peasants kept them in their yards. The bird did not display its tail, only dragged it along the ground in a long train, stopping every now and then as if to spite the spectators. It did not pretend to be looking for anything on the ground with its beak, but was unable to prevent its neck from being iridescent blue mixed with copper, a wonderful zigzag which assured attention. At a certain moment it might have wanted to fly above the netting, it measured the height with its eyes, the ends of its tail feathers fluttered nervously, or rather swept the ground, after which the bird turned round to the opposite direction, took another few steps and stopped.

The still searching eye of the camera now slithered over the front rows; necks, backs, heads again flew past as in a frieze by Picasso, strange shapes, notched, buxom, jagged, mocking, crowd upon crowd, crush upon crush, until suddenly among the throng of heads a blank appeared in my view-finder, and there were the honoured guests. The District Officer of Krosno and his wife. They sat strangely stiff in the front row of the chairs arranged for notables, both dressed in black, and this detail surprised me. Mrs Kirchmayer was, as I had heard, in mourning, but he? Did he share his wife's mourning to such an extent, or was this the attire, in his opinion, appropriate to the dignity of an official representative of the state? Together they formed a very large stain in the colourful crowd. They were reflected from the background, creating a peculiar subsidence in it. I waited for a moment's break in the music, made my way towards them, introduced myself and entered into a semi-official and semi-sociable conversation, in accordance with Aunt's intentions, but moved by curiosity as well.

Mrs Kirchmayer rose from her seat with difficulty in her very advanced stage of pregnancy, attempted a conventional smile from which her face assumed even greater pallor, and she emanated an almost infectious sadness, unsuitable for the occasion. Perhaps only the older women felt solidarity with the mother-to-be. Some of them tried to make her more comfortable with a large cushion which she received with embarrassment and the false commonplace that she felt very well.

The District Officer turned out to be a grave and reticent man, but conversation with him seemed to pass beside every subject, while for me it was awkward to talk about cemetery gates at a harvest festival, so I postponed the matter until another time. There would be time for that; the flame of Prometheus could wait. I did not know how closely were lurking other flames not in the least mythological which would destroy this whole world.

Meanwhile Mrs Grzesik was already experiencing her own private disaster. I sought her out among the singing, the choir, the dancing, the general movement, in the very midst of the festivities, in order to say goodbye. I came across her in the hall of the pink house, and her eyes were fiery with tears which she was now openly drying with a handkerchief as huge as a tablecloth, muffling a sob with all her strength. "Mrs Grzesik, for the love of God, what has happened?" I asked, startled, and my choice of words could not have been worse. Mrs Grzesik seemed to go up in flames for good and all.

"'For the love of God' you say, miss. That's just it! It's all precisely for lack of love, for people I mean, for honest folk, you know everyone here, what've they done wrong? That jailbird doesn't count, it's nothing to do with him, he's been back in the village again for years. It's not him that counts. It wasn't him the priest was talking about from the pulpit, but about us, about our House-wives' Circle, saying we're some socialists or other, ungodly, that some of us don't come to church every Sunday and that we probably won't be bringing the children to be christened. He didn't exactly say it like that but he did give everyone something to think about. What is it, we're some anti-Christs are we, for him to abuse us like that?

"'Some people have gone mad,' that's what he said, and everyone understood very well that the Reverend Father was preaching against us from the pulpit. That we'd founded our Circle on our own, without the permission of our good master. And that's why this harvest festival's so unsuccessful, because some folk are looking and looking to see what sort of creatures we are, as if we didn't come from here, but from God knows where."

"Aren't you mistaken, Mrs Grzesik? After all, Father

Krzyb is the very soul of kindness."

"Oh yes, him and his kindness! He considers it kind-hearted and his spiritual duty for nothing to take place without him, and anyway you don't know everything yet, miss, because they won't have said at the manor."

But what 'they won't have said at the manor' I was unable to discover. Deep sobs, no longer restrained, flowed and tumbled out of this woman, and she flapped her hand a few times to signify there was nothing left to say.

"And by the way," I added, "a peacock like that, it might seem as if it was deliberate malice against the parish priest."

"A peacock you say, miss? It was only at the very end, when he'd shouted at our delegation, because we sent a delegation to the priest after that sermon of his, it was only then that Wojtek Koszutski borrowed a peacock from Mr Przyluski who fancied the idea. And Mr Przyluski wanted to add a peahen but because she was sitting, he couldn't do it. But I think he only said she was, because where do you ever get chicks hatching out at this time of year? Anyway, this harvest festival of ours hasn't turned out right the first time, so it won't be successful next year either."

"You're mistaken, nowhere is it written that it won't be successful. On the contrary, I'd say. You'll see, Mrs Grzesik, that it can be completely different."

It was different. It was the last harvest festival in pre-war Poland. That was probably also the last time before the war that I saw Kostek. He was with a brunette, stamping loudly, having a good time, his hand lifted in the air, exactly as in Stryjenska's depiction. Clearly he was going to have a good night. I envied him.

"I envied you then, you know," I told him after so many years, in London.

Because it was a night not to be alone, like mid-summer's eve. It lay in the nature of things to experience love on a night like this. A few of the young house guests generally disappeared after supper and young girls, if they happened to be on their own, did not have a pleasant evening. On a night like this, older people were overcome by melancholy and bitter memories, and did not care for the cakes or wine. But all this was never talked about.

From the terrace came the voices of flirting youth. The whole world lay at our feet. Whatever might be said in the daytime, for whatever reason, the core always remained untouched and good - the charm of life on the manor. A charm unaffected by any argument; on the contrary, it was precisely what constituted an argument in itself. The pleasure of being here and now was thrilling to the marrow of one's bones. The gravel shimmered in front of the steps of the house, all iridescent with fires of quartz, the edges of pebbles. There was something glistening in the gravel, always changing, as if the eye were coming across hundreds of eyes, each knowing something, seeing something, benevolently or maliciously, who knows, as if it were different from mere broken stones on a road. And if so, then here it looked like an encrustation of something pretty laid close beside the greenery. Maybe that glitter was in gratitude for being so elegantly placed. So the gravel, too, was glad that it was here and now.

Gravel met lawn at an even, cultivated border. The grass, trimmed short, did not lean over its boundary and, dew-sprinkled and combed, it also seemed glad. The grass gave off a scent, that gift which gives ceaseless pleasure unawares, which people forget about in the city and immediately repent as soon as they arrive in the country and regain the benevolence of grass.

Lifting up my eyes from the lawn, I discovered the

graciousness of the ornamental shrubs. They were beautiful and varied. Under the night sky different ones edged forward from those that came to notice during the day. The hour of the agaves was approaching; they received little praise and were always overlooked by day in favour of the colourful islands of hydrangeas or smoke trees or even the 'hepi' of foreign origin. None of the guests knew its correct name; that was what the gardener called it. In the catalogue it said that it was a difficult and fussy shrub requiring much cultivation and good attention, and therefore only for the happy few, which was where its name came from. An ornamental shrub although it seemed modest to look at. Small flowers gathered into a cluster, like a cluster of grapes, pink and apricot. At night they huddled together as if sleep were sucking them in. It cast a huge mobile shadow, this shadow never slept, it swayed and mounted guard on the canvas of the lawn. Above it only the sky or sometimes the moon standing on tiptoe, rising here. It set above the gate, deeply hidden, the far gate not visible from the terrace. Right next to it was where the agaves grew. Like twisted forks or octopus legs. But their shadow was always the same, like a statue.

Then the rich deciduous trees. Few of the guests could distinguish a beech from an ash, an oak from a larch, though there were also landowners among the guests who talked least about such subjects. Conversations about the charm of parks, manors or agriculture would be unnecessary here. Nor about reform either, although there had previously been so many complaints. Parks, our eternal teachers, stood for history.

Ours became a teacher too, although thinned, changed, continually felled. In 'New Poland' the manor was turned into a school. Which trees and shrubs survived my mother did not write to me about. But I was interested in the wood and the people who had lived there. What could we do from here, how could we rescue them? Protest, just protest all our lives? Who can that be enough for? Make the world aware that lawlessness and a political mistake had taken place? Yes, but I did not believe in any immediate change in politics, and our fate depended on that alone. To work for mankind? Mankind, well then, ah...

22

As I was showing Kostek out of the front door at Harrington Gardens, I recognised a silhouette standing in front of the house a few steps away. It was Weissman. He stopped indecisively, as if embarrassed at unexpectedly meeting me. I decided to go up to him.

"Mr Weissman, I've got nothing to say to you about this affair. Your presence surprises me."

"I understand that it surprises you. I apologise to you. I hope you don't think that I'm doing it to spy on you or that I want to bother you. I'm well aware that you can't help. But you see, it's a strange thing, when I leave the house - I walk around town a lot - at a given moment something draws me regardless of my will towards your house. How shall I put it, I don't understand it very well myself, but it's as if the very fact that you were there at that time and in Bern itself, for me it's like a magnet, or a thread through the labyrinth."

"A thread," I interrupted him impatiently, "that leads nowhere, Mr Weissman. I've nothing to add to our previous conversation. Except that I lived in Bern whereas this terrible affair concerned, as far as I remember, Zurich."

"Zurich or not, Switzerland is so small and so dense in wartime. Matters like that aren't settled in one place alone. And the legation was located in Bern only, so if any documents were involved then it's obvious that it's precisely in the legation, or, more likely, in the consulate that they could have been..."

"Documents?" I replied in astonishment. "Forgive me, but to ascribe that terrible business which has nothing to do with the official representatives and institutions of Poland to anyone whatsoever of the people who worked there..."

Weissman was so intent that he grabbed my elbow.

"Definitely not, no, that's not what I wanted to say, it didn't even cross my mind. Except that it's like this with people, you want to be close even to the shadow of a shadow, even to someone who was in that place, I meant to say in that country, in all that turmoil."

He was sincere. He was close to tears. I was sorry for him and at the same time I loathed him. Him and Kostek, all the people who detained me with things that had passed, one of them with former joys back home, the other with recent atrocities.

"I'll kill you."

A terrible thing happened. I said these words in a quiet, distinct, cutting whisper and Weissman could not fail to hear them. Something irreversibly terrible flowed over me and over the surface of my skin and hardened into dismay. How could I extricate myself, how could I save myself, what could I say to save myself as well as others whom I had ruined together with myself once and for all in this man's eyes, making him the witness of a nightmarish untruth. For he could interpret it in one and only one way.

He was silent. He was still holding me by the elbow and was looking at me, with an awful silence.

"You can't understand. What I said. I know what you

think, but it's not that. No."

Another moment of silence which seemed to me like a mute but terrifying verdict. I do not know how long this moment lasted. Until at last from this muteness the man's words started to reach me. I did not grasp them immediately; I heard only a soothing sound, transfixing me.

"I don't understand, you say. Why should I understand one thing but not understand the other? I'm well aware that nearly all our young people, mainly the ones at the universities, they were in favour of exactly the sort of change which has come about, they said, 'revolution, reconstruction, revolution, reconstruction', they said it quietly, and loudly too, they did time when they fell foul of the authorities, but I understand that as well. You think that they weren't well-intentioned? They were. And when such an exceptional political situation came their way, you can't be surprised that they seized the chance they'd dreamt about. Sure, every Jew is a theoretician at birth, because if not, then how could we have survived these two thousand years? You'll say that a wise person can see how theory turns into practice and what the result is. The result is the opposite, sometimes exactly just the opposite. But the Poles themselves thought the same way in olden times and things really turned out different from what they'd imagined. I know them very well, these people of ours who rule Poland now. And I regret that they're so determined to do what they think is right and also - let's be frank - to take revenge, although that's not the most important thing for them. You don't believe it, do you? I might not believe it either if I hadn't seen from close up how the one and the other were linked in their minds and what they thought and why. But as for me, do you think that every Jew believed in this system, really wanted communism? *Bih-me!* Not every one, not every one. And I'll also tell you that..."

He was really going on. A long exposition and I wished it would last as long as possible. The relief of a revoked threat was flowing over me, an averted moral catastrophe. The relief of a misunderstanding not put into practice. I relished Weissman's words. So he did not treat my awful sentence as anti-Semitic. It was not that that he suspected me of. He took it to be my reaction to the political power which his fellow Jews, or rather his cosmopolitan co-religionists, had taken such delight in when they had wanted to impose their ideal picture of the new reality on the whole nation. It was this that Weissman was talking about, it was this.

It also dawned on me that maybe he knew something else about me, maybe the Baums had told him. He could have heard about me in Switzerland; I believe he was well informed about Polish circles. Various contacts and assistance for families in Poland were dealt with by factotums in the consulate who had, as they said, 'ways and means everywhere' and knew how to give good advice in situations very difficult for their own kind, since for the duration of the war they had lost the right to change their surnames. Or perhaps this Weissman knew Stempowski, perhaps he had sought advice from him in this terrible investigation. Perhaps. After all I did not ask Weissman about his Swiss connections and acquaintances, although perhaps I should have done. Besides, he must have come from around Lwów or nearabouts, what with that *bih-me* of his. Where had I ever heard that outside of Lwów?

Gradually everything was returning to a state of correctness. I peeped out of the snare and listened to Weissman who, it was his turn now, thought that he had reached the heart of the matter and that I had had this political subject in mind when I had said 'I'll kill you' through my clenched teeth. Because he became loquacious good and well, good for me and for him. It must have been a burning question and fundamental problem for him. Another suspicion - perhaps he was afraid that the Poles, now harbouring a different sort of prejudice against the Jews, would not want to help him, and so he had to assure them that he himself, Weissman, and others were opposed to the Communists and were engaged in the conservative political activities of émigrés.

Of course he could not know that nobody had seen these idealistic Jewish Communists at close quarters better than I had, not students with theories, but the workers of Lódz and Bielsko who had escaped to Lwów from the Germans and there at last had taken a deep breath and, chests free, inhaled their beloved idea to the very depths of their lungs. Poor and dirty but morally as clean as a new pin. They also occupied a fair bit of room in my book, conceived in the boat on the Thames. They formed the backcloth and the revolving stage of their own later tragedy. No, Weissman could not know that.

So Weissman could be in the jaws of distrust, having various doubts in the Poles' goodwill. He could be, but he could just as well be voicing his real convictions. It seemed to me that he was one of those Jews who were building capitalism from the foundations, from the very simplest grains of pepper bought and sold, and for whom trade was a real mission, the tool of their battle for existence but also a matter of intimacy among his own people, although they always considered themselves as of greater worth, more deeply initiated, the first people to speak with God, and no one could deny that.

I had known them so well from my earliest childhood because we had spent our holidays in a small provincial town in my grandmother's house with its huge garden and orchard. These Jews were an eternal element and part of the landscape of all small towns and even smaller suburban wastelands. They had always and would always speak Polish badly; any thought of assimilation would be outrageous to them. They were particular people and concentric like fruit stones, enclosed in their own lives as in a stronghold. These strongholds were generally very shoddy, often simply miserable, houses made of wood or half-timbered, covered with roofing felt or corrugated iron, rarely with tiles. Not necessarily in the suburbs either. Houses like that grew almost immediately beyond the last chestnut in our garden, right next to Domaslawski's carpentry shop, and as I often crossed that way I used to pass one of them. It was banal like its neighbours, but was adorned with 'Jude's barometer', the likes of which I have never seen before or since.

This barometer was a curio. Whether it was a well-known or typical article I did not know. Its pointer lay in a small board painted with oils in the design of a spreading tree, schematically, bough after bough, branch after branch. Each of these branches bore underneath it a white strip with an inscription, like a genealogical tree. Yet the inscriptions were in Hebrew and it cannot have been one family's tree but a chronological description of a historical tribe or subject. I did not find out about it at the time and now I will never know. Jude's barometer was considered to be unusually veracious, and my grandmother's servants referred to it, correctly reasoning that fair weather or foul did not lie within Jewish influences. Some days the barometer was not visible; when the windows were opened, the window frame covered it and then 'those there Gutwins' were to blame.

Some autumn or winter evenings, on the Sabbath, a lighted candlestick and the white covered table could be seen inside their window. It always reminded me of my favourite but extremely rare moments when the electricity went out in town because of a storm in the mountains. Then candles were lit in our house too, diffusing a brownish yellow snugness everywhere, secret intimacy, happiness itself. Walking round the room - it was out of the question to do anything - one could delight in the sudden loss of identity, being at one with the furniture and objects, as though of a different world. There was also unintended mimicry because from the kitchen, past the garden all naked in winter, one could see the Gutwins' distant, flickering window.

There were many windows with Sabbath candles like that in town, and of course I never gave it much thought; they were ordinary and ancient. Who asks the wayside trees where they come from and how long they have been there? Yet when the war annihilated them, the ghastliness of this destruction and the incredibility of evil cut off any and all reflections about those windows and candles. As if the feudal Old Testament and the egalitarian New had not existed at all.

23

These windows returned to me in London, not so much as memories of childhood, as an attempt to escape from an unbearable snare. The dead world must have known what the ways, secrets and ambushes of all emigrations are, and it stood like a post at a crossroads among walls and yards like these, on the point of collapse, in these stunted streets. There people knew how such strange turns of fate as resettlements, settlements and exiles of various types should be dealt with. Only now did I become aware that nearly all of those very poor people who had become one with the town for evermore had a relative or close friend who had settled abroad, trying for a better fate.

Letters with foreign stamps came quite frequently to

Gutwin, for example. Twice a year he made a present of them to lawyer Stein, a well-known philatelist, in exchange for legal advice. Once he gave a stamp from Assisi to our teacher of religion, through the good offices of our Marysia the Fifth, the washerwoman who also did the priest's washing. I often used to see Gutwin at the post office before the postmen set out on their rounds. It was said that he did it on purpose in order to appear important, because whatever business or important news could someone like Gutwin have, but 'the way he always comes out of the post office, you might think...' They were evil tongues, Jewish ones as well, in fact.

The news he was waiting for concerned no matters of business, and people held that against him as well, but he did not care. He was one of those pious Jews who prayed and communed with religion daily, and there were many like him in our town. They formed a separate caste, usually the poorest. The Polish provinces with their landscapes were well suited to slow and patient deliberations about the most fundamental questions. That was probably also the reason why, having settled here for centuries, they did not want to wander further. It was easier to put down roots of piety in this ground than in the large cities which they viewed with mistrust. In reality they considered themselves inhabitants of Israel although at that time a state of their own was only a dream. So, in the name of peaceful contemplation they knew how to endure poverty, which was often extreme and known only to those who had seen it; and they knew our Polish faults, some of which, paradoxically, might have been educational or even life-giving. They knew that for centuries they had been condemned to their own tolerance and that of others, because one has to live somewhere, and there will be people everywhere who feel at home. Perhaps that was also why they meditated in such detail, with such obsession and metaphysical tonality on what existence means and how it should be lived, while ploughing their own furrow, even the worst, always regarding it as miraculous.

Lawyer Stein openly said that he felt at home, but he was already one of the Polish intelligentsia. He did not go to synagogue, although he was not an atheist. Yet he was a severe critic of 'his Jews', as he used to say. He accused them of various faults and shortcomings and also declared that "Jews aren't able to be really wise because their intelligence prevents them." Whether he regarded old Gutwin as intelligent or as wise I will never know; both Gutwin and the lawyer are no longer of this world.

It was because of them that I heard a conversation about modern emigrations for the first time in my life. Stein was telling my father that old Gutwin lived in a daydream and that no arguments would do any good. "He believes that his son will come back after a few years and he'll have made enough for them to be able to start producing sweets here; they'll hire two people to carry on the business while he and his son will be able to devote themselves to reading the Old Testament and the books of the prophets. He doesn't want to believe me that you don't return from exile. That Joszek of his won't ever come back here, and even if he does come, it won't be for good. He also doesn't want to admit that it was him who encouraged his son to go away, and it's eating him up. He'd like me to give the young man a job in my office because then Joszek would throw everything up and return. But you know yourself how well lawyers are prospering in this town."

And Stein, slim and elegant, spread his hands in helpless regret. He was right, the town had thirty lawyers for only 15,000 inhabitants, and several were eminent ones, from the epoch of prosperous petroleum businesses which had already folded. So the old Gutwins were threatened by the shadow of defeat. Gutwin collected small packets from the post office, mainly books sent by his son, and immersed himself more and more deeply in his communion with the Holy Scripture. They must have lived on what their younger son earned; he was the local middleman, so his earnings were small and irregular.

'You don't return from exile.' These words reached me in London, from the world of the dead. It was only 1946, and our exile was only just starting. Perhaps the lawyer used to talk like that because of his animosity towards people who had torn themselves away to go into the world. Was it envy? Or wise experience which said that the hardest thing is to become eminent among your own people? He himself stood in both worlds, the Polish and the Jewish, like a dowser who knew how to find grounds of common good in relationships and avoid slippery and dangerous ones. But, it is true, the emigration of Jews who could find their own people almost everywhere was one thing, whereas ours in a place like England was another.

More memories: 'The Assyrian'. In a corner of my town, in an old house near the parish church and the road to the cemetery, there was a shop with papers and household goods. A narrow shop, long, dark, full of all sorts of articles. The owner was one of the wealthier traders. He was called 'the Assyrian' on account of the unusually thick, black curly beard and facial hair that enveloped almost the whole of his face. His hat rested on bushy eyebrows and from beneath them shone eyes that were almost without whites, immobile, inhumanly grave.

When we were children we were scared of him. In fact he was rarely to be seen. Two slim, neat daughters in red sheepskin coats and laced shoes bustled in the shop, both of them merry and not looking in the least like Assyrians. When I went to the shop once - it was far from our house but had the best selection in town of photographs of film actors - the owner came out to me in person from the depths of his accommodation. He silently leafed through in front of me the thick pages of an album of screen beauties, which became, in his hands and under his gaze, a more and more stupid and preposterous nothingness, a trifle not worthy of attention, a compromising fancy. I was ashamed that I was bothering so serious a person with such a frivolity, so I hurriedly chose one Laura La Planta with Raymond Keane and one Greta Garbo and left with a feeling of general dissatisfaction with myself and the whole world.

A few days later I learnt that the Assyrian had been lurking like that in his shop from morning until evening for a while now, though he had not done so before. And that the reason was a family drama. His eldest daughter, who was married and lived in Prague, had emigrated with her husband to New York, but it was said they had previously converted to the Protestant faith although the father had not been told. Perhaps he had heard rumours, perhaps he was only pretending that he did not know. It was enough that he had shut himself into himself. He took his other daughters out of the shop and, in order to seclude himself from the family, spent whole days behind the shop counter. The shop and the business did badly out of it. The Assyrian did not have the gift of attracting customers; being proud and dry, he actually drove them away. After a year he decided to pack his bags and emigrated in turn to...Rzeszów, and he never returned.

And I recalled him for the first time only in London after so many years, after my conversation with Weissman. People said that it was not so much his daughter's emigrating that broke her father as her change of faith. To forsake one's religion was in his eyes something even worse than disowning one's nation was in ours. For him it meant shattering the reason for existence and for the future. When it was said that Jews were Orthodox and from the old order, one forgot that theirs was the Order of Expectation. People who wait always have a deceptive superiority over everyone who lives in the past perfect, and so the Messianism of the Jews had furnished them with a sense of superiority and that eternal patience which irritated us so much - until we ourselves became once more the nation chosen for political negotiations and balances.

We were starting to wait for Poland once more, for a war between nations and for changes in the world. There would be a period of migration before returning to the lost land. Returning? Those lands now seemed almost sunken into geographical non-existence, a remnant neither of the world nor of time, and we once again a people of wanderers, welfare workers, supplicants and champions of lost causes. We were starting to assume both a superiority and an inferiority complex, to battle with requests without response, be subject to alien laws and customs and alien landscapes, but there was no Rzeszów that I could escape to from this.

A ready-made model of the long-suffering Pole was already waiting for us abroad, as before; in other words, everything was returning to normal. The Polish fate, most fated. We ourselves were becoming an old order, demanding justice and independence, that is, unimportant fancies. Not for us. Although some of us had already changed our names, were erasing our origin, migrating to the USA or elsewhere in a state of diluted individuality, like a 'new element'. Like the Assyrian's daughter from the corner shop.

That shopkeeper and his shop had already disappeared into the mythology which had quickly started to suck in and cover the whole Jewish nation, as if the reality of what had happened could not bear its own self. Myth is not born in the course of time, but at a flash of lightning. Myth squeezes its way in to sustain us, before the real truth is lost too suddenly or too terribly. Myth-making gauges were already reaching out for us, in exile, although we were witnesses of the epoch. So I had to remind myself quickly of the sights, words and history of people before they shaded into apotheosis or nothingness.

By London I had already forgotten exactly how many houses descended towards the river and at whose fence the willows started. They grew in a fairly crooked line along the old road, once a field path and later almost a street, approaching the first of the town's buildings. Willows, slender records of the Polish landscape. But in spring their withes were cut right down to the very trunk for making baskets, transforming the trees into likenesses of old people, hunchbacked, with large heads nestling on their shoulders, exactly like the Jews walking to synagogue on Sabbath evenings in their ceremonial clothes with fox-fur hats on their heads.

The synagogue stood at the bottom of town against the few buildings there. Above low roofs the willows stretched in a black line, larger and smaller. The sky behind them assumed all the colours of the dusk and almost always at this time the clouds, if there were any, thickened into longish smudges. The evening wrinkled and folded, and then pleated until it lengthened into night glimmering like velour.

Among the photographs my mother had sent me, there were also some of Jaslo ninety-seven per cent destroyed. German reprisal for the rescue of prisoners from the local jail and the Home Army's 'diversionary actions', particularly intense in this town and area. The majority of my schoolfriends were deported to Auschwitz then, and in the pages of the souvenir Centenary Book of King Stanislaw Leszczynski Grammar School there are many familiar faces, often of close friends, with shorn heads and in striped concentration camp garments. Ninety-seven per cent.

Of the three per cent that survived after a fashion, I recognised near our house the fragment of a wall where in past years I had become used to seeing little Bramek, a child with quite an unusually lovely and happy face. He was called Bramek; I do not know if it was a diminutive of Abraham or because the child was always running out in front of the gate, called a *brama*, of the inn rented by his grandparents. He would stand in front of it looking at God's world, pulling the springs of his side curls with his hands and chasing refractory hens into the yard full of wooden porches, steps and outbuildings. All the charms of miniature figurines were concentrated into this boy's small form. He looked like a living trinket, and even our servants were pleased to see him in our yard when he was bringing back our cat - said to be the strangler of their hens - which somehow usually happened on a Thursday, when it was our day for pancakes with rose-petal jam. Bramek's favourite delicacy.

He of course could not teach me how to adjust to my new life when I was already among a diaspora - a fatal word, diabolical. Little Bramek's only emigration was from the ovens to paradise.

But I remembered something else for the first time: little Bramek always knew how much eggs cost, how many hens strangled by our cat (although perhaps not by our cat) were missing, and the cost of this loss. And he was always right. It was me who was not. It is hard to believe in rightness which is not of this world. From where that child might be laughing at me. With a pancake and rose-petal jam.

24

Next day I saw completely different roses. Some English people - no doubt rich - wanted a frieze made of ceramic tiles which would form a counterpart to one built into their corridor wall between the dining room and the drawing room. It could not be ordered without my seeing the original. I found the house in far-off Ealing, near Mathilda Mews, and rang at the front gate at four o'clock.

I rang with pleasure. I liked the house. I liked these quiet, seemingly modest mansions, the decorated narrow door, the window with its gratings, and the short-haired lawn where grew just two bushes of what was for me an exotic plant, signifying the charm of a seat belonging to the happy few. A garage stood slightly back, adjoining the house; next to it climbed a rose, lofty and lordly although more of a wild rose, and above it, like a short fringe, thick shiny ivy hung down. Along the wall was a small wooden trellis, now bare, but carefully prepared for its springtime foliage. I could hear resonant barking somewhere, so suited to the decorum of this place, and someone tall and broad-shouldered came out from the house towards the gate, immediately giving a friendly greeting. When he had opened the gate, he shook my hand as if I were an old friend.

"Come in, please come in."

He introduced himself as Geoffrey Curtis, the man who had phoned our studio. He looked different from what I had imagined. His face was very suntanned, as with people who always live in the country, and he had flaxen hair and moustache. He must have been about forty, although the onset of stoutness made him seem older.

He immediately started doing the honours of the house. He had the tact not to ask where I came from, which my accent betrayed of course, and I liked replying to the usual, unavoidable question. But it was not asked. My host was very pleasant and rather amusing in his efforts that I should sit down in this armchair and not that one, "This one is more comfortable, and you're at the age when women don't avoid the window. Men generally avoid it, haven't you noticed? It's a legacy from the last century - the window is good for women doing embroidery, a gentleman shouldn't steal the light and should always be nearer the exit, shouldn't he? To defend the home fires and for personal freedom, isn't it?"

"For the personal freedom of the gentlemen the window also came in useful at times."

"You're right. Absolutely right," Curtis stopped in the middle of the room as if nailed there by this inspiration. "What would you like to celebrate your discovery with?" he asked and laughed. "The national drink, or perhaps you pay tribute to more continental traditions?"

I was faithful to the British national drink, and taking a glass of whisky from my host, I involuntarily glanced at the wall opposite where a large picture attracted my attention. Still making small-talk, I congratulated my host on such a beautifully composed interior.

"Really?" Curtis was pleased. "Of course everyone says so, but everyone who does gets close to me. You've no idea how much it cost me to acquire this house and then arrange it as you see it now. But I was ready to trample over corpses in order to get hold of this little nook."

"And as I can see, you've got a corpse as well. But I

admit I don't know that painting. It's not Cranach, is it?"

"No, it isn't and besides it's a copy, not the original. Excellent, though, isn't it?"

It was. In a very ornate frame hung a large reproduction of a painting depicting a young naked woman in the company of a decaying corpse standing next to her in a fairly aggressive pose. But in contrast to the horror of such company, the woman's face was filled with an expression of sated satisfaction or even deep, slightly restrained joy.

"Baldung's *Temptation of Eve*, Hans Baldung, also known as Grun, little known in England, an Alsatian painter of the fifteenth century. It's a painting only just discovered last year in London thanks to an expert named Clovis Whitfield, and it remains in the possession of Messrs Thos Agnew and Sons. A wonderful thing, probably the best of Baldung's works. He returned to this subject twice, at various times in his life. Do notice the mystic relationship between Eve, the Serpent and Death. Eve is holding the serpent which is holding Death which is holding Eve. Please do look at the expression of delight on Eve's face. It's almost provocative, don't you think?"

Yes, 'provocative' was probably the most appropriate word. I went up to the painting and contemplated Eve's smile, which was as enigmatic as the presentation of the subject. Eve was holding an apple in her hand, but moving her hand toward her back, while in her other hand she was holding a coil of the serpent which was appearing from behind a tree. A hideous corpse, its body decaying to shreds, was closing its veiny and already bony fingers onto the young woman's shoulder. Both these figures, girded along with the tree by the same coil of the reptile, stood in a macabre but fascinating harmony.

"Death's feet finish with a hoof. One doesn't often see that."

"Exactly," Curtis was pleased, as if that perception

gave him personal pleasure. "I was waiting to see if you'd notice it. The majority of my guests turn away from that figure with disgust instead of examining the details. That one is important. It leads some specialists to conclude that Baldung considered death in itself to be the devil or hell, an act of condemnation. That would be contrary to the spirit of the times. There's no help for it, it has to be read as a punishment for pride, one of the mortal sins. The pride of knowledge and recognition. And retained for herself, for in that movement Eve looks as if she's about to hide the apple quickly. Pride leads to sin which leads to death which leads to hell. But Eve shows no sign whatsoever of fear, only joy, probably joy at possessing the truth. One can either ascribe heroic cynicism to her here or, by contrast, boundless confidence in the grace of redemption, some day later."

"I wouldn't go so far. Perhaps she's simply pleased at her own youth and beauty. What's more important in life than that? She's not thinking about death, death is thinking about her, and the serpent is God's representative in the created order of things."

Suddenly I started chattering away. I told this unknown but interesting man about my former collection, about my childhood liking for a superstition of the Middle Ages - and of the Renaissance here and there - the serpent being depicted as having the head of a woman. It entertained and charmed, frightened and amused me. I used to cut out all likenesses or reproductions of old paintings, engravings, illuminations and pictures, holy and unholy, where the serpent entwining the tree appeared and spread into the torso of a woman, which sometimes, on very old and worn bas-reliefs, like the ones from St Bernard de Comminges in the south of France, looked like three bulges, the face and two spheres of breasts.

This collection started over the years to assume an increasingly precise nature, numbered and subscribed but without a commentary which I kept 'for later' if I were to elaborate the subject into a monograph. Yet all the same a biggish notebook, a common squared one, grew out of it. It perished, like everything else during the war. I knew that I would never return to this subject or to this collection. In the same way as I would not return to anything that used to be in that place once upon a time. Our Helcia was pleased that it had perished. She had considered the idea unsuitable, even wrong, not to mention sinful, and asked: "What does Janisia want it for? Whatever for? You'll be dreaming about it at night."

Wikcia had a completely different opinion. She was older than Helcia by a whole generation and had found her for us. Wikcia considered, in a way that was relentless and vehement at that, that this serpent-cum-original-sin-cum-woman was completely in keeping with the truth, that it expressed what was 'woman's spawn, the soul of harlotry and source of all evil in the world'. She had proof for it, 'from my own experience', and I knew very well what she had in mind: her brother.

I knew her Pietrek. I had once even been to his place, and I remembered where he lived and how. I had also known him before because he hired himself out for day labour in gardens in town or for chopping logs. Tall, thin, very dark, with traces of smallpox, like Wikcia, on his whole face and hands, silent and sullen, sullen for evermore. He had been through a great drama with a 'flighty hussy' from another town nearby, and it must have been a serious matter. He wanted or tried to kill her; it ended up in court. But he was not sentenced, the girl retracted the charge, although she ruined the lad's life and everybody knew it. He grew wild, cut himself off from his friends, lived in one room on his own and despite the long years that had passed, did not enter into a relationship with anyone.

All he did was go to work and return to his cottage. He

cooked for himself and did his own washing, if he did any washing. The room did not even have a kitchen, only an iron saucepan on an iron tripod in the corner and also a spirit stove, a few plates and evenly arranged hewn wood, one chair and bedding which should really be called a lair since it had the shape of neither a bed nor a sofa. A table, yes, he did have a smallish table and on it moreover a blue enamel jug with a twig of lilac. An interior for Cézanne, but I was not to know that then. It was not dirty there, only untidy, a colourless and shapeless jacket hung on a peg on the door. I think he never removed his hat, or rather his peasant's cap with a small peak - only once did I see how he shook the cap off his head in order to straighten it, and then unexpectedly fine and abundant hair shone for a moment, slightly wavy, a real adornment.

People were generally surprised by the fact that he did not drink, except when offered one by an employer, and then only in order not to refuse. Once someone was said to have joked about his solitude, saying: "He chops and chops, so he's probably gone and chopped something off himself accidentally. Or on purpose." And then Pietrek got up without a word, seized him by the collar, and squeezed him so hard that people had to tear the unfortunate joker out of his hands, fearing he would not escape alive. Pietrek did not say a single word, no swearing, no insults, no shriek of rage, and that was exactly what scared people. Since then Wikcia had conceived such a hatred for womankind in general that seeing it in the role of evil incarnate as a serpent's head suited her most of all.

I once accompanied my father to Pietrek's. My father had some papers for him and pretended to be just passing by, so he called in to deliver them 'as I had the chance'. I assumed that he did it so as to go to this man's place in person, stressing in this way that he did not consider him to be a reject or of minor importance, and I think Pietrek understood. But he did not have the courage or the desire to suggest that we sit down. My father commented, "It's warm here," and stretched his hands out to the fire, rubbing them as if he really was frozen, and Pietrek responded, "I bought the wood," in order to avoid the suspicion that it was taken away from someone. They started a conversation about the sorts of timber, that is, it was mainly my father who did the talking, but the host did respond a few times about this subject which was, after all, his specialty.

Pietrek came back to me, here and now, in this gentleman's extremely foreign house full of curious and rare objects. That room belonging to black-haired Pietrek stirred and poured into me. What was his name? I had forgotten his surname and I rooted in my memory for a while, sipping my whisky very slowly. That was it, Tabor. Like his sister. *Peter from the Height of Tabor*, it sounded like the title of a novel. 'From the Height' because suddenly, experiencing this memory in such different surroundings, I felt that I had the advantage over it. I had the advantage over reality, the present one, I was above it, I had the power of transferring myself to those other sights and people and the power of bringing them here where they would sit down around me, unseen - they are already doing so. Pietrek from the Height of Tabor and everyone close to him. And far, all of his and all of mine.

Yes, this was a victory. For the first time I felt the taste of victory in this exiled sub-existence. Therefore... I could do with Pietrek's axe to smite the serpent, the firm muscular flesh of its body which was seizing Eve and Death and was therefore superior. Was it, or had it simulated this superiority? It had conspired with Death, that was obvious, Death bore its mark, the goat's hoof, like the nobleman's right of citizenship, and therefore belonged to it, in other words *point de rêveries*.* It was rare to see Death in the company of an angel anywhere.

While looking at the tiled frieze, which was the purpose for my visit, I kept thinking that no sport can replace the one and only coil and recoil of chopping wood. I remembered Pietrek in our yard when he was chopping large logs into smaller ones for use in the kitchen, an excellent blow following a huge arc in the air, then a dry cracking, the pinkish white wound of the riven wood, its immaculately clean and fragrant interior.

In Curtis' house the thought of wood gave me the idea to paint individual ceramic squares with the leaves of various trees and winding serpent-like ribbons bearing their Latin names. My host-cum-client was very pleased; it really did form a counterpart to the frieze opposite, as if interpreting it in detail and conferring a scholarly botanical nomenclature. I suddenly realised that I did not remember the exact Latin name for beech. Was it *fagina silvastica*? Or *silvestra*? I would have to check. I asked for an encyclopaedia. "Because there's one name I want to check at once, I'll verify the others later in the studio at work, they can wait."

"Why are you in such a hurry with that one?" asked Curtis, reaching to the bookcase. Unexpectedly I told him the truth. "You won't believe it, but for some time now I've been renting a place on an old unused motor boat on the Thames, so that I can work on the water and not on land."

"Are you painting a river scene? Oils or water-colours? If I'd known you before, I'd have suggested you use my yacht. I've got a small one, not for the sake of economy by any means, only I don't like large yachts. There's something in their nature which in my opinion requires

---

* *Point de rêveries* alludes to the reply given to a Polish delegation in Warsaw in 1856 by Tsar Alexander II as a warning against exaggerated Polish political expectations.

small dimensions. A yacht is always a very young man, if you know what I mean." He said 'a very young man' but I thought only of a slip of a lad. Why? Was it the refreshing breath of the water?

"Yes, I know very well." I told him that it had no connection with a river scene in oils or water-colours. That I was writing certain things there that I did not want to write on land. On dry land.

Curtis thought about it. His nonchalant way of being a dandified gentleman, which suited him so well, suddenly left him. All of a sudden he became serious. "It never entered my head that one could write differently on water than on land. I didn't know about a difference like that. If it's not about a solely marine subject."

No, it had nothing to do with any marine subject. Only about not becoming anchored. "I didn't want to feel settled, you understand. Water is more..." Here I lacked the English for 'navigable'. I said: "The river is more everythrough," using a word that does not exist in English and Curtis gave a warm and friendly laugh.

He understood. I had explained the reason, however strange. After all, in reality London or the Thames, doesn't it all boil down to the same thing? But perhaps the English have a greater feeling for matters aqueous, or else this person was endowed with uncommon imagination. He understood.

25

Entering the house at Harrington Gardens, I found several people in the corridor speaking in the puzzled undertone of people in trouble. Two men got out of the elevator, one of them in policeman's uniform. Something had evidently happened and I found out what, without even asking, from Angus Dean, who was eager to tell me.

"Do you know what's happened?" he asked, pleased at imparting sensational news. "You must've known that Norwegian from the room next door. He's been found dead. He committed suicide. He shot himself. But it seems he wasn't Norwegian but German. He used Norwegian papers. The investigation probably won't be difficult or complicated, but you never know. They've just taken him out of the house. The police are talking to the tenants."

The young supposed Norwegian had taken the room that I had previously occupied on the first floor. He had the habit of leaving his door open or ajar, and when I passed I could not avoid seeing the young man lying on his bed. He always lay fully dressed, and holding a cigarette in two fingers bent far from the rest so that it looked as if his hand had two parts. A few times I saw him running down to the front door when the postman was due. Obviously he was waiting impatiently for some news, like nearly everyone else at the time. There was nothing strange in that, and I felt sorry for him every time there were no letters for him. He greeted me wordlessly with a stiff nod of the head; he had probably noticed, with envy, that letters arrived for me every day, sometimes in both posts, morning and evening.

So, this stranger whom I occasionally saw through the half-open door, usually with a book in his hand, had concealed his true identity. He might have been a deserter, which would no longer be relevant, or he might have entered England as a Norwegian after the end of the war for other reasons. As for me, I had lost the habit of being surprised at anything. But suddenly the person of this unknown young man (how old could he be? thirty, at most?) became important. So near to me, a few metres of corridor, two small steps and there was his door behind which a drama had been played out. The door was wide open now as well, and someone was just leaving, probably one of the policemen. He scurried down the stairs towards the other people. Impelled by a sudden reflex and not knowing the reason, I entered the room.

It was empty and fairly tidy. A large stack of books stood on the floor to the right of the gas fire, and others lay on a low table under the window. I was curious what the books were; they might help me learn something about the man. I was also curious what would happen to them. He must have intended them for someone, perhaps he had left a letter and instructions. On the pile of books on the floor right next to the gas fire (the house was full of them, it had been split into separate rooms for renting, but had once had real fireplaces), there lay a small and fairly thick notebook in a black cover. It was slightly open at a place where a corner of the page was dog-eared and was covered in small close-set writing. I did not hesitate for a moment, I took it there and then, left the room with it, and entered my own. No one would know that this notebook existed, in the event that it was looked for (but for what purpose?), I would always be able to leave it somewhere, there would be time to think about it. From the book spines I could read only two, lying on the very top, Rilke's poetry and a volume of Husserl. Most of the books were concealed by brown paper covers; obviously he was a reader who looked after his books. Or else he did not want the titles to be read at a glance.

Once in my room, I placed the notebook, which looked like memoirs or a literary notebook, behind my identical gas fire, although I was sure that they would not search the other tenants' rooms. Anyway, Angus Dean was my witness that I had been absent from the house at the time when the police were dealing with the deceased and his belongings. I did not associate him with the word 'neighbour'; that organic, earthy and social word did not suit the stranger. I thought of 'him next door', but that also contained the meaning 'right next door', as if it created an aggravating circumstance for me, the proximity of human affairs, unyielding and inaccessible.

At least there's no sun, I don't have to put dark glasses on. I find it increasingly hard to bear weather like that. I get the impression that it's laughing at me. Cloudy weather or grey light are nearer to me, almost vital. Götterdämmerung. *Besides, from the time of the first campaign I'm probably allergic to that sort of weather, although the* Hitlerwetter, *as the Poles called it, was propitious to us. Everything was propitious to us, and I laughed at Helmuth, who considered that such an easy start was a bad omen. He preferred obstacles, hand-to-hand fighting, he imagined these things like they were in the past, he really wasn't overjoyed at this mechanical war of ours. I'm thinking about him today because 'Helmuth's birthday' and his Bavarian address are written in my diary, so it would be his birthday if he was alive. How stupid to die at the very end of the war and in such a terrible way.*

He had an exceptional cult of beauty, he considered it the leading idea of Nazism. Different from the ancient Greeks. With them beauty was an abstract idea that they yearned for. The Greeks, as is known, were physically ugly, but they knew how to compensate for the ugliness in their art. I always admired them so much for it. Rilke understood. Our correctness in France was distance, none of your fraternité.

Thermopylae. I don't know who's already said it about the Nazis, that every battle in this war was like Thermopylae. Not for strategic or territorial reasons, but for the camaraderie. Humanity, unisexual and conscious of its impending destruction. In fact, from 1943 we all knew that we wouldn't manage to win the war, some had forecast it much earlier still. There were others too who, on the contrary, had the problem of 'what will we do with victory?', and I think I valued them most of all. But few people talked about it out loud, it was considered rather indecent. I still don't know for what reason I always felt that talk of die neue Ordnung in Europa seemed to be limp and didn't elicit real resonance. But I always liked the saying about Thermopylae, although our commanders didn't like it, after all some of the men among us were married, were even young fathers of small children, they took pleasure in the letters from home and the family.

We prized the war because of this exclusively male company and because it imposed a situation on us that was independent of ourselves. Weren't we most ourselves then, to be perfectly honest? Women hinder men from real fulfilment, war helps. Sport too. Elimination and sublimation. Although sometimes the order is reversed, sublimation comes first. To turn every birth's thoughtless adventure into sense, sense of the senses, give it the dignity of an absolute and sacred ritual. The first years in the Party at once elevated and enhanced us, but there's been nothing to expect for a long time now.

Perhaps in France I saw for the first time that the danger is in ourselves. The way of life there seemed to loosen our sense of cohesion and superiority, that's why we had special instructions and orders for France. But not everyone understood that our faultlessly polite behaviour in public places was a lesson and picture of die neue Ordnung in Europa. In general the French don't take care of their own history and it completely astonished Helmuth. He was right. Those wonderful eighteenth-century palaces in the Le Marais district, neglected and misshapen, contained the miserable work-

shops of small craftsmen, insignificant dirty factories
employing whole families, usually Jewish, establishments
producing buttons, tailors' requisites, hosiery and haber-
dashery. Also those disgusting thirdrate canteens and odd
works, inside which to my great astonishment one could
come across traces of old paintings, often remnants of
emblems or coats of arms, and even whole allegorical
figures. Helmuth was astonished at this lack of reverence
for former aristocratic seats, he was shocked that Paris
didn't respect tradition and disregarded centuries of
achievement. It destroyed historic and interesting buildings in the most unexpected way in order to erect
something new with great enthusiasm, as if burying
former beauty was no crime.

In Paris the famous continuity of French culture
looked like perpetual transience, a passion for the
fleeting and short-lived, and this passion has degenerated
into adoration of trivia and the dictatorship of fashion
and has thus raised the fragile and the ephemeral to
values of the first rank. They hypnotised the whole world
with this, and even during the war, they valued the
pleasure of the moment above all else, while truly great
matters seemed to happen behind their backs. Could they
dissemble to such an extent? The French give me the
impression of being a great nation through distraction.
Would it be proof of their inferiority or their superiority?
Are their famous light and quick minds a virtue, or, on
the contrary, a vice? Frivolous and vain, they possess a
resilient strength, a gift of perpetual regeneration which
Helmuth called a source of condensed energy different
from ours. They lost the war, they capitulated, but some
of us are wondering whether this capitulation wasn't a
kind of trap for the enemy. Personally I don't believe it.

I stopped reading at that point; it merely repeated
what I had heard elsewhere. I remembered the English

woman, Mrs Fryer, declaring loudly that there was one thing she wished for the English above all - to be occupied by the Germans for three weeks. "Then and only then will they understand the situation other people are in," but I did not react, and no one higher than me in the legation hierarchy reacted either. It was obvious that in England the Germans would behave completely differently than in Poland. England would never see the true face of the blond beast of Nazism, just as *la douce France* had disguised its nature and did not experience what we Poles suffered. But the Poles always exaggerate, *n'est-ce-pas*?

The French Resistance started late and how few of the French it attracted from the start. Fascinated by their failure to defend themselves, I privately asked some of them: "How did you imagine the future if it weren't for de Gaulle's military action? Didn't you foresee anything?" The young official in the French embassy with whom I could permit myself to be sincere replied with surprising but, for him, natural conviction: "We'd have devoured them. It would've taken a while, but they'd have been Frenchified, it always ends like that, doesn't it? We French, we're only really interested in civil war. If it hadn't been for the whiff of civil war, the Resistance wouldn't have succeeded. Only your own people can be really dangerous. And so they are." I remember his smile very well.

From time to time I returned to the notebook which contained many calculations of all sorts, loose words and sketches of heads. I read it haphazardly and was always accompanied by a feeling that here was a veritable war trophy, and also of course by embarrassment at my indiscretion. Apart from the sketches the slim notebook with many pages torn out contained some attempts at poetry, starting with *Diese unheilige, unstille Macht*, an awful travesty of the well-known German carol, a long commentary on the words of Yliaster, Yliastrum, components of the cosmos. It always brought to mind the inscrutable riddle of the duality of German nature: the fragility of our civilisation, and its unextinguished primitivism.

Weimar had turned its face of *Kunst und Wissenschaft*, art and science, towards me. I could not fail to remember, however, that Goethe was the author of the famous sentence 'I prefer order to justice', and that present-day Germans often quoted it. Yet Goethe was no patron of the present age; he was too distant and international.

Every Friday an old German, stout but hale and hearty and wearing thick glasses, called in at Borkman's printworks where I worked as a print designer after I left Poland for Germany. From his behaviour I could tell that he must be an important customer who was treated seriously. He always came in connection with his monograph on Goethe which he was continually correcting, revising, caressing, never insisting there was any hurry to print it. The foretaste of this little work must have given him more pleasure than its realisation. His tedious corrections displeased and wore the staff out. He was reputed to be an eminent expert on heraldry, but there was an imprecise unpleasantness about him despite his constant smile.

One day I discovered why Borkman disliked him so much. Having seen him to the door of the office, he exploded loudly, despite the presence of three people in the room: *"Aber so ein Schwein. Mein lieber Gott."* He was wiping his neck and forehead, sweating with rage, talking and throwing his hands about all the time: "To blackmail your own son like that, it's beyond belief. That young Heinz, maybe he was too cocky like all of them from the Hitler Youth and he didn't respect his father, and so the father, a cunning piece of work, he had his revenge. He gave him to understand, because he didn't say it straight out, that Heinz shouldn't be too sure of his own origin because his mother 'had an affair, who it was I know very well, that's my business, but it can't harm me any more while it could do you a lot of harm, a whole lot.' Naturally it hit the young man like a shot. His mother's been dead for a long time, so our Wende had a good hand to play. And the son looks just like his mother."

"But how do you know about all this?" I asked. "The son won't have said a word to anyone."

"How do I know? I know it direct from the father, from Wende himself. It was him who told me 'in secret', pleased that he's found a way to get peace and quiet in the house now. The son's cold but polite and doesn't invite his friends home so often which was what used to annoy Wende so much. Sure, he's found a way." He laughed. "I could teach my Fred as well when he gets away with too much, but what, I'm not a pig and anyway, the lad's as like me as one pea to another. What's more, my wife's still alive." Suddenly he stopped laughing and scowled. "Only I'm surprised that he told me. What did he tell me for? What do I care about other people's family secrets? There's nothing good in them."

And I understood that a silent secret web of blackmail was being stretched over the whole of Germany and that it would forever remain an undisclosed weapon, that it was their national taboo.

As for me, I had the Elefantenhaus, the famous hotel where Mickiewicz and Chopin had once stayed and where their profiles hung in the main salon together with other notables of the age. In the Elefantenhaus I allowed myself just the once, just the twice, the luxury of drinking a cup of coffee. Thus metamorphosed, I felt almost like a foreign tourist, a normal European, a cosmopolitan.

But it was not cosmopolitanism that bade me approach

the portraits. I felt something like reverence with a smile of gratitude. The fact that they were here, that they were reigning, that the ways of the world were not solely the ways of exile and torment, but also European salons, weights and measures appropriate for everyone, the breath of man. My own breath. I was moved with unexpected joy.

Naturally I did not think about the fact that they were people from post-partition Poland, the one I had not wanted to talk about in school, the one with its martyrology. On the contrary, I, who had so disliked the history of the Great Emigration, now came to understand its brilliance, its services rendered in building Poland supra-aerial and eternal, and my soul repented for my presumptuous conceit of a child born in freedom. I apologised to the Great Emigration. I gave thanks for our great Romantic bards, Mickiewicz, Slowacki and Krasinski, and for the ordinary rank and file exiles of those times. I revered their poverty and fortitude. It is simply unimaginable since we will not be exiles, the war will end sooner or later and we will return to our own country from the purgatory of war, better, wiser, experienced, capable, meting out justice and...

In the meantime I was not allowed to stroll along all the streets, but I was able to become acquainted with this charming, still nineteenth-century city, where a carriage passing by would not have surprised me. In fact I actually saw one, a carriage for children placed by the park exit, and there it rattled and shook on the spot, not in use at this time of year, tossed by the wind. The slender and elegant silhouettes of trees completed the likeness to old engravings which often hung on walls in Poland and always seemed to originate from someone's family travels abroad.

A Singer treadle sewing machine, the same as my grandmother had, often clattered in the room which I was allocated in the apartment of the ageing Nazi Party member Frau Helbing. The patterns were still brought from Vienna. The machine was the first to react with a special shudder at the first sound of the air-raid siren and then it remained all alone. All the inhabitants of the house dashed to the shelter in the cellar in orderly fashion. The air-raids were particularly heavy and persistent here - Weimar contained Gustloff Works, a factory producing ammunition and military equipment, a very important target. Sitting in candlelight among the others, I thought that it would be singularly bad luck to die from an Allied bomb.

26

I decided that I ought to visit Kunegunda Grzesik, who had her own restaurant here in London. She was not the first example of the thrift and energy of Poles in exile, already being talked about more and more, a real hatchery of organisational talents, yet when I finally went there I was astonished.

Above two windows and the painted green entrance door ran a large shop sign, as laconic as could be: Grzesik. Huge letters, unpretentious, all the better. Kunegunda is a brave woman, there's no denying it. How on earth do the English pronounce her surname? Grezik? Greysy? Jesick? I presumed that she was not counting on an English clientele, only a Polish one. I was mistaken. The premises were unexpectedly large, occupying two fair-sized rooms separated by a door, and both parts buzzing with people.

I entered the first, larger room, closely arranged with

tables for four. Along the wall ran a long table with a bench in front, as in a Polish inn, covered with a dark striped oilcloth. Rounds of drinks were frequently served there, wisely located close to the bar. On the wall hung a wooden plate carved with the head of a man from the Tatra mountains in a hat decorated with shells and a feather tucked in diagonally and a pipe in his teeth. Round the edge of the plate ran a very blackened inscription: 'Our cottage is pleased to offer all its wealth'.

My God, I thought, encompassing everything from earth to sky. I looked at the throng of people and not without difficulty found one free place where someone was just getting up. I sat down, pleased that it was far from the door to the kitchen which I guessed to be on the other side. I wanted to have a good look at the new Grzesik establishment before meeting the owner in person.

Mobile patches of faces and hands manipulating food or gesticulating in conversation, here and there tables pushed together formed a clump of human earth, which was precisely the right term to describe these humans concentrated in the act of the most basic need of all. My countrymen were guzzling. However I viewed them, whatever I thought, I was one of them; in the bottom of my soul trotted a poor sense of community, and I could not shake off the thought that what I was seeing would probably be long-lasting, for years. Odious history, forever faithful to us like *diabolus qui semper in exilio est.*

Yet for the first time, pity. Without anger; disinfected, as it were. We were going to attack each other again, some of us high, some low, before we were consumed, the ones who had survived, by ordinary nothingness falling to our share. The sight I had in front of me fell to today's share: the fundamental and characteristic physical features of Poles, just like an object 'made in Poland'.

Thick and heavy skulls, protuberant foreheads, concave and wide cheeks, with the features spread as if generally incomplete, as if unpolished, or again, exaggeratedly sharpened, almost aggressive in their subcutaneous structure, good faces for 'after death'.

They reminded me somewhat of the history of the earth, marked by tectonic movements into hills and hollows, the boorishness of birds, vegetable gnarls or volcanic lumps, and a common muggishness was reflected from the way we so often looked, suggesting nothing to the imagination, fleeing the eye, a real commonwealth of man. Perhaps that is why the Germans killed us with such alacrity and eagerness, because we are not a beautiful race. Perhaps what my next door 'neighbour' had written simply contained a physiological basis of hatred for what lacked logic and grated by its distance from the model of imagined Aryan beauty. Perhaps they were even angry with us for being Aryans, because the word meant something more than merely 'racial purity'. Why should it be pure if it cannot be beautiful, of its own accord, from its distant, prehistoric layers which should already have produced a better and amended edition long ago?

What did all these people do? They looked as if they were already working somewhere, not unemployed. They were probably staff in the service industries, as workers generally ate in their canteens. But there might have been a workplace or workshop nearby employing both men and women. There were many women, almost all of them very colourfully dressed in clothes bought here. I noticed only two who wore large woollen flowered scarves thrown over their shoulders, from Poland without doubt, but with the fringes cut off. Yes, of course, easier to wear and wash without a fringe. Here and there I could see a vividly coloured flowery hat, but bare heads immersed into thicker or thinner scarves round the neck were in the majority. There was no cloakroom in the place; the backs of all the chairs were covered with coats or jackets. Large shopping bags of assorted shapes lay almost everywhere on the floor next to the tables, or where men were sitting, crammed briefcases, with their locks rarely fastened.

These briefcases, by which Poles could be recognised from afar on the streets of London, seemed to be an inseparable part of their bodies, as though grafted onto them. They deserve a separate monograph and history; they knew all the fates and fortunes of the freshly settled newcomers. It intrigued the English. Whatever do the Poles carry in those briefcases? They can't always be going shopping? Kostek used to laugh at the habit, but he himself never stirred anywhere without his 'mycum', as he called his haversack, christened like that from *mecum porto* ('I carry with me'), and he swore that only a haversack is suitable and decent for exiles. "At least you won't lose your military fashion, seeing as you're going to be 'politicals'."

Little of this military fashion remained, but among the customers I did see a few dyed battledresses, some with the shoulder-straps cut off. No, they should not have done that, even if they had dyed them. A striking characteristic was the general neatness and cleanliness, different than in English eating-places of a similar sort. The shaven and carefully groomed company ate quietly but talked loudly, mainly the women. A short silence would descend every so often, when a plate of hot soup or a steaming dish was taken from the hands of the waitresses, and then everyone smiled at these young women.

In fact it would be hard to call them waitresses; they had a familiarity and solidarity with the people they served. Reciprocity without acquaintance existed between them, a routine far from impersonal. They worked quickly, efficiently and patiently - Mrs Grzesik must have known exactly how to train her staff. She will have treated them well and paid them suitably. I watched with pleasure these young faces often adorned only with their youth, but always with a purely national grace, and their neat movements, energetic but fluid, never angular. Not without emotion I ordered some *bigos*. The national emotion, the national dish.

It arrived. It was brought by a girl whom I had not noticed so far. A dawn of a girl. She who was standing at my table looked like glory itself. Glory be to God, if it was really He who made creatures like this: pinkness blazing from within through a white complexion almost transparent but in fact enveloped in down, wisps of very fair hair wound round the top of her forehead and then, tightly combed, her hair embraced her head like a helmet. A short thick plait behind, eyes steeped in blue under a long line of straight brows, and in the middle of her face smiled well-defined unpainted lips. The short sleeves of her blouse showed equally white arms as slightly plump hands placed the plate in front of me. Where could she come from? In what part of Poland are girls like that born?

"I'm from the Krosno area," I heard in reply. "It's in the south."

"Just like Mrs Grzesik and it's from there I remember her."

"You know Gran? My gran, from before the war?"

"Gran? So you're her grand-daughter?"

This was a revelation. How was it possible? At that time Mrs Grzesik still seemed a young woman to me. So how old could this grand-daughter be?

"I'm nearly seventeen, this autumn."

Which meant that the year the war started she must have been about ten. True, Mrs Grzesik did have some children, the oldest, a son or daughter, could have been a father or mother long ago, only I had known nothing about it. I was already a generation cast aside. What about this girl's parents?

"Dad be not coming back from the war. Mother was in a camp, but she's not with us now."

Short is Poland's history. As if a skirt had fluttered in a farmyard. But the girl had said 'Dad be not coming back', a form of speech used in olden times about old people. How had it happened that she had retained this form which I might never hear again? Her father must have been a young man when he died.

The dawn disappeared. She must have been working in the next room because her voice reached me from there. I could distinguish the words: "If you want to follow me." Obviously English people ate there. It was true that Polish restaurants were very popular with the English. But I was in no hurry to see what was happening on the other side of the wall. What for? I felt more relaxed here, more peaceful, I did not want to move on quickly. Dinner here was like a national chorale, I thought to myself indulgently and very carefully, so as not to spoil this moment.

Even the ashtray was friendly. Plain and thick, good-natured, unbreakable, 'Utility' manufacture, round, with hollows for cigarettes, serviceable, almost sanitary in its whiteness, not even carrying any advertisement. It could just as well come from Cmielów. It did not, I knew. It would be enough to turn it upside down to find that it was manufactured here. But don't turn these ashes over, woman, you don't know what thoughts they contain, respect these people's butt-ends.

They reminded me of ashtrays in rooms similar to these where I had an audience when I toured every single camp for soldiers interned in Switzerland with the Puppets' Crib. It was not my show, but a nativity play, a very successful production with which I crossed the whole of Switzerland. We were accompanied by three soldiers who formed the permanent cast: the huge, almost two metres tall Jan Dziadek from the guard of honour of the president of the Polish Republic, tiny corporal Blicharski, and plump black-haired Uriasz, the accordionist. The carols we sang were unknown to most people, not traditional, but original folk pastorals, some of them from the Polish mountains. The audience did not consist of Polish soldiers alone, but also the local Swiss, since the Nativity subject needed no translation or explanation.

We could give our swollen knees the credit for our repeated success because manoeuvring the puppets was done in a kneeling position. What requests, pleas almost, we received from the leading surgeons of the clinic in Leysin in the high Alps to repeat our show for other sick people who depended only on the radio and were deprived of any contact with people and live art. These spectators made a terrible impression as they entered the room. They were all in complicated mechanisms keeping their limbs in various artificially twisted positions, like the victims of cunning tortures. We suffered the horror of normal, happy young people seeing the ghastliness of incurable disease, and we acted with unnatural intensity, as if it were possible not only to entertain but also to cure these people. In the interval Uriasz played our folk-dance tunes briskly on the accordion, completely drenched with sweat, while Jan Dziadek quietly repeated the 'Our Father'. I did not know whether he was praying for those unfortunate people or thanking God for his own health. It is good that I experienced those moments of pure service, long weeks in snow and travel, unrepeatable and invaluable. Very likely I too should have lit a candle in the clinic chapel, and later as well.

Unrepeatable? The *bigos* disappeared from my plate and my cigarette enveloped me in smoke. Why was it unrepeatable? Something similar could be done here in England even though it is a Protestant country. Done differently. One can imagine a van stopping in the square of small towns or the London suburbs, or at the crossroads of quiet streets. Announced, awaited, it stops where young spectators have gathered, generally with their mothers. The back wall of the vehicle opens, a makeshift theatre takes shape. The guiding star and searching shepherds introduce the action; the English have old texts which could serve the purpose and their own Christmas carols which could be staged with a puppet theatre. Tola Korian is in England, she is a brilliant actress, scholar and specialist in this genre. I should meet her, show her the photographs, consult and discuss with her. Dig around in libraries, dig up what was needed, start something different again. Even if I left England later.

Unexpectedly I saw Mrs Grzesik from afar. I sensed rather than recognised her. She came out of the back, gave instructions to the person working near the bar, then briefly cast an expert eye over the room. Our eyes met for a second, but hers did not stop on me. She did not notice or recognise me. I would have to go up to her a little later when she was not so busy; now she was at full swing and could not come out to the guests. Or perhaps she did not want to. Perhaps instead of boasting of her achievement, she did not want to see me. Why? I could not believe she had any personal dislike of me, but perhaps I passed in her eyes as one of those who 'were guilty of everything'. She remembered the harvest festival. Never mind the fact that I was not personally guilty.

My desire to see the owner of the premises left me although it had been my purpose in coming. I can do it next time, another day. What could be simpler? The dawn did not appear again either. She stayed in the room next door and disappeared, although I sat for quite a while. Finally I paid another girl and went out to the street, where a very fine rain hung in the air and was impregnated with a sweetish sickly smell and taste. It started lashing more strongly at the crossroads, where I also met an odour of grease or petrol. Walking quickly, I passed three side streets. A small stretch of road separated me from the underground station, but I took the opposite direction, quickly passed two more streets, and then turned into the right one.

It was the street where I used to eat dinners in the Polish woman's private apartment, where the stranger came with the map of an uninhabited island near the English coast said to have been bought by the Polish government. I do not know if he still went there, perhaps simply out of friendship if he was a personal friend, for meals were no longer served there.

I often walked as far as that house. It was the purpose and extent of my walk, a strange and really non-existent purpose, as if I could still find a trace of that lunatic and his companion there, his good friend, whose compassionate look I had noticed and remembered. I never saw them again. But I was drawn in that direction like a compass needle, almost unconsciously. Sometimes, when it was not raining, I used to walk right to the end of the street and back. Once I phoned a number I knew from a telephone kiosk there, but when someone's voice answered, I replaced the receiver. When I picked it up again, I did not dial any number and nothing responded in the void full of dry crackles and murmurs, unlike the voices of any river or sea or island.

27

I decided to change rooms. The neighbouring room had not been rented, and its emptiness held something disturbing. Yet my thoughts kept returning to that tragic room which I did not even want to discuss, above all not with Angus Dean. He wanted to. For him it was a sensation, confirming his theories about castaways and displaced persons of various sorts and about the consequences of great historical catastrophes. But those conversations bored me.

I did not believe in the value of what Angus wrote or said in the lectures with which he toured political clubs in the provinces. Anyway, even if his sociological opinions did have any value, they presented the British point of view, in other words, did not disturb the new post-war world order - the consolidation of the Left and the new tasks of the Labour Party, in which he saw the panacea for nearly all the suffering and difficulties of the present state of affairs. From the British point of view there may have been some validity in this, but it was not my concern. For the time being I could only look backwards in order to seize the fugitive past disappearing for evermore, and to try to face the equally fugitive unknown tomorrow.

My work was going badly. The book, two-thirds finished, suddenly started to sway and break harness on the most important side, psychological veracity. Quite unexpectedly my protagonist disobeyed me; he started leading me instead the other way round. My Jerzy Plawicki was splitting. He was a witness of events but was starting to be a witness too conscious of his testimony. He seemed to feel and understand that his role and intended vicissitudes and characteristics did not suit him. He was so much at the very core of daily life that he did not want to control or comment on it. True, the protagonist of a novel should not serve for appraisal and judgement, rather for action, even if it mainly takes place inside him. But Plawicki switched off. He was escaping. He was dissolving into something blurred.

Obviously I had unwittingly grafted on to him my own present state of mind, and my own convictions or moods had filtered into him, which in the time I was describing were already becoming anachronistic. He sojourned in Lwów during the first September, October, November and December of the war, through all the dramas and tragedies of those days, but he was already putting them aside for future reflection, and I did not want that. It was still too early for that. We did not know then that an irreversible change was taking place, that we would stop being the inhabitants and masters of this city and these lands. September was still trembling with the dynamism of battle. And to the invaders, in their big tanks and with their bayonets at the ready, the revelation of these lands and people was in itself first-rate literary material. It could be.

So at times I regretted that I had chosen him, Jerzy Plawicki, a young Polish intellectual, as my central figure, and I was more tempted by the person of our compulsory tenant, a Russian. His surname was Tiedov, his given name Lev, Russian for lion, in obvious and amusing contradiction to his behaviour. His wife was called Talka, probably from Natalia, and they had a child, Grigorka, who was about seven. At the onset of the requisitioning of houses for members or officials of the Soviet secret police, the NKVD, and also for military personnel, a tall and severe *komandir* called by to inform us that he was billeting a family with us. He wrote down the name without giving a precise date and immediately left without looking at any of us. We, no longer surprised at anything, deluding ourselves that by way of politeness we might succeed in getting my brother freed from prison in Sambor, started carrying all his personal bits and pieces out of his room.

Suspended from the ceiling on a thread was a small metal ball with a lug which Bogumil had hung up just like that, for no known reason. When we were taking it down, it seemed that the earth's globe was being severed from its place in the universe. We did not talk at all, and only Helcia, dusting the chairs automatically, said loudly with the gravity of a prayer: "May God only grant them to be decent people."

She made the bed carefully, and perhaps her sigh was uttered at the appropriate moment because the married couple who arrived the next day did turn out to be 'decent people'. They were young and gave the impression of being very scared. They quickly and quietly spread their bundles out over the floor. The man showed my mother a piece of paper with some seals, said "*Spasibo*", and entered 'their' room, after which a silence lasting a day and a night descended there and continued throughout the next two days and nights as we became more and more surprised.

In accordance with the agreement with the *komandir*, these residents had the right to draw water in our kitchen ('entering through the porch from the yard', as my mother specified), and they also had access to the wash basin. The bathroom, fortunately, had not been mentioned, so we all breathed a sigh of relief. Our Helcia thought up a good idea, out of politeness, as it were, and placed two buckets of water on the porch in front of the kitchen door. The buckets were taken in in the evening, and the following day they were standing empty in the same place. This taking of the water was the only sign of anyone's presence in my brother's old room.

As for other needs, they must have used the garden, in which there were no longer any railings. These had been missing since the ammunition trucks, still Polish ones, drove into our yard and the whole area, including the garden, was covered with square wooden boxes as pale as butter beans.

We meant to repair the ruined fence after the war, but from the time these Russians settled into our house, although nobody said it, we all felt that the place was like a badly healed scar. A few broken railings still lay there and no one had moved them, as if they marked some grave or other. We liked it when sparrows sat on them, and then when scant but strong grass pushed up from underneath, although the yard was paved with large cobblestones. Later the snow cloaked them like shapes in a cemetery, but that was much later.

The Russians moved in at the beginning of October. 'The month of October', as old Wikcia, Pietrek's sister, always corrected us. I did not know why only this one month had to be pronounced as if it had a first name and surname, why this one and no other. I realised only later that October is the month of the rosary and that was why it should be distinguished from the others.

The traditional repetition of 'Hail Marys', which ought to be accompanied by an internal vision of the experiences of other people, their joyful, painful and laudable moments, was linked to the business with the Tiedovs. A strange business. Perhaps that is what I should have chosen as the subject of my book, their history and not the experiences of one of us, a fellow Pole of my own age. But the intention would have been over-bold, the expectation too great, a temptation to see everything differently, to detach myself from my own background, from the authenticity of people and their familiar, because visible, problems and fate. While the fate of that Russian couple...

One day they disappeared from our house. No one removed the buckets of water from in front of the kitchen door. Helcia informed my mother. We all in effect simply shrugged our shoulders. There were by now so many refugees staying in the house who sometimes suddenly disappeared, leaving a message to say that they were going somewhere because they had a chance to leave Lwów, that news about the untouched buckets of water was of no particular interest to anyone.

It was not until the evening of the third day that my mother knocked at the door facing the stairs opposite our entrance hall. No one answered. The door was not locked, nothing had disappeared, and the tidiness would have seemed unnatural if anyone were living in the room. No note, no sign. Only a small thin net curtain still hung over half the window, obviously left behind as unwanted. The bed was made slightly differently; the dishes we had lent them were cleaned and stood ostentatiously on the table in military array, irrevocably. In other words, there would be a lot of trouble for us.

We ought to inform someone, do something about this absence. But before we took any decision (best to inform the caretaker to start with), three people arrived by car, two in uniform and the third a civilian. The civilian spoke Polish and made an unpleasant impression as he kept tapping the end of his pencil on his closed notebook and did not remove his hat. He tried to speak sharply, clearly wanting to frighten us. It was Helcia they watched most suspiciously. "You say that it was you who brought them water, comrade," he was asking for the third time while the faces of the other two were like ice. Helcia became irritated: "I didn't bring them water, I only left it in buckets because that's what I was told, but what they did, where and when they went or not, then I don't know that. Their door faced directly onto the stairs, don't you know? So ask the caretaker, maybe he'll tell you something."

"Perhaps you think that we've poisoned them and buried them in the garden, gentlemen?" smiled my mother, most inappropriately, and - as I was told - this smile offended them all. The Soviets were shifting from foot to foot, 'and they creaked in those leathers like at the saddler's'. My mother said, "You can search the house too if you want." A dangerous bluff, for some of the refugees might have arms in the house.

Helcia revealed later that she was seized with fear then because she knew that Mr Olenski (the one who had struggled all the way from Krynica to Lwów wearing just the clothes he was standing up in, a coat and tennis shoes, and was looking for his wife and daughter here) had a pistol or revolver in his pocket. "If they'd found anything here, Jesus!" Fortunately they did not start a search; they realised how absurd it would be in this case. However, the one in the hat pulled something out of his pocket and thrust it under Helcia's eyes: "Well, what's this? Who's this from? Not from you? It didn't turn up on him from nowhere."

He shook a fairly long dark rosary, winding and unwinding it without taking his eyes off Helcia. She denied it: "Not from me. I didn't give him anything. He didn't come into the kitchen, we only saw him when they moved in." But she was saying it, as she later admitted, with dread. She recognised Paraska's rosary. Paraska was no longer our servant, but she still came on Sunday afternoons for tea in the servants' room.

"So if you found it on him or else on them, then obviously you must know where they are and what has happened to them," my mother calmly surmised, and I can still see her raised thin eyebrows as she was saying it. Then Helcia was seized by a sudden inspiration, 'the

212

Holy Ghost's inspiration', as she later described it.

"So what if it's a rosary? Perhaps he only wanted to
see the world and show his folks, his wife and child.
Rome," shouted Helcia, "he wanted to see Rome and he
picked up the rosary from somewhere or other. Maybe
you don't know it, but you can see the world in here,
there's a glass here, look, it's here, where you can see
Rome."

Later I thought of Mickiewicz's famous line 'This inn
called Rome' and we all laughed at such an excellent but
perverse dramatisation of the words. The Russians
showed real interest. First one and then the other took
the rosary with disbelief, lifting it up to the light so they
could 'see the world'. And see it they did.

If the Tiedovs had indeed managed to escape and
cover their tracks, how did they feel, what did they think,
in a world so new to them? When had they taken the
decision to leave the army and their own people and
attempt a new life at the risk of life itself? One would
have to imagine something like the creation of the world,
a newness never known before and perhaps impenetrable
to the understanding, a beckoning from a direction
unknown.

28

Everything looked different now, as if a total eclipse had
taken place. That was probably why I could not move on
from where my book had foundered. I would have to
turn my back on my way of life and reach for other, more
successful, tools. Higher, superior, like the eye of
Providence within a triangle in an old engraving. I

remembered one in particular, in the form of a huge iris. Pythagoras was holding it and commanding his disciples around him to believe in metempsychosis, to live ascetically and to aim at perfection, like the perfection of his theorem. Like the admonition to be courageous in his Golden Verses.

Be courageous. Courageous. Courageous. Did I lack courage? Rather, its object. How could I assume my obligation and discharge it here and now, when I was seeking a secret exit from this darkness full of snares, unknown voices and entreaties, as in a vast forest. At this very moment Polish forests and woods were swarming with people who were being hunted, or who had decided of their own accord to emerge into the light of cruel day.* Yes, their every minute required courage, if only to die. What would happen to them before they died. Which of them knew the limits of his endurance? Kostek believed in his cyanide. But what if for some unforeseen reason he did not manage to take it in time?

Courageous. More courageous. Most courageous. What obligation was there to discharge? In the months of October, November and December, the time-frame of my novel, courage had been needed simply to wrench oneself out of the cauldron that was Lwów in order to reach the war which was just starting. Why could my protagonist not bring himself to do it for so long? Christmas was approaching, it was high time.

Yet leaving Krakow is different from leaving Lwów. The men and women who left Lwów knew that they would never return. They did not say it. On the contrary, they pretended they would return. Because leaving Lwów

---

* Polish Home Army soldiers, whom the Communist authorities considered to be reactionaries, were persecuted after the war. Some took advantage of an amnesty proclaimed by the government and came out of hiding, i.e., 'emerge[d] into the light of cruel day'; others remained in hiding in forests.

meant leaving the world. The weights and measures between mortals and the gods were already being measured out here, in this city; a mound was being raised in praise of the gods of Union and Reconciliation for yesterday, today and tomorrow, to the end of time, but the gods had turned away from mortals and had surrendered them to fratricidal linkage.* The war was not yet over, but the fate of the city was already rending its garments.

Pathos, that's what hero Plawicki was afraid of. Pathos. As if the crafting of words to express human feelings and affairs could make them even worse and subject people to ridicule. Because people are not created for misfortune, which contains a more or less flagrant indecency. That must have been why Kostek had thought up a twisted reversal of the two syllables, calling everything that was happening in the city 'the national *thospa*'. Lwów's merry wave had ended,† *thospa* had arrived. But before we get used to it... well, well, well.

In order to move on with my stalled novel, I decided to write the most difficult part, at least to sketch it and rid myself of the phantom. Later I would manage to pick up the thread in the right place, but I would already have the most difficult bit behind me. That should help me. At least one version of the moment when they say goodbye. Then I would see everything more easily, the irritating anxiety would disappear, it should disappear, surely. So I shall cross right through, I shall step over the *thospa*. I tackled the moment of parting.

---

* 'Linkage' refers to the Soviet plebiscites organised by the NKVD, predecessor of the KGB, and held in all the Soviet-occupied territories of Poland in 1940. Lwów and the surrounding area were incorporated into the Ukrainian SSR.

† Lwów's merry wave alludes to a program called 'The Merry Wave', transmitted by Radio Lwów and very popular throughout Poland before World War Two.

The scene takes place in the Plawickis' home: *In a room on the first floor next to the Russian's room, Jerzy said goodbye to his father. Szymon Plawicki grasped his son's hand, squeezing it hard to conceal the shaking of his own. He smiled, seeking in the smile a support for his trembling lips. He restrained himself with all his strength so that he would not be broken by emotion, and this battle absorbed his every nerve, the veins on his forehead played from the exertion. His eyes were red and puffy from sleeplessness.*

He hugged Jerzy hard and slowly, as if afraid that this contact would shatter something in him.

'*My son...*'

He took Jerzy's head in his hands, felt beneath his fingers its long regular shape, similar to Teresa's head. He felt that he ought to say something, something of supreme and utmost importance which would stay with his son, but he could not find the words or thoughts. He passed his hands over his son's neck and shoulders and embraced his arms above the elbows.

Jerzy shook his head. He smiled like his father. Like his father he could not find any words.

'*I'll be waiting for you here in Lwów,*' *whispered Plawicki. They kissed. Jerzy leaned down to Szymon's hand but he removed it quickly.*

'*Stop that. What now?*'

This small gesture of opposition did him good.

'*Jerzy, stay well. Goodbye.*'

He raised his hand as if saying goodbye for only a short absence.

'*I'll stay here in my room, I'll be at the window. I'll see you as you go out.*'

He suddenly turned away and Jerzy was alone. He left on heavy legs, slowly, sagging more and more as he went.

'*I'll be waiting for you here,*' *he heard mentally as he went downstairs step after step. Mechanically, auto-*

matically, something was repeating the sentence in him, the engine of that last moment was still turning and throbbing. He did not feel anything, did not remember anything, did not think about anything. With his hand on the banister he was transferring his body from one stair to the next. His heart grew small in him, minute, and almost disappeared. It was travelling through him somewhere, it wanted to stop somewhere, it must stop somewhere. Finally a thought struck him, specific, just one. How true to talk about legs of lead. Six more stairs, only four more, now just two, now the last one.

I did not change anything in the text later because I did not know how. It referred to me personally as well, with the difference that writing it in London after the war I already knew the outcome. I remained all alone with history's *instrumentum diaboli*, and to my misfortune I did not believe in the devil. Good luck to people who do believe in him, for much shall be simplified unto them. As for me, nothing.

I cannot have been the only one with this problem, although nobody spoke about it aloud - everyone who intended to leave and travel to other countries stayed here in England, which was a mixture of the most precious and the basest metals, in no set proportions. Sleep fled first of all. I comforted myself with the fact that London was said to be notorious for sleeping badly, but it was not true, not our truth.

'The world's waiting room', England's capital was called in those days. It contained something electric, with internal incandescence and concealed energy, an inflamed state of all the power and strength of men to become masters of their fate and choice, all the while aware that they are merely throwing the dice. Rather like the woman who tossed half-crowns instead of deciding.

Kostek laughed at all this, armed with his ready-made

cynicism and authentic humour, for which I envied him. He could laugh naturally and with superiority. Striking the gesture of a waiter, one arm bent at the elbow, he showed me what we are like as a nation: 'ever on a salver', because we can always be served, removed, jostled, spilled off the map of the world. And so on, and on and on. I had turned solemn and was easy prey for his ready jokes. Kostek was right to scold me, most of all for betraying humour: "Life shouldn't be taken seriously, but not everyone is given the talent," as he put it.

"Do you remember how orphanages were laughed at before the war? Orphans don't have 'father, mother or relations, so they're brought up on quotations'. It's always worth knowing a lot of quotations because there are always a lot of orphans. Well, as many as there are now, we didn't foresee that. When I return to Poland, I'll try to become director of an orphanage in Pomorze. It's said to be a good business. People are paying directors privately so they don't have to disclose they're parents for a while. In the present mess everything's possible. Besides, I like little kids."

He said 'kids', a word which was in common use in Poland but was only just beginning to be accepted among Poles abroad. For a moment the thought flitted through my head that perhaps this return to Poland really would be a success for Kostek and that he would feel - despite everything - better there. My country, right or wrong.

A shadow of envy flitted over me, as short as a heartbeat.

29

The ceramic tiles were ready. I was pleased with the work and again found myself in the little drive full of varicoloured greenery in front of Curtis' house. He greeted me like an old friend, found the tiles 'wonderful' and we started to experiment. They would look better on the wall if some miniatures nearby were moved somewhere else. The glass top of a small table reflected the horizontal line of the ceramics, distorting their proportions. So perhaps we should move the table. One metre further would be enough for the reflection to vanish. In its new position the table attained greater clarity, and each object on it acquired a stronger effect. I moved back a step to gauge it better and was struck by an unexpected sight: a goat's hoof in low grass appeared in the glass tabletop, next to it the plump foot of a woman, a pink calf, full thighs encircled by one of the serpent's coils, Eve's womb, and higher up, small widely spaced 'Gothic' breasts and a hand removing the round fruit on a stalk. Whitish brown strips of rotting flesh dropped off the bones of Death whose head, like Eve's, was not visible; the edge of the mirror cut off the top part of the figures. Only the serpent's head could still be seen in foreshortened profile among the green thickness of leaves.

A fragment of Baldung's painting on the opposite wall lay wrong way up before me.

Curtis was delighted. "What a charming surprise," he exclaimed warmly, catching sight of the reflection just after I did. "It's an excellent effect. Only I'll have to put completely different objects on the table, something connected with what's reflected there. It'll be fascinating. Different objects will give different combinations, and interpreted in various ways, they'll assume a different significance. Splendid. Instead of a nineteenth-century table for spiritualist seances, it'll be a true 'speaking table'. You'll see, but I'm already sure that it'll be really original, unlike anything I've ever seen in anyone's house before."

"You'll be in paradise when you're choosing these knick-knacks."

"Just like in paradise. Of course, this paradise is already endangered, but not yet lost. The apple picked, but not bitten. A really exceptional moment."

"I imagine that you believe in Baldung's scene like the gospel."

"Well, I don't believe in the gospel so much," admitted Curtis with some hesitation and discreet scepticism, "Different people wrote it differently. But I'm a firm believer in temptation by the Devil. I've never doubted it. His presence has never been up for discussion, it's a certainty."

"Certainty? In this picture, in the form of a serpent, naturally."

"In this picture in the form of a serpent, but of course in life he appears in completely different shapes, or rather he doesn't need any external forms. You don't agree?"

He turned towards me with this question and stopped, with a crystal decanter in one hand and a glass in the other, just like in a film. The situation was amusing.

"Perhaps you're a lover of so-called forbidden fruit. It's said to improve the taste. I really believe there are people like that. I even envy them. It explains a lot of things in the world. While..."

"But his non-existence would diminish us! I'd feel reduced to zero if I stopped believing in him for a single moment."

The sincerity and spontaneity of this exclamation was disarming. Perhaps Curtis also conferred on his way of life one further feature of originality with this rare virtue, so different from the majority of people, similar to elaborate - dare I say, devilish - coquetry.

Quercus sessilis, populus alba, fagus silvatica, carpinus betulus, ulmus, castanea, I recited the names of the painted trees in turn, arranging the ceramic tiles, one next to the other, on the mirrored tabletop. So the picture of the serpent, Eve and Death disappeared, chased away by my leafy woods, my every *quercus* and *populus*, *betulus* and *carpinus*, my passions arboreal, my silvan matter, my republic of trees, my most faithful love since childhood. And suddenly, from nowhere, Cicero's fourth oration against Catiline: *Tantem in vobis fore diligentiam, tantem auctoritatem, ut omnia opressa, illustra, vindicata esse.* *

Where had Cicero suddenly come from? Along what path? Probably a wooded one. Since trees were now sheltering people, whoever confided in them believed that the war was not over, that everything would be vanquished and delivered. Believed that despite realpolitik, despite official negotiations and pacts, the fate of the country could still be changed. The woods remained. They know how to be silent, people can conceal themselves more and more deeply in them to survive for a long time and travel a long way through them as well. The woods alone will not betray or denounce anyone, will hide the traces.

Woods, and here their leaves, in a delegation of individual varieties, their academic, universal language of botanical Latin. Political frontiers traversing woods. Nothing made us more ridiculous than these artificial

---

* "You will possess so much diligence and authority that everything that is vanquished will be clarified and delivered."

demarcation lines of man's settlements on earth. And nothing was more necessary, since our natural state is fear and defensiveness. *Cuius regio. Cuius regio. Cuius regio.*

Curtis could not know where my soul was wandering and when. He could not know the splendour of woods, although the English are very familiar with botany, nor could he be aware of the political role of the wood in the Republic. But he was greatly pleased with the changes and novelty in his drawing· room. That afternoon he placed in a bookcase, glazed in the English fashion and locked like antique silver sugar caskets in the Polish manors of old, an inscription-cum-motto in black Indian ink on a white slip of paper, *sapienti. sat.*, 'enough wisdom', which put him into an even better mood. The paper was only card, a base and impermanent material, so he asked me to make it in porcelain, kiln-fired for eternity. But black or gold? What a problem!

We started talking about the symbolic colour of wisdom, different signs, emblems of increased quality, decorous calligraphy, the gravity of antiquity.

It was almost evening. Curtis wanted to drive me home, but I preferred to walk. My walking mania had not left me and I liked walking alone. I stopped here and there and admired some of London's ruins, commendable testimony of not surrendering to the aggressor, which made the special landscape of the city close to my heart. The evening was pleasant, slightly foggy, and warm. Facing towards the rising moon, I walked along the route of my bus so that I could meet it at a stop if I wanted to. But I had no idea that I would meet with something so strange as what happened.

"Good evening."

"Good evening."

This greeting surprised me, but since London was full of Poles, it was always possible to come across someone you knew.

The street was empty, the fog was already thickening, the contours of the houses were becoming more and more blurred. Only around the moon was a smooth scrap of sky visible, as if it had a pearly lining.

I recognised the face immediately and replying with my 'good evening' I almost extended my hand in greeting. However, at the last minute I realised that this gesture would be inappropriate and started pulling on my other glove. My companion tactfully pretended that he had not noticed this manoeuvre.

I knew him only by sight. But I had heard about him while he was still in the presbytery in Siedlicze. The Siedlicze parish priest, Father Krzyb, found himself in trouble because he had been given 'a portrait' of the Devil, seeing as it would not do anyone any harm in a holy place and could even look like a trophy from a successful exorcism. I do not know who the donor was, probably one of the local landowners with an earthy humour. The parish priest, a pleasant and good-hearted man who had only recently taken up his position, kept the 'likeness' for a while, probably not knowing what to do with this slightly embarrassing gift, and when the opportunity arose he got rid of it with sincerity and politeness: "It's not very suitable for me as a cleric to have a thing like that in my house, but it's different for you, you're a layman and educated, besides, you're a lawyer."

"So the situation will be reversed," laughed my father, "not *advocatus diaboli* but *diabolus advocati*."

My father took a liking to the picture. Actually a lot of people liked it. It belonged undeniably to the kitsch species, but was of the species closest to good painting and therefore hard to dismiss. Painted with technical skill in a naturalistic style, the portrait was a good representation of what the Devil's attributes were generally considered to be, and that was probably why it was successful. It depicted a man's face, beautiful, narrow and sharpened with an aquiline nose. Turned three-quarters to the front, he eyed the beholder with a suitably diabolical smile of mockery, cunning, flattery and even a certain cajolery. The eyes were green, of course. It was that green which irritated me most, the stereotype which recognised only black or green as the colour for Satan's eyes. "Why doesn't anyone paint the Devil with blue eyes?" I criticised, "Or even grey. If Dürer could paint the Madonna in a fiery red dress covered with a no less fierce purple cloak." But what Dürer could do...

The picture hung suitably on a Pompeii-coloured wall in my father's study. It was the colour of bright rust all over, and only the eyes bore the weight of contrast, obedient to the artist's intention. In the top lefthand corner, against a completely dark background, was a lighter, irregular fragment of landscape, almost a minia-ture. Two thin, bare trees and a bend in the road which disappeared beyond the frame. This small detail, placed here as if accidentally, elicited a familiar reminder of the poverty in the Polish countryside, to some extent the work of evil forces. Unexpectedly, and perhaps uncon-sciously for the artist, these few strokes sketched in the corner contained a likeness of daily life. Yes, such bends in the road do exist, trees do wind into the sky like that. Reality is like that: nothing stands in its way. Roads, like an inexpressible promise, are often cropped just like that.

At this time my father moved from Lwów to Jaslo, near the sub-Carpathian oil wells with their promise of business. Just then, and quite unexpectedly, these hitherto blossoming businesses collapsed. French capital was transferred from Poland to Romania. Long and hard discussions about it created a gloomy atmosphere among the family. The idle pit, the ground not flowing with life-giving oil, the rock providing no petroleum - nature seemed most unnatural. Only the Devil on the wall was smiling.

Grandmother, my father's mother, decided to kick the newcomer out of the house. She was angry with my father for hanging it in his study, and citing his professional setbacks, the voice of both piety and superstition cried out in her. She said that the picture should be destroyed, not given to anyone else. Destroyed. Deep conviction resonated in her voice, which amused my father, who shrugged his shoulders. Grandmother's attitude angered me. I liked superstitions, charms and spells of every kind, and I noted them down with the pleasure of an ethnologist; but professing and practising them in real life shocked me deeply. We found an agreeable way to settle the matter, however, in true Solomon fashion.

Our local council had decided to initiate an art exhibition (who knows, perhaps it would be transformed into a museum afterwards and raise the prestige of the town dignitaries), and Grandmother sent the portrait of the Devil to the exhibition, where it was given the title *Head of Satan*. My father commented wryly that our Devil had received a promotion from the local council. Grandmother must have thought that the nature of public property would remove the picture's demonism and that its power would be wiped away.

"Yes, that's exactly the way your honoured grandmother thought," said my companion, newly met in London. "She was convinced that the more people looked at the Devil's face, the more quickly it would disappear. She believed it."

So he had guessed my thoughts well. Guessed or knew? But I was grateful for having my conjecture confirmed and for this authoritative information which issued from someone who knew and determined the truth without hesitation or mistakes.

"You recognise me, don't you?"

"Of course."

It was not difficult. The same inclination of the head, the same angle of his face turned towards me, the same pale green eyes. But his expression was different. *Unde malum?* - whence evil? - the famous obsessive question asked by theologians of all times, perhaps for ever unfathomable, now, in this street already losing the outline of houses, in the slightly unreal, diffused half-light, seemed natural.

The clouds thinned, then gathered more thickly, the moon hid itself, then looked out again. I noticed that the newcomer's head was not covered with a rust-red hood as in the painting, but an ordinary hat with a narrow brim.

"Shall we sit down?"

"Yes."

A bench I had not noticed stood close by. There was not a lot to see from there, but all the charms of a solitary walk had gone to the devil anyway.

"Maybe not all," said my companion.

"Sorry. I forgot you're a mind-reader."

This presented a problem. A conversation with someone who knows everything we want to say beforehand stops being a conversation. It was a troublesome and strangely awkward situation.

"Don't mind it, please," Unde immediately replied. "It's my form of courtesy to let people speak. People have to have their say. Otherwise it'd be difficult to reach agreement."

"Exactly. At least I can learn something from you."

"You'll learn something for sure," he replied and bent his head slightly. At the same time he reached for his hat, took it off and placed it next to him on the bench. Only then did I see that his hair was completely white.

"My God," I thought silently, but this time my

companion did not react, as if he had not heard. He was right: on his forehead were two vertical furrows which had not been there in his old portrait.

"You'll learn many things from me. How this or that really happened. The majority of human fates and fortunes are always distorted at the time, or later, whereas my version accounts for the whole truth. Since you write, I'd have only one condition, let's say, a certain proposition."

"Oh yes? You can't want me to give you my soul or sign a pledge," I laughed sincerely. "It'd be very dishonest on my part. I've nothing to offer, you know that, don't you?"

"Yes, I know, of course. It's about something else. I'd simply like you to write about this meeting with me. Write and publish it in a journal; I leave you to decide and pick which one."

"In print? Publicly? To write that I met you, that - that..." He nodded in silence. "No, I can swear to you with certainty and with a clean conscience. I won't do it. I'll never write about it. Nor tell anyone. It's not true that I saw you and that we talked. No."

"I could render you some service."

"No. I've simply drunk one glass of whisky too many at Curtis's, that's all."

But of course I had not.

30

Rummaging through my documents in search of a clean sheet of paper, I came across a bookmark cut out of stiff card once upon a time in the good old Bern days and read on it the words of a short burlesque which I had completely forgotten about. Evidently it was a literary riddle.

> *The angel of prose has left me and Puck's comfort-*
> *ing and ironic words addressed to the audience*
> *come flying at me:*
>
> > *And, as I am an honest Puck,*
> > *If we have unearnèd luck*
> > *Now to 'scape the serpent's tongue,*
> > *We will make amends ere long,*
> > *Else the Puck a liar call.*
> > *So, good night unto you all.*

A bookmark. Made once upon a time, long ago, perhaps two years ago. I could not recognise myself; those moments of good humour and relaxation seemed incomprehensible. Now I was saving myself however possible. Helplessness is the mother of absurdity. Now I turned this riddle over in my fingers as if it were a menacing, unpaid bond to blackmail and frighten me. I must escape somewhere. Escape! I felt safe only when hidden. Safe because anonymous.

I became convinced of this one day in the newsagent's nearby. A small shop, but it always had a few copies of *Le Monde*, which I read regularly. I had been waiting quite a while at the bus stop with a copy in my bag when someone unexpectedly addressed me in English, with a wide smile on his face.

"So you are French. I've been telling myself for a long time that you're from the Continent, from France, from France of course. I always see you on this No. 30, it's my bus as well. It goes all the way to Kew Gardens. Have you been there too? The famous botanical garden; everyone who visits London goes there."

The chap wore an English check jacket, with a hat, and a waistcoat of worn and shiny suede. The short, light moustache above his deformed lip as well as a prominent, bony chin made him look the epitome of an Englishman. And he probably was, in the gentleman-farmer edition or something similar.

I did not deny it. I smiled the Continental smile which the locals value so highly and replied that I knew Kew Gardens already, that it really was a delightful place and that it was not at all surprising that it attracted so many foreigners, and that oh yes, I had seen a black swan there for the first time in my life. With a red beak, just as it should have. Oh yes, there were many interesting things in England.

After which the chap started praising *la douce France:* life is so beautiful there, even outside Paris one lives differently, Provence, ah, Provence, he had been there twice; apart from that he had been to Nîmes, he knew Avignon, he knew Mont Saint-Michel and Biarritz, of course, and he even knew Pau in the Pyrenees. I nodded.

"Before the First World War, Pau was the true capital of English tourism. Not only tourism. Many people, rich of course, settled there for good; Pau has the European record for beautiful weather. To this day the tailors and outfitters are more attuned to men than women. Last year a shop called 'The New England' opened opposite the historic 'Old England'. It went bankrupt before the year was out."

The conversation continued for quite a while in this vein. The stranger envied me that I would probably be returning to my country shortly, what a beautiful country, ah, beautiful and so fortunate.

I nodded with the discreet smile of indulgence for someone who did not have the privilege of being born in France. Not a word that I was not French, that it was not my country. I got off after two stops in an area I did not know, at a small, badly lit station. I walked with quick steps as if I could feel that they were numbered.

So that was what betrayal looked like. It lets itself be committed so easily, it comes so naturally, it says hello, asks no questions, understands everyone and everything, a toast come true although the words are not heard clearly.

I bought myself a very old map from a shop in Chelsea, a fanciful map where Boreus blew in the upper spheres of the chart, Mistral and Tramontana in the lower, and the signs of the Zodiac encircled the terrestrial globe. They influenced man's humours or disposition. He depended on them, and whatever happened to man was written into an astral configuration of their exhalations, attractions, forces and reactions. The map seemed to be a kind of horoscope which one need not believe in to find amusing.

This naive arrangement was cruel and final in its infallibility, arranging the world and the universe like this and not like that and therefore arranging man's place like this and not like that. Yet its naivety was also soothing. Very well, so I too am contained, or foreseen, in here somewhere. I will not rebel, but smile. I will learn humility, humility, humility, or at least enter into the way of this narrow virtue. I must try to educate a new nature for myself.

What if the author of this map was only a copyist? If he had made this engraving feeling no personal involvement at all in what he was engraving? What if he made a mistake with some detail, not difficult to do, after all? Perhaps the real truth lay between the creator of this map and its executor, and was slipping away? If I were entrusted with preparing such an Image of Heaven and Earth, what would I make other than a faithful copy? But everyone makes mistakes. What then? The oldest profession is not the prostitute's, but that of astrologers and fortune-tellers of all sorts and has lasted until our own times. The era has been particularly conducive to it - various exiles, affected by the disaster of uncertainty and the Unknown, seek the advice of clairvoyants and soothsayers as in the Stone Age, well, perhaps a little later. It's human after all.

These superhuman maps include the presence of man, as if the cosmos treated him as baksheesh for Earth's being in its place and fulfilling its obligation. What and to whom, the map does not say. Lo and behold, Sun and Moon, both with human faces, favoured this human kind because although the Winds also blew with human faces and the animals of the Zodiac's belt were carefully drawn, yet Sol and Luna towered above everything with no legend to clarify them.

Flumina, the rivers, raised their semicircles underneath, trying in vain to complete a full circle, condemned to fail eternally. Under the waters a narrow strip of red appeared like a dishevelled fringe; it might have been a volcanic layer but more likely it was hell. There had once been a name for this place, but the old map was torn exactly here. This was probably why the price was within my reach. I felt like a satisfied hunter who wishes to tame rather than kill his quarry.

My room assumed more and more personal traits, and I thought unwillingly about leaving it. To settle, be able to settle somewhere for good, was my greatest desire. A three-week visit to France unexpectedly resulted in a change in my situation: when I returned to England my 'unconditional landing', as it was called in my passport, was no longer accepted, and I was allowed to stay in the United Kingdom for only three months. The Home Office demanded a declaration from the embassy of People's Poland that I did not have the right to return, a paradox which I repeatedly sought to explain to a young and unpleasant civil servant.

"I have the right to return," I said emphatically, "except the Republic of Poland doesn't exist any longer. The present government is not a legal government but an imposed one. There is an agreement about the status of people who refuse to return to Poland in the present political conditions."

After I had explained this clearly and emphatically, the civil servant, not looking me in the face, repeated what she had to say and so did I. The deaf speaking to the deaf. Until at last one day at the Home Office reception desk, an older civil servant spread out his hands and told me that if I was not in possession of the documents from the Polish embassy, then his woman colleague would not receive me. My helplessness must have been visible, for the official whispered a few words which were to be my life line. He whispered: "Write. You have to write it." And I understood. While verbally we were encouraged in every way possible to leave Britain, a written request could not receive a negative reply; that would be contrary to the rights guaranteed to exiles. Kostek also confirmed this in his humorous way, but he also felt, although it did not concern him, that the wheel of history had now turned round for us, 'whoever goes up must come down'.

Though he comforted me, he could not conceal his own worry. He had received letters from Poland containing bad news. His younger brother had run away from home and was known to have joined the partisans. Sometimes in the evenings he managed to steal up to the house of an old railwayman who had once been one of Pilsudski's soldiers, and he supplied him with food, him and the others, which surprised me. What was it really like? How much food could that old man supply, and how many of these others were there? Immediately behind the station the road entered the woods, so he could leave something regularly in agreed places; he was said to be one of us. But then his daughter-in-law moved in with her young child. She was gaunt and greedy, not in the least one of us, and from then on it started getting difficult for the railwayman. Kostek bit his lips; perhaps he was leaving something unsaid.

The room where the young German had lived was still empty. The owner of the house was worried; an empty room brings no income, or perhaps she was gnawed even more keenly by superstition not clearly defined but obstinate, despite her Protestantism. One day someone came looking for a room. Mrs Dengs brightened up and showed the prospective tenant around. When he had seen everything, he said that he would phone that evening, but then gave no sign of life. So the room still stood under the mark of death. Personally I preferred no one to live there, although I could not clearly define the reason.

I did not look again at the deceased's notebook, not through lack of interest nor any sense of discretion, although... No, it was postponement rather, delaying my confrontation with the contents, until such time as I would be stronger, less shaken by the passion of anger and hopelessness. I did not want to lose the stranger's notes, as if they could open a door to an inaccessible world which I lacked the courage to enter but which could disclose itself to me any time I wanted. If I wanted.

How happy my neighbour, Angus Dean, would be if he could get his hands on a document like that, although it was a kind of rudimentary diary of a strictly private nature. But I did not say anything to Angus about my 'quarry', and he became more and more engaged in his own work. I was irritated by his unflinching zeal and conviction that the new socialist world would make everyone happy, if only it was not vanquished by outbursts of mindless nationalism, and this he did not consider unlikely.

"In that case there could be no hesitation," he insisted,

"it would be necessary to resort to force." So an outcome of this sort did seem possible, although officially peace had to be praised at any price, and my neighbour excelled in exactly that.

One evening I wrote about various kinds of emigration.... Take Lot's famous wife. She looked back, then called out for help, but she could not move from the spot, slowly solidifying into a pillar of salt. She had to swallow the salt of her own tears, while her pillar became a border post to act as a warning for our own times. It had already passed into history while history passed by next to it. And continues to pass by.

I gave Angus an ironic text like this but much longer, in the form of an article, asking him to correct my English, which was the most natural pretext for acquainting him with it. As I imagined, he was interested in it from the professional aspect first and foremost. Was I considering devoting myself to journalism? And where did I intend sending something like this, did I already have anything on the horizon? In London?

"Oh," I made light of his questions, "it's only a specimen with no value. I'm just interested to know if my English is good enough. Who can advise me better than you?"

He turned the three pages of manuscript over in his fingers and, despite his surprise, managed a smile. "I'll read it carefully. I'll make comments in the margin, or if necessary, on a separate sheet. OK?"

"OK."

"A title would be useful; a title is important."

"Oh, I've got a title," I immediately replied, "I want to call it 'A Suit of Sables'."

Angus was surprised. He did not see the connection.

"It's from Shakespeare. Do you remember Hamlet's words: 'Let the Devil wear black, for I'll have a suit of sables'? I wondered whether to use the first part of the sentence: 'Let the Devil wear black', and omit 'for I'll have a suit of sables', but on reflection I changed it and just shortened it to 'A Suit of Sables'. It's better, isn't it?"

Angus did not remember this quotation from *Hamlet*. Bitter and perverse laughter crowed inside me as I remembered other words from Shakespeare: 'Everyone can master a grief but he that has it.'

From the time of this conversation Angus spoke to me differently. He even encouraged me to send the text to one of the journals, and received my assertion that I had no intention of doing so by sticking out his lips in his characteristic way. He did not believe me, which is precisely what I wanted. Not obols but sables, we will not always be crying sorrowfully over our fate because it is sure to change. My pretended self-assurance helped me and surprised him, maybe even gave him food for thought – historical dialecticalism does not always allow the future to be foreseen, surprises do happen.

And my own behaviour on the very same day came as a surprise to me. When I was leaving the house, just outside the front door, I met a person with a piece of paper in his hand looking up to check the number of the house. Smiling myopically, he turned to me to ask if the room to rent was still free: "Yes, it's this address and it must be this house."

"Yes, but the room was taken this morning."

The oldish man, wearing a typically English raincoat and holding the piece of paper next to his eyes, said, "Oh, I see," after which he added, "thank you," and trudged away.

I had carved something out of time and space. Probably not for long; the room would be rented tomorrow if not today. And I experienced a very strange satisfaction as if the emptiness left by that man next door had built an invisible tomb.

31

Kostek brought me a jar of his home-made pickled wild mushrooms. They had become famous and had sold well throughout 'Polish' London from the time they were placed on a shelf together with books, in a spot visible through the window, and despite the reluctance of the bookshop manager, who considered it a profanation of the Polish nation.

Kostek is said to have settled the matter briefly: "For three days. Only for three days. If you haven't phoned me on the third day, then I'll take my jars away and make you a present of two of them, all right?" And so the mushrooms entered into that world of the Polish word. Kostek was beaming with pride and rightly so. "At last literature has really come in useful for something," he laughed, probably aiming his gibe at me. He did not know that I would not oppose him, since cooking too is an object of our national pride.

He had barely enjoyed his triumph to the full when he decided to start writing a cookery book, and in it how to prepare 'nostril of bear and leg of stag', but I was completely unable to help him in this, and I still do not know if any Pole knows this recipe. Before gathering the material for the book, Kostek unexpectedly struck a jingoistic vein. He thought up a small ornamental breastplate cut out of tin cans with a picture of the Mother of God painted in the middle. Even the chain was made of hand-cut shavings, twisted strips of tin, but this turned out to be too laborious when production was increased and was replaced by a red and white cord. He was supplied with tin cans by a friend who worked in a food shop, a Polish one at that, and his manager undertook to sell these products among the Poles. "They're nice," she said, "and people will buy anything with the Mother of God."

So that was to be my commission, a picture of the Mother of God, composed in such a way that it could easily be reproduced. From Czestochowa of course and Ostra Brama, 'for the folk from Wilno and thereabouts'. The beautiful one whose memory I had personally always cherished from the moment of delight when I first saw her in 1936 and which will remain with me for ever. A bright point of emotion.

I made Kostek some designs which were easy to reproduce, and he came for them three days later. He had lugged something else with him, and at the threshold he said, "I won't bother you with this, I've only brought something along to show you."

Taking it out of a leather briefcase, he put it on the table, carefully moving the papers aside.

There were two wooden crosses, flat, about twenty centimetres long, covered with battledress material that was fastened with small nails in such a way that the edge of the wood was visible. At the transection of the cross was an army stripe with 'Poland' written on it.

"Of course they're not being produced for sale. I made them for myself, that means for everyone very close to me in my regiment. I'll take them to Poland, one for the church in Jareniowka, you do remember it, don't you? The second one is intended for my own home. I'll probably get married and live in a place of my own after all. I only wanted to ask which one you think is better. Because as you can see, they've got different proportions, and also this one is of lighter wood, that one's darker. And do you think I should fasten the battledress with nails, or wouldn't it be more attractive to fix it onto the wood, something like encrustation? More work of course, but it might be nicer."

Kostek did not know, could not know, what memory would open before me the moment I looked at his work. The sight of the huge factory hall, almost empty, the hall of the former spinning shop in Langner's factory where I worked then, in the second month of the Soviet occupation of Lwów, the hall which was to be made into a canteen for the workers.

The current canteen was not big enough, and the need was becoming more acute every day. The panes in this part of the building had almost completely survived by some strange chance although the floor was covered with rubble and plaster that had fallen off the walls and ceiling. Just next to the entrance stood my table, serving as an office, where I was to sit and enter the amount of raw materials delivered and details of various categories of manufacture. In practice they did not differ at all, but the very fact of record-keeping increased the prestige of the production which was just starting up.

One day Kostek turned up, to my dissatisfaction. Giving his true personal details, he asked for a work card, explaining to me that in this canteen he would get the best idea of what 'they' needed most, and that he would undertake to supply potatoes, cabbage and even cereals. Nothing came of it; the Congress of Trade Unions took care of supplies, which everyone grumbled about even before they found out that they were right. The local union was in no hurry for regular supplies because it was still at the stage of organising itself, just like our factory. But one thing they assured us of every day: bread. The people in administration swore loudly that the ever growing register of workers was 'not a register but a racket'. After all, they knew very well how many people had nothing to do with any textile industry, 'and their papers always got lost somewhere in the turmoil of war'.

Whether they worked or not, there were many people present. Every evening (evening fell early then), each person leaving the factory received a loaf of bread as black as sacred soil and heavy as the grave, yet it was bread without waiting in the queues in the city. Once a week half a kilo of yellow sugar and two packets of shag tobacco were also distributed. I started smoking it and, like the whole factory, became infused with its smell and saw everything through the thick fog of its smoke.

Almost every day I used to find on my table, next to the typewriter, small objects or fragments of objects brought here by anonymous hands - small holy pictures, sometimes a rosary or part of a rosary, photographs, sometimes pictures of dead people with a prayer underneath, shells with the inscription 'souvenir from Zakopane', or other bits and pieces. This did not surprise me. I was, as it turned out, the only Polish woman in the huge and constantly changing crowd filling the factory.

The factory was named after Comrade Khrushchev and attracted a lot of attention in 1940. It served above all at this time as a place for propaganda meetings, during which the limelight was occupied by Mieczyslaw Buch. He was then in the prime of his life, outshouting everyone and exuding an authentic and fervent faith in the triumph of Communism. He had always been a Communist and was notorious for an extraordinary piece of bad luck which surpassed every anecdote: he was so short-sighted that when his apartment was being searched, he handed the policeman his Party membership card instead of his student card. Of medium height, very slight and inconspicuous, he attracted attention by his tirelessness and the unusual endurance of his voice. His voice was inappropriate for a tribune's; thin and high, it absorbed all the man's bodily energy in order to pierce the jungle of voices and noises.

Sometimes a merciful hand would give him a mug of

hot tea, as if to a patient. These people showed humanity and solidarity; the majority had participated in the famous demonstration in Lódz demanding 'five zlotys for a day's work'; the majority were real paupers, and Jewish poverty in Poland was not widely known about. I had never been to Lódz. For me it was a symbol, a terrifying place depicted in Reymont's novel *Promised Land*,* like a nest of inhuman contrasts out of Dickens. Yet I had not really wanted to believe in the lot of these people until they were cast in front of my eyes by history and I saw their ranks in my town, their physical presence like a geyser exploding from under the earth. *Proles - dolores*. This was our country's very depths, its lowest stratum, speaking not my language but Yiddish, which I understood with difficulty.

One day I saw them in a different light. One of them had been waiting a good while by my table. I knew him fairly well because the second day the factory was open it was he who initiated me into how to use the spinning mules which were always getting stuck in the same place. He was called Zylbersztajn. His eyes were always red and watering, he was never clean-shaven, but did not have a beard. The cap pulled over his forehead had grown into his skull so much that it was like a part of his body. This time he pressed the cap down even harder, wiped his eyes with an habitual movement, then wiped his fingers on his dyed ex-army greatcoat, and was somehow awkwardly silent, which surprised me. "Have you got some business with me?" I asked finally. "What's it about?"

"It's not really my business," he said at last, "it's a factory matter, comrade."

* *Promised Land* is the title of a novel by Wladyslaw Reymont (1867-1925), winner of the Nobel Prize for Literature. It depicts life in the industrial city of Lódz towards the end of the nineteenth century.

"A factory matter? What is it, am I in the factory management that it's me you're approaching?"

"Because it only concerns you. Only you."

"What? Why only me? Can't you say clearly what it's about? I don't understand you."

Quietly and timidly he said: "Cifix."

"Cifix?" I didn't understand.

He started to wipe his perpetual tears again, and without turning round he pointed at the back wall behind him. Slightly upwards.

High up, almost under the ceiling, hung a cross. Of large dimensions, slightly larger than the ones which hung in schools, bearing a mass-produced, almost official figure of Christ, which was now covered in flakes of fallen plaster and dust.

"You do understand, comrade," said Zylbersztajn, "it can't stay here now. Times are different now, comrade. Well, it's different, you can see for yourself. It's better for you to remove it yourself than anyone else. Isn't it better? That's what I think."

I understood. And I immediately replied, or at least I heard my own words, "Yes, you're right."

I got up like a wound spring. I left my table. And only then an attack of reflection. How is it better? What am I agreeing to so spontaneously, how could I say this, 'Yes, you're right'? Suddenly immobilised on the spot, leaning against the table in the infinite clarity of what they wanted from me, what they were demanding, and also in a limitless void. Through the smoke of my own cigarette I noticed his look which was still concentrated on me.

"People will help," he said, as if to comfort me.

Because it was high. I had to get there somehow to take the cross down. But let the others do it. I should not put my hand to it. It's impossible.

So why had my first reaction been agreement? With the instinctive feeling that yes, it would be better for my hands to do it than theirs.

"You do understand," he repeated again.

Maybe that is why I said 'yes' then, because it was said to me with goodness, even with the correct tact. If it had been the brutal tone of a command, I would probably have said 'no'. I shall never know. Never.

"Well."

After all, it was not personal piety holding me back. But that cross had been looked up at hundreds, and hundreds of thousands of times by people who had worked here over the years. Maybe they were just passing glances, unconscious, but now they grew into a huge mountain. The Order of this world, both Old and New, so it was believed, was made by the Creator, redeemed by His Son Jesus Christ because He took this sonship upon Himself, accepted it, recognized the God of the Old Testament as His own Father in order to link the Old Order with the New, buy off all the evil of creation at the cost of His own torment and death, and transform cruel Jehovah into justice and mercy. Since that time people could swear by Christ's wounds, and there is no call or oath or scream greater than these words. It was not the depiction of Christ rising from the grave that came to represent the profession of faith, but a tormented man stretched in agony on a cross. Hanging there under the ceiling of a factory shop, as it had hung until now throughout the country, in every church and in almost every home. Until now.

I understood that the world was now leaning on an invisible axis. It had moved from its place, and this was how it looked in its human likeness.

"People will help." And Zylbersztajn added, as if to get me started, "I'm not talking to you without *verstand*. But with *verstand*."

Something tore me from the edge of the table in the same way as it had been holding me until then. As quickly as possible. Now. Now, because...

I had not noticed until then that a lot of people were standing behind the shop door, densely packed and silent, looking on. Cheek to cheek, everyone curious, some with smiles or frowns that seemed to harden and then disappear, they pressed down their caps and lifted their heads.

"Well then, I need a ladder. Have you got some scaffolding? There's scaffolding in the spinning shop."

"*Stimmt*," sounded the voice of one of the people by the door, "but it's too big, there's not enough room, it won't go in."

They were not behind the door any longer but were filling the space near the entrance to the shop. Then they dispersed inside, stood in random groups, or sat down on the floor here and there on their own.

There was some movement near the entrance. They must have foreseen everything beforehand; almost immediately three people brought in a long straight ladder.

"Haven't you got an extending one," I shouted out at the top of my voice. "What kind of factory is this not to have that sort of ladder?"

"What are you rattling on about?" laughed one of them, others followed. Quiet conversations started, and louder ones too. I did not understand, partly I simply could not hear.

"There was a ladder like that, but they stole it. We can all see what the gentlemen factory owners left us, just rubbish and nothing else."

When the ladder was placed against the wall, it seemed even shorter.

"On the table with it. Give it here!"

And the person who shouted this out kept repeating the same words louder and louder, 'give it here', as if there were a fire.

The shuffling noise of the heavy table being dragged

across the floor, then sudden silence as they placed it by the wall. Everyone could see it was too low and that the ladder still would not reach the cross. Then someone in the crowd called out that there was another table. So they brought it over with difficulty because it was full of drawers. A soft grey rag was poking out of a drawer which was not fully closed and they pulled out the rag and the drawer. Then they pushed the first table aside and placed one on top of the other. When they had finished, they tried it out to see if it was wobbling. It did wobble a bit so they put a piece of wood under one leg, and when it was secured, several of them assured me that I could go up without fear because they would be holding the ladder. They had also brought what I would need to take the cross off its hook. Maybe it was simply hung on an iron peg, as was usually the case. But one of them thought that perhaps it would be too heavy for me and brought a rope. He tied it to the top rung of the ladder, and from my arm they hung someone's tool bag.

I stepped onto a chair, from the chair to the top of the first table. From there I saw many hands stretched down towards me from the people standing higher up, and they lifted me higher still, sufficiently high this time. They held the ladder tightly at the height of their outstretched arms. Then I threw the gloves out of my jacket pocket. They were getting in my way, and with my foot on the first rung I looked round. The gloves fell quite far, straight to the floor, into a space between groups of people. I could see them clearly. They were thick, fur-lined gloves that kept their shape. They fell palms up, with the fingers bent forward a bit like two open hands, one next to the other, parallel. Like pleading hands, mute and isolated. From my height, I alone could see their terrifying gesture. I also saw someone walk over to pick them up. He held them up in the air to show me they were not lost and that no one would steal them. He was slapping the inside of his palm with them mechanically, as the thought went through my head that until today they had been ordinary good winter gloves but that they would never be the same. Maybe when I put them on again, something would cut my hands off.

At last I turned my head away and stepped onto the next rung and the next again, now concentrating on getting there as quickly as possible and then coming down. The fifth rung was rotten; it seemed to shudder under my foot. The next six did not shudder; I could feel under my fingers the nerve of the wood pulsating from the hands of the people below. They were starting to seem distant; mist and smoke mingled under the ceiling in an almost tangible weave. A stream of cold air blew from my lefthand side into my face, cobwebs trembled all round, and then I noticed that the top pane of glass, right under the ceiling, was broken near the frame and that the cold flowed in from there. At the same time a red spot flickered indistinctly not far from my head, quick, airy, from the left, the right, now here, now there.

A robin, I thought, or maybe I even said it, though not to myself and not to the bird. It must have flown in through the gap in the pane and couldn't get out. Don't fly out yet, you're my companion at a time like this. I'll always remember that you showed up by me now, that you were here with me now.

Like a benevolent ray, this darling bird of winter, symbol of Christmas and New Year's greetings, adorns and comforts homes and courtyards. It fluttered silently, I could not catch sight of it, but its very presence seemed miraculous. My heart beat out of gratitude, thank you, thank you, repeatedly.

It was not a robin after all. It was someone below casting up the beam of a pocket flashlight. Under the ceiling it was getting darker and darker. I suddenly understood. The light had struck a tatter of coloured paper left over from a garland at a dance, but I could not see it clearly from where I was.

With my fingers I felt the arms of the cross. Years-old cobwebs wound round my hand as I searched for the place on the wall's lumpy surface where the crucifix was attached. I leaned with both hands on the wall in order to catch my breath for a few seconds after this journey up the ladder, then I started to search, feeling with my fingers again. At last I touched the place where it hung. The cross was secured fast, it hung on an iron peg, but behind the place where the arms intersected I felt not the roughness of brick but cold smooth cement. I could see that over time the peg had become loose in the wall and had been fastened again. This was an unexpected blow. No tugging would be any good here. I reached into the tool bag hanging down from my arm, felt for a hammer and a carpenter's wide chisel.

Someone shouted to me from below, but I could not make the words out. I hit the cement once, twice, ten times, something seemed to crumble, but the cross did not even twitch. I started to hammer with all my strength; with the strength of desperate rage I was banging the place where the brick bordered with the cement groove. I counted on being able to rip out the whole resisting lump, tear it out of the body of the wall. They had given me good advice; the rope did come in useful. I tied it under the arms of the cross, made a loop on top, hooked the loop over the right arm so it could not fall down, only slip. The flashlight from below still wound round me. Suddenly it became brighter; evidently the direction of the hand holding the light had changed, and at the same time another rope flickered in the air with a whiplike movement. They called to me to grab hold of the end and pull it towards me. There was a flashlight attached to the other end, but I was scared to lean over the ladder, so they handed it to me on a long iron rod.

By its light I saw a crack which I was able to enlarge by driving a spike into it, wobbling it hard, turning it in all directions. Lumps of cement poured over my fingers. The hammer became springy; I could feel that it was being embedded into the drilled opening slowly but evenly. I pushed it into the wall almost up to the shaft and leaned on it with all my weight and strength, but it stuck. I tried to pull it back towards me, fighting with something that gripped it from inside the wall. This battle with an invisible obstruction lasted quite a while, until I heard a grating noise inside the wall.

One blow and then another at the wall above the crack, until splinters and fine sand came spurting out over me, turning my hands white up to the wrists. I stopped using the iron spike and leaning with my elbow against the wooden end of a wide chisel, I started to chip at the other face and slightly below the peg. After a moment the chisel's blade must have hit the mortar between the bricks; a sort of softness opened up. Lumps of crumbling mortar fell down the surface of the wall, not touching me. The brick seemed to shudder. I stopped using the chisel and tried a small-gauge drill. It entered deep, but the peg would not let itself be knocked out of its secured position; it moved only up and down. However, the uneven and narrow crack looked big enough for me to slide my hand in, folded like a fish gill. Grazing my skin badly, I managed to slip my fingers over the sharpness of the crack, and with the tips of my fingers I almost reached the brick's back edge. I started to lever it out with a jerky pressure as my concentration became impatient. But the resistance proved more obdurate. No, I'll never be able to overcome it, it's impossible. If just one brick, precisely this one, yielded its place, let me get nearer, I could hammer from the other, invisible side of the wall. If only I could manage it.

My jacket was lined with fur which seemed to mat itself

onto me, like a damp animal skin. The next moment I seemed to be pierced by cold, so I tightened my belt and raised the collar of my sweater almost as high as my chin. To rest, disappear, become nothing, not be myself. Home, my home, the world, suddenly became an unreal paradise, something which would in reality never exist. I could not see the people below clearly. They were veiled by cold mist and increasingly dense smoke. When I get down, I'll light up as well, but when will that be? Probably never.

In the tool bag I found a short thick hook whose purpose I did not know but now it might come in handy. I hammered it in beneath the brick as deeply as possible, jerking it at the same time. The brick's red body appeared, its edge, then a piece of plaster fell off and down. I levered the brick. The wall coughed powder and splinters, and I knew I was on the right track. The hook banged perpendicularly into the wall and split the brick in a crooked line similar to a short flash of lightning. Hammering at it I knew that I would overcome the resistance. The left part turned over like an opening door. Very slowly, after a few blows it fell out of its own accord; beyond it appeared an opening the size of two fists, black, slightly smoking.

The second part of the brick resisted longer. It did not crumble, only fell backwards on the other side into a space I could not see. Beneath it was that clot of cement, revealing its upper outline. I could hit it through the gap I had made by putting my hand in, but before I tried doing so, the lower brick yielded under the weight of the ladder, surrendering unexpectedly, and the whole wall shuddered. I pushed, and it rolled down towards the interior of the shop, hit the table, fell onto the lower table, and got stuck between the table and the wall. I kept hammering at the cement obstacle, regularly and loudly, until it was surrounded by a crooked oval contour that became darker and more and more distinct.

I transferred the rope loop to my back and suddenly what should have happened did happen. The cross shifted, its shaft wavered. I pressed with my hands only. One more effort, two, three, and the whole length of the Crucified bent towards me with a slow, slanting movement. I stretched out my arm to let it rest in the crook of my elbow, lifted my other hand to receive it, leaned my elbow against the top rung and almost immediately felt a weight in both hands. I anticipated the force of its falling. Now I had hold of it, now it was mine. The bottom end of the cross I placed on the rung, but I had already felt that it was not too heavy a weight. I put my arms round its arms, hugged them in fact, and started freeing the cross from the rope. It fell down, and a tall column of dust rose towards me.

Next to my shoulder I could see the head of Jesus covered with a thick cap of age-old, encrusted dirt, like a bird's nest. With difficulty I started taking off as much of it as possible. The face inclining onto the chest was not dirty, only covered with light powder. This powder was whitening my jacket, highlighting the impression left on it by the crucified man's figure. I held the thick leather buttons of the jacket closed with my left hand and felt the edge of the ladder with my right. We started to descend.

It was a slow business. A thick and viscous silence formed below, then a shuffling. My feet in their thick felt boots from Zakopane lowered themselves from rung to rung as if falling of their own weight. Deprived of my sense of balance, I pressed my knees to each rung. Evidently my unsteadiness was obvious because I felt someone's hands touch my back. Then when I was close to the crowd below, I turned the crucifix round to face them. I must not have done it carefully enough because, turning the cross round, I noticed one thorn was missing from the crown of thorns. Where it was broken off, white plaster was shining, a veritable eye glaring at me. I covered it as quickly as possible and started rummaging in the breast pocket of my jacket, among the buttons and pocket flaps, for that broken piece so very small. At last I found it tucked in above the buckle of my belt. Still holding the figure in my left hand, I descended onto the smaller table, wobbling a bit, then, pulling my tight skirt up over my sore knees, onto the larger table. No one was helping me any longer, no one approached me. At last I jumped to the floor and walked straight towards the door, my one-person procession ending at the shop's exit.

I went through the exit which led into a dark corridor, cold as the grave. The panes were smashed, and I recall that some ragged clothes lay or hung at the end, old protective coats dumped there haphazardly in a heap. I knelt beside the pile, placed the cross so it was leaning against the wall and with both hands sorted through the materials that were heavy and stiff from cold. I needed a flashlight, but did not call them to bring me one. Finally I picked out a fairly short and not too thick coat, wound it round the cross firmly and quickly, tying the sleeves like a strait-jacket. I had not forgotten to bring the rope with me, and I made a good job of securing the bundle. Some people passed me by, but did not ask about anything; maybe they already knew that it was best not to ask anyone about anything. I was wrapping it on the floor, forming a flat oblong object which acquired the shape of a biggish rhombus and looked like the cover of a musical instrument.

Then we went out. I did not think, did not even remember, that lately in the factory it had become compulsory for every departing workman to be checked at the main gate. When I noticed the guard's silhouette, I prepared a verbal barrage so that he would find out from factory management what I was leaving with. But the guard did not detain me with a single word. He was pacing to and fro, most people had already left, and the empty street gave his outline a silver-black background, steaming in the evening mist, so that he looked as if he was inside an aureole. His small head, beneath a cap pushed back off his forehead, kept appearing then disappearing in a spot of light from a distant lamp post, while from under the cap a trace of smoke ascended, first darker, then lighter, as if a single seam which slowly dissipated and rose again was linking him to the world. It was then, instead of going out at once, that I made my way straight towards the guard who was pretending that he could not hear my steps. Maybe he really did not hear; a tram screeched outside the factory wall just then.

"A cigarette."

"A cigarette," he repeated and with his tongue moved his own into the corner of his mouth. He pulled a bundle out of the depths of his wide stiff sleeve, moved the rubber band aside and with his fingers in woollen gloves pulled out a cigarette. "There's two but one's broken, so you'd better pull one out yourself because I can't see which one's whole."

"Quickly, man."

At last the cigarette in my mouth, at last the flash of the lighter on its hempen cord, at last the first gulp of smoke right down to the bottom of my heart.

I do not even remember if I thanked him, but I probably did. An unimportant trifle but irritating, based on the conviction that nothing was the same any more and did not have the right to be the same as it used to be. At that time this certainty was exhaled with the smoke in the most natural way, there and then.

I righted the position of my load, reminded myself of the words 'my burden is easy' in an almost mechanical way - and out we went through the tall factory gate. I could again hear a slowly approaching tram a long way down the street, which after a moment became visible. Those days in Lwów, to see a tram meant the start of a dramatic battle to get inside or at least to hang onto the lucky ones already hanging onto the steps. I had no hope of managing it. I decided to wait for the next one. Wait? I recovered my senses, struck by the absurdity of it; the next one would not be any better. I would have to do battle at once.

I ran up to it as it was just moving off. Someone on the rear platform stretched out a hand and grabbed me. I managed to jump onto the edge of the step and to squeeze through the jungle of people towards the outer part of the platform. Its iron barrier gave good protection to my parcel, which was less exposed here to the crush of feet and bodies. I leaned my hands against the arms of the cross. Standing, and holding it tight, I started this journey through the frosty dark city in the deafening clamour of rails and bells.

32

The journey seemed endless. To my right and left the city was unfolding its winter sheepskin, a historical garment which had again become commonplace. In front of houses, here and there, I could see Soviet trucks and scenes that had become usual by now, reminiscent of paintings and summoned up again. That flash of light clipped by someone's shadow in the depths of a gateway, that fragment of a street, bags and bundles, someone's embraces, someone's words, once in a while someone running, situations from the painter Grottger which I had already become accustomed to because I saw them almost every evening when returning from the factory. This time I saw them as if I were absent.

I was afraid, terrified, at every stop of a new inrush of people. In fact, squeezed into the very corner of the platform I had a space more or less secured for my holy luggage, but not so much as to avoid being jostled by the surge of passengers boarding the tram. The nearer the city centre, the more there were. To leave the tram also meant battling through the crowd on the platform to extricate myself, and I waited for it to be less dense so that I could jump off at any stop whatsoever and continue on foot. Anything to make it quicker.

I reached home at about eight in the evening. Entering this house invariably gave me pleasure, particularly during the war. It was all so sensibly and pleasantly laid out: an extensive hall, no narrow corridor this, and from the hall rose massive wooden stairs where one floor up a door opened onto an outside porch to the courtyard. The porch surrounded the house and freed the building from a second, kitchen staircase which my mother disliked so much. This well-to-do house with large high rooms and slightly uneven parquets belonged to the university. Opposite our front wall ran a low and picturesque wall on the other side of the road; behind it lay the botanical garden inaccessible to the public, with the walls of the old university visible inside. Ours was a quiet romantic street housing the Institute of Chemistry and, at the end, the home of professor Romer, the eminent cartographer. His place was 'the end of the world' according to our Helcia, who was friendly with the professor's servant and knew that home full of maps, strange instruments and incomprehensible photographs.

This time Helcia's end of the world became the end of the world for me as well. Because the selfsame Helcia, upon learning what was in the parcel I had brought, lifted her hands to her face and went out of the hall without a word. I later discovered that she had been seized with terror. "Fancy bringing home a crucifix," she said to my mother and sister. "There's enough trouble every step you take. It'll bring disaster on us. A home isn't a church, after all."

A conference started in the hall, where I had sat down on a trunk, sapped of all strength. "The church really would be the best place," said my mother, utterly unaware of how tired I was. "Better sort it out at once. Father Kajetanowicz won't be asleep yet, and if he's not at home you'll find him somewhere in the chapter house."

Then, listening to these ordinary and sensible words, still holding on my knees the package no one wanted, not having any strength left to relate how it had come to this and what had been required of me, I experienced for one single second, one single time in my life, something that could be called fervent prayer. A short circuit, a flow of electric current, exultant but fleeting, unlike any feeling I had known until then and untouchable with words. Indescribable. No longer than a split second, but jostling time both internal and external.

"Right. I'll go to Father Kajetanowicz. If you'll just give me a cup of tea. I'm frozen."

I received a cup of tea, quite strong for those days, and drank it, scalding my mouth and throat. I stood up. "If I've got to go I'll go now, at once."

So I grasped my bundle again, throwing it over my shoulder this time, and we set out. Just as we were at the very end of the stairs, my mother's voice stopped me. As luck would have it, someone was about to drive in the direction of the market square about the piano, so he might take me. "I utterly forgot about it. I was going to tell you this morning, but it slipped my mind."

Yes, just in time. I knew about the intended sale of our piano, but at this moment all that mattered was that I would get there sitting down.

Anyone who does not know the Armenian Cathedral and Square in Lwów cannot imagine the splendour of the architecture, transferred piece by piece from Armenia, including the gold and blue mosaics of the apse. The stone church exuded the endurance of centuries. It was arrayed with godliness past and present; nothing could disturb its gravity and majesty.

To avoid Sunday high mass, my mother used to play the organ there every day at low mass, at seven in the morning, when it was said by Father Kajetanowicz, who was a family friend. Despite the early hour, I understood the pleasure of being high up in the choir and filling the church with the resonance of music, and I well understood my mother's regret when we moved out of Grodziecki Street adjacent to Ormianska Street.

Yet it was not Father Kajetanowicz I wanted to meet in the chapter house but the younger Father Alladzadzian, with whom I could probably settle the matter more quickly. I was driven by car to the market by a fat bolshevik in a great hurry, who spoke to me only once, and in Russian: "Do you speak Russ..." I interrupted him immediately and then he fell silent and very quietly crooned a tune whose words I could not understand of course. He let me out in the market by a corner house, opposite the well-known Atlas Café, and I walked down Grodziecki Street to the Armenians. It was dark everywhere; only a distant street lamp removed from the gloom the twists of the old courtyard and the large side altar standing outside the cathedral, whose shapes of supernatural size rustled with dried ivy and hawthorn, imitating movement. I had always been slightly scared of them.

Above all, I was worried whether I would find anyone here. I banged for a long time unanswered on the side door through which the church was always entered. So I ran round the cathedral as far as I could, and from one place I spotted a window inside the highly complicated building. I was sure that my memory had not failed me, that the window was one of several in the meeting or conference room, and that it was in there that the renowned Armenian balls used to take place, snobbish, refined and slightly pompous. At the last one, the previous year, I wore a dress of whitish green organdie and green silk shoes. This memory, so grossly inappropriate, made me redouble my blows on a tiny side window perhaps a metre above the ground, firmly nailed shut. This hammering was louder than my knocking at the door and was not in vain. At last someone opened the door a crack and asked, "Who's there?" I gave my name and the priest's. The door was opened for me and I entered.

It was a nook of nooks, so abundant within the Armenian Square, a wooden entrance full of various doors and short staircases, lit by just the one candle held by a dry old man with a blanket over his shoulders.

"Reverend Father. I'm sorry, I didn't recognise you. Please forgive me."

"My child, my child," he whispered with his finger to his lips. As he bolted the wooden bar of the window awkwardly, I helped him, seeing with sorrow how his small and shrivelled hands were trembling. He was a very old man.

Wordlessly he showed me the way up a short staircase behind which rose another, more steep, and I stopped in front of a slightly open door. He pushed it carefully, and I found myself in a room I did not know, although I knew at once that Father Kajetanowicz's room had to look like this. I was struck most by the coarse boxes tied with ropes, clumsily and thickly; almost all the furniture was pushed into one corner, and only the dark crimson curtains at the window, from floor to ceiling, had the seal of gravity and dignity. Again all the light was provided by just a candle, in fact a pitiful butt slipped into a small jug.

The priest glanced at me, and I understood what he was thinking.

"No, my father isn't worse, he's as before. I've not come about that." And I told him tolerably concisely what had brought me. I should have been relating this in a different way, in a more plaintive or dramatic tone, because the priest bowed his head low, his hands covered his face, and I heard him weeping quietly, and although it was sudden, I could tell that his sorrow had probably been building up for a while, as if someone new whose presence I could clearly feel had entered the room.

"So I've brought it here," I said very quietly, not knowing what else I could add. "But a huge pale mark stayed there on the wall."

The old head nodded, tormented and furrowed. The lids of the huge black eyes with treble pleats stuck together for a long while. The priest was praying.

Then he started telling me, or rather, he simply waved his hand round the room. "We've got everything packed. We've got the most of the relics and really sacred objects hidden in safe places, but I'll never see them again. I've got no illusions. I regret that I've lived to see times like these, although it's not right for a Christian, particularly a priest, to say that. It's not right."

He wept again, but it was different now, like a stream's source in a flat meadow, the very essence of life.

"We're expecting to be ordered to leave the property any day now. And the cathedral of course. There was a man, an art professor so they said, he's one of them, he talked to us, he promised that as for the frescos and the mosaics, he may have some influence, he can try. He even asked us not to imagine that they're barbarians or an unenlightened rabble. But let me tell you, my child, that the unenlightened rabble will at least regret the loss of what's sacred and take pity, while the doctrinaire won't. Besides..."

He gestured with his fingers, opening them wide, as if all time was to flow through them.

"Just three weeks before the war someone pawned a watch for me at the Communal Bank, a gold watch with a chain, my private property, because there was someone I had to save. It was a souvenir from my ordination, and something told me not to do it. But I did, and now everything's lost."

People were still redeeming articles from the Communal Bank. I saw them every day, after all. Should I suggest it? But when could I go there? Perhaps I would find someone who could deal with it.

"We could still try," I said vaguely.

Those old hands were looking for a blue slip of paper, the pawn receipt, as he gave me a soft smile, not believing that such an extraordinary thing could succeed.

"If I don't find you, Reverend Father, I'll give it as an offering."

"Where, my child, where?"

What did 'where' mean? Did the priest not foresee any place of worship in the whole city under the new authorities, or did he simply think that everything would be plundered?

"I must go now. It's late."

I kissed his hand, again showed him the package placed on one of the larger boxes. The priest nodded his head, and then said that I should thank my mother from him for playing the organ at morning mass.

"I'll always pray for her. Tell her not to worry, she will believe."

I did not ask what these words meant. I was in more and more of a hurry, and Father Kajetanowicz sensed it. He embraced me strongly, made the sign of the cross on my forehead and led me downstairs, again with a candle, which surprised me, for there was no lack of electricity in the city.

Despite my hurry I ran inside the courtyard again to cast an eye over the ballroom window, vowing in my mind to remember it, and everything, even my green shoes from the last carnival. Not yet knowing that I was of the first and last generation to have enjoyed themselves in free Poland.

That was the epilogue of the 'cifix' from the factory on Janowska Street, but like the event itself, I did not put it into my book. I did not know how to write it.

I entrusted Kostek with the blue receipt, proof of a pledge at the Communal Bank, since he already had something to deal with there. He redeemed the watch for the money the priest had given me, but when I hurried to the Armenians again three days later, there was no one there any longer. I discovered that Father Kajetanowicz had been deported together with the others; the cathedral was closed, as was the whole area. The information was proclaimed in a large notice in Ukrainian issued by the authorities of the new republic.

33

Every visit of Kostek's in London brought me more and more details. He flooded me with them. I had to defend myself against getting completely bogged down in them because they were still moving. Again I felt terrified about whether and when I would be able to master them. Master? That means carry them inside me and with me, leading a new life abroad, sail somewhere and learn new service. It was all words. Even convictions. Our patriot predecessors had already known this, but our situation differed from all previous exiles. Learn new service. But even if we do, will past time fade in us and subside? Time did not pass for us. It had been cut off for us - unrealised time. What exactly was our new service to depend on? On convincing the West that it was suffering from colour-blindness? On working to extricate ourselves from being politically second-rate? Western culture had shown us what it was capable of being. I had seen the films shown in Bern after the discovery of the concentration camps.

Curtis had a new commission for me. He wanted to have 'something' which would illustrate the aphorism defining man's eternal fate: 'birth, copulation, death'. He set great store by it, in the same way as other people desire a *memento mori*. I wondered what intrigued him most in these words that reveal a perverse pleasure in negation and in reducing human beings to so brutal a simplification. The pride of knowing that although we can change nothing, we humans are aware of it all the same? Or the bitter awareness that whatever values we serve, in no way is death's fundamental violence diminished? Or the longing to pass into another form of existence, discarding these three thresholds on earth as an insignificant, transitory stage? Maybe he believed in 'something' after death and wanted to communicate to death his scornful contempt for its supremacy.

I accepted the order with a sort of pleasure, since these base moods spoke to me most strongly, these tentacles of horror by which my epoch expressed itself, casting their infinitely long shadow over everything else. All joy in life had sped, become a duty of recompense. Having survived was such a privilege that it seemed to deserve commendation.

In my own case this privilege was so manifest that it almost cut me off from my generation. Slowly, slowly it pushed me aside. I was unable to understand this all at once. Maybe my first steps towards understanding were two conversations with Curtis on the subject of his new fancy.

"The expression 'copulation' seems to me superfluous. Too optimistic. After all, in the last war millions of young boys and girls perished who had never participated in this act. They simply perished, not knowing what a kiss is, an embrace, an erotic experience."

"There have got to be three stages. It's the form of a classic triptych; it can't be reduced to a diptych. Your comments are correct, there are ascetics and people living in celibacy, as well as those who died too young, but all these are historical matters, therefore changeable, not typical; whereas the word 'copulation' expresses the ceaseless continuity of life and death, the sense or nonsense of continuing the species. So it can't be omitted."

"You can call it something else. Simply: being. So it would be 'birth, being, death'."

"No, 'being' can refer to lifeless things and not solely to living ones. Why are you opposed to plain 'copulation'? Aren't you happy in your personal life? Naturally, please don't consider this a question that requires a reply."

Such an indiscreet question certainly did not require a reply. But my laughter was so sincere that I placed my glass on the coffee table so that it would not hinder me from laughing to the tips of all my fingers.

"I don't agree with you entirely," I said at last, returning to the subject. "The word 'being' can be taken as an insult to life itself, robbing it of character and chronology: childhood, youth, maturity, old age. It doesn't suggest any completion either, any value, and that's what you mean, isn't it?"

"Do you think so? I'm not sure."

Curtis considered it. By force of contrast I was reminded of a sight so very different, perhaps associated with a movement of Curtis' shoulder, which revealed the quality of the wool of his jacket: soft, tight, falling into characteristic folds with a wavy line as if the material found pleasure in demonstrating its quality. It drew my memory to the other wool, from earlier days and another place, and for a moment I could almost feel its roughness on my fingertips.

The sticky wool clung to the fingers as the workshop carding machine pulled unwanted fibres off with every stroke. Swellings of the textile formed in the teeth of the machine and were combed off with an iron comb, initially with a quiet grumble, later with the resignation of habit. Two foot pedals snored unevenly. Being slack, they hit against each other time after time. The shuttle running through the warp dragged a thread of the weft, and here and there the material became thin as if it had already been worn for a long time. But no one worried about it and no one cared, although all the workers watched and fingered the roller winding the woven merchandise, smacking lips full of delight and tobacco.

It was impossible to cure anyone of giving the name 'merchandise' to the lengths of cloth being woven, and the factory brigade leader, Rud Akiba, reviled his comrades in vain as 'bourgeois flunkeys' whenever he heard the expression. Many of them simply did not understand Akiba. 'Merchandise' was the word they had used in Lódz, it was their word, they knew no other, they had merchandise in their blood and everything could be expressed through it. So, don't they weave merchandise in the Soviet Union? Well, what do they weave? Akiba himself used the expression at a meeting when he was briefing his brigade.

My workbench stood just behind the door that stayed permanently open beside the shredder because there was no window in the neighbouring hall. Shredded wool billowed through the door as various people moved around in the fog of thick dust. The shredder, known as 'the wolf', growled deafeningly, and a thick cloud of wool dust always covered all our faces. Chaja Unger, working in shifts with me in the workshop, very attractive and conscious of her beauty, covered her face in cream and advised me to do the same - the dust settled in the fat, and made a kind of mask which could be removed more easily later, after work.

"It protects you from the dirt," she used to say, and in the evenings proudly sported her fine pale face, smooth as satin. Her eyes glowed at the men then. They looked at her with pleasure, and also with gratitude for the symbolic triumph of her beauty over toil. Chaja would throw back her head, and her plaits wound round her head gleamed like a crown and her snowy teeth glistened. In the evening she would stand by the baskets in the canteen and distribute bread to people as they were leaving. She seemed at those moments to be all trembling with joy and pride; the black earthy loaves of bread flickered in her hands like links of an invisible chain. To every loaf she added a smile and often a dashing word.

No propaganda poster - and there were so many of them - could compete with the radiance of this girl at the prime of her life. Not only hers. She shared her idealist zeal with zeal for love. Her partner in love was not so much a handsome, as an interesting, medical student, and their partnership seemed to me most natural and appropriate. They met each other and mated, every evening, in a small space, a niche rather than a room, not far from the mules, on a temporary and shapeless bed where they both threw themselves down, not bothering that the door never closed.

And so once, passing in the corridor with other workers, I glimpsed these two in the act of love. Chaja had not removed her skirt; she had snatched it up, and she looked like half a woman turned into a statue. Her thighs squeezed together with the black heart of pubic hair, thrust slightly upwards, thighs so full in their ellipse and so pale that they seemed to contradict the dark matt opalescent shade of Chaja's shoulders and hands. Her body thus divided by colour into two domains, upper and lower, startled me as if there were a camouflage for visible or invisible matters.

Only now, in this rich Englishman's large drawing room, did these genre scenes from the Communist factory in my city appear before my eyes. I would have to write about Chaja in my novel, not let her perish in anonymity, recreate her, let her be resurrected. If the word is flesh, then the flesh subsists through the word. Even an image sculpted or painted or sound recorded will not return to life if it is passed over in silence and no one transfers it into words. Art is acquainted with death; it dies heart-rendingly like man. It is not eternal though it has the chance to become eternal. Stempowski and I often said that sado-masochism is probably best experienced by artists who destroy the work they have conceived and accuse it of betraying, deceiving and leading them astray, of being a flight too low to uplift them or too high for them to reach and thus elevate themselves and their world. It is a heroic deception to think that we will prove equal to a task whose dimensions and composition we do not know. Nor whether anyone, anytime, anywhere...

"I beg your pardon?"

Curtis had been saying something quietly, at length, and his sudden silence restored my attention.

"I was saying that every time I've been in close contact with it, I never believed that it could have anything to do with me. I was always sure that it would find someone else right beside me more interesting. I was always proved right."

Yes, true, we were talking about death, the one in general and the one to be painted. Gazing into the corner of factory buildings where Chaja Unger was making love with her partner, I had not been listening to my host's words but had remembered that one day the door which never closed disappeared completely. Had someone stolen it, or was it done deliberately against the lovers? Out of envy? Out of idealistic prudery? Maybe it was out of prudery because once someone came out of there carrying on the end of a rusty pipe the blue scarf which Chaja often wore round her neck. Afterwards I did not see them for a long time; perhaps they were promoted to the Congress of Trade Unions. Probably neither is alive today. Copulation. Death.

They had little chance of surviving when the city passed under German control. They will have risen in the black and yellow air like stars sewn onto the sky, they will have been one of those stars, huge sacks filled with wool sailing next to them, small shreds pouring out of one sack like flakes of snow, above them a lamb's head turned backwards and flowing from its back a black and white striped cape, perhaps striped concentration camp garments, perhaps liturgical dress, flowing onto a ramp or a balustrade, and pigeons, pigeons, pigeons sitting on it, but they will have been ring-necked doves in a rainbow nimbus, while in the distance, from far away and across, welled up a shape not completely distinct, white and long, neither Chaja's thighs nor the Tablets with the Commandments, the moon swelling huge above them with a child's hand reflected flat, perhaps the shadow of a hand. Perhaps the shadowy hull under it was the body of an Orthodox church with its cupola of a head, neither the bead of a rosary nor a bubble of a sigh?

Further on, just above the ground, an oil lamp in a halo dotted with tiny insects. An oil lamp like one of the many in my grandmother's house. One of them was said to have been obtained from someone to whom Ignacy Lukasiewicz had personally given it as a present. It had a cylindrical metal body and a shade made of a strip of matt glass as wide as a hand. A lamp.

So my circle was closing in this way. I was constantly returning to the part of the world where I had come from and to its glory. The line 'I gave you light from the ground' kept recurring. Lukasiewicz' fate was the converse of Prometheus', and it pleased me that in my great countryman's achievement there was nothing of morbid pleasure derived from the recollection of past suffering, nor did it thrive on anyone's pain. It thrived, grew and lasted through endurance and seeking. This seeking is commanded us for ever and is an innate need. Therefore it was a value. But then was a time of building values and of faith in their existence. A pleasant time. Apart from copulation and death.

Now Curtis was deliberating over these three stages which had been our destiny for ever and ever.

Ever and ever was of no interest to me at all. Yet ultimately I could imagine absurd and absurd. I could try to nourish myself with it, at least try in the quietness of my spirit and for my private use alone. The use turned out to be summary and very practical, because it suddenly dawned on me that I ought to give the Polish church in Devonia Road a present. Flowers, but flowers in a cup-shaped vase, richly decorated with ornament among which would wind the inscription 'Blessed are those who believe for they shall possess heaven and earth'. No, impossible, it is discordant and audacious; I cannot add of my own accord to the holy text of the eight beatitudes. Perhaps it should be different: 'Happy are those who believe for they shall possess heaven and earth'. That was really what I thought. Yet if fate, through this business with Curtis, was making me into an illustrator of moral quotations, principles or generally accepted beliefs and 'golden thoughts', then at least I would be useful to mankind in this way. I would always find shops or bookshops with customers for things like that. I would always find mottoes or golden thoughts which would not arouse my own protest.

This vision of such a disappointing career contained the seed of self-humour. I recalled what Kostek often said about orphans brought up on slogans and quotations. There was nothing I needed so much in those days as a dash of humour, and if I was already becoming an idealist exile in my ancestors' tracks, then let their maxims be fulfilled. I did belong to the 'late grandchild' generation after all.

In London I felt most at ease at Curtis' house. Perhaps because never once did he touch on the political question, nor on my own position as a dispossessed person. Nor did he mention any troublesome subjects, so my difficulty was purely professional. More of a problem than a difficulty.

What did surprise me was the return of precise moments, seen pictorially, from past provincial life in Poland, or fragments of events in the greatest contrast with the interior of this house. Last time I was here, I thought to myself, I saw Pietrek Tabor; next time it was that Chaja from the factory in Lwów, then the wells and Lukasiewicz's lamps. Why did these memories visit me here? Did they need me in order to be at rest? Did they need me to feel I had found myself beyond the brackets of all fundamental torments? Did they need conversation about universals like Curtis' three acts of life? These acts invoked, like Warlock in *Forefathers' Eve*, former existences and non-existences and intermediate spheres. Whatever did they want of me? They were urging something.

34

Boat crafted of beech!
You who bore Priam's
Fair-faced shepherd
Upon briny waters
To Eurus' crystal shallows,
What sister-in-marriage
Have you brought
To Priam's worthy daughters,
Noble Polyxena and
Seeress Cassandra?
In whose wake, their trail direct,
As tracking a fleeing slave,
Rapidly they follow,
The hunt to complete.*

Is the boat to blame that the chorus addresses it as if it were a wrongdoer? It was built of the best timber, of beech from Mount Ida, where the most magnificent masts were chosen and finest vessels constructed. Is the boat to blame that it was burdened with criminal plunder? Paris, son of Priam, condemned to death by his own father, was secretly saved by the officer Archelaus and entrusted to the river banks to be brought up, so it is no surprise that the boat assisted him, not knowing what he would do some day.

This passage addressed to the boat always astonished me. We too were now set down on the banks of the river

* From Kochanowski's Renaissance verse drama *The Dismissal of the Greek Envoys*, translated with the assistance of Krystyna Kimbley.

so that it could 'educate' us. We had been taught mythology. We knew Latin, and because of it we imagined that we belonged to the West. And what happened? Mythology has ridiculed not a few of us, the ones who survived the hell of war, but each of us must now start to build something out of the remnants, if only a raft.

Along the Thames at Battersea Bridge, where the old landing and 'my' motor boat *Wings* had been, no vessels or anything navigable remained. All that was left were two stout poles driven into the ground, leaning slightly. The river bank had been strewn with flat stones. In one spot an iron rail had been fitted so that no one could cross that way, but the area did not invite walks anyway. Large trucks rather than elegant limousines drove over the bridge. The opposite shore of the Thames was constructed of huge, heavy factory or administrative architecture of the old school. The buildings were so bulky that they must surely contain something important, must surely serve something that does not die, that is needed generation after generation. I looked at these massive walls that attached no importance to beauty; I was not interested in their real name and function. I was meant to be thinking about the representation of death, how to paint it on the tile and which aspect to emphasise. Contrary to tradition, I did not want it to be depicted on Curtis' classic triptych as a menacing skull or with any traditional attribute like a scythe or an hour-glass.

I wanted it to be young and beautiful. Not with its eyes closed, but open, just like when we die; with its mouth half open, just like when we die. With a worm emerging from the corner of its lips, still fairly discreetly, but a bold one, first among equals. Should I do a second one perhaps, since everything was in pairs? Birth was shown as a baby being delivered by Caesarean section, according to an engraving of a work by Paracelsus. Copulation was a dark shape, two-headed, four hands with fingers entwined, like 'Janisia's dead bodies' from my childhood. Death still remained to be done. I would have to do it at last.

My return journey from the bridge crossed Drayton Gardens, a small peaceful street not too far from where I lived. I remembered that Hania had mentioned a pub in the area where she would try to find a job if her other plans fell through. She had said when we met that I should go there some time 'just in case'.

The day seemed appropriate, one of those grey days that stimulate new initiatives. At this hour the pub should be open but not yet crowded. I found it without difficulty. It turned up in front of me of its own accord, and I was slightly surprised at its low windows and its authentic old-fashioned and plebeian look, as if snuff-soiled. It had inner and outer double doors. The second set were swinging doors; they were half open in front of someone else who was entering and scooped me inside as well. From the very threshold I noticed some way off a light point which was Hania's head. The interior did not correspond to the view from the street. It had been altered and modernised, which was probably meant to result in more custom. For Hania it was undoubtedly an advantageous change.

There was a large rectangular space separated from the rest of the room by a wide bar counter, all lined with dark wood and glass, rather quiet. She'll be all right here, I thought with pleasure. Partitioned from people, a barmaid is not a waitress. Barricaded with polished metal, a shining row of tumblers and glasses in front of her and a wall of bottles behind, she was in a very colourful place, full of sheen, cleanliness, and reflections. Whatever she touched was cool and smooth. Ah, so this is her glass house. She is to enforce obedience and maintain order within it.

As backdrop she had signs from the most famous English taverns and inns: a chess board for 'The Chequers', a flower for the 'Rose and Crown', and a ponderous head for 'The Bull's Head', ran diagonally towards the green 'Royal Oak' on a white field. On the left side 'The Black Horse' rampant, on the right 'The Red Lion', whose movement was so very similar to the one on Lwów's coat of arms. Yes, this company of emblems put me in good humour; the naive drawings and names sounded as if they had come from a children's book.

As for the living, apart from Hania, there was the owner himself hovering around, stout, with a greying moustache, in a velvet waistcoat: presumably Mr Hedder, the one who had bought the pub from his incompetent brother-in-law, as Hania had told me. I also knew from her that he would pay a young lad more as an assistant because he considered that self-respecting pubs should have only male service. So she assumed that the job would not be permanent. In the meantime, high among the bottles, Johnny Walker was smiling in his ceaseless march across the world. He looked like a good guide, imparting courage.

Before approaching Hania, I surveyed the customers who were now flowing in a small but steady trickle through the swinging doors. Others, obviously regulars, had already settled down on small hard stools and a long bench that was probably ancient in front of which stretched an equally old and narrow table. It drew to mind a row in a concert hall, except that my eye fell on their faces, the individual faces of these people. Not only the ones on the bench. All the faces bore the seal of isolation and a silent decision to withdraw into oneself, or else to retreat from one's own affairs. It seemed as if they had come to bide their time and to extricate themselves from their own existence.

A shudder ran through me at the sight of life so frozen that it no longer seemed suitable for any human community. Or perhaps every human life settles into this kind of solidity after many years, and that is exactly what the human condition looks like. After all, there were hundreds of identical or similar pubs in England alone, probably not hundreds but thousands. Statistical humanity touches no nerve. But these particular people...

They were not poor in the strict sense of the word. There were no signs of poverty; some of them even looked fairly wealthy and middle-class. But they gave off that stench of solitude or seclusion, a Beckett-like aura or plasma. Probably a plasma, if they sit for a bit longer in this immobile drinker's position, then... A grey fossil silently settled everywhere. Silence hung over them, smoke circled above their heads for a while, thicker and thicker, before it dissolved halfway up towards the ceiling. Surprising that the people themselves did not dissolve, but they adhered to everything and everyone, and in the greyness of these figures, in their rigidity over their glasses there might be, there had to be, an internal quarrel with the unavoidability of fate which I had keenly observed.

I kept examining them carefully; actually I wanted to investigate this state of affliction. So that's what they were like. But if I worked here, then in wiping glasses, in arranging them upside down in rows, in my polite readiness to serve would be concealed an indifference as coarse as the world. And at the same time something like conceit. The species of our problems and our dramas of a people without a country towered above ordinary people like that. We could have no tangential points, no common perspective forwards or backwards.

I suddenly understood and experienced that 'pride in misfortunes of a higher order' which Dostoyevsky so cruelly mocked when depicting Poles. It had previously seemed repulsive to me. But now it did not lie so very far away, although an English pub is not Siberian penal servitude. So it's like that. This presumptuousness of Poles with their higher order of suffering, so intolerable to foreigners, can it happen to me as well? I must take care. Not slip into the same mechanism which governs these people. Fear overcame me. Was I, a daughter of *Serenissima*, to contend with such foul thoughts? Could I descend to this?

I decided to stand a beer for the fourth man on the right, by the wall, the most doleful of the lot. His glass was almost empty. What else could I do to recover a degree of ordinary humanity in my own eyes? At least make a gesture.

I felt sorry for Hania. A moment ago I thought that she would be all right here; all was so clean and smooth around her. Immediately afterwards, however, I was stung by the disproportion between her light familiar head, the only point of light in this dark gloom, and this surrounding strangeness. There is a mute key which when pressed gives out no sound but a shudder. People who travel frequently know it and instinctively raise their collar, not for fear of a draught, but because of the particular need to protect their camouflage. It works efficiently. So as to be preserved, not to scatter, not to vanish.

But Hania showed me an agreeable face. She noticed me only when I stood up to the bar and ordered a whisky from Mr Hedder. Whisky in hand, I greeted her through her metal barrier. She was wiping glasses, and her fingers had the warm damp touch of river creatures. She smiled a Hania smile, and again the golden swatch of hair caressed her face every time her head moved.

"You already know, don't you?"

"That you work here? But you told me yourself."

"I don't mean that. But you must know already.

You've seen Mrs Drymmer. She's been searching the whole of London for you because, can you imagine, I lost your telephone number."

This news was like a shot in the heart. Mrs Drymmer was the wife of the former chief of protocol at the Ministry of Foreign Affairs. If she was looking for me, it was in one matter only: the Second Corps was returning.

"Are they in England already?"

"Not all of them yet, but she's arrived and is contacting the families of men in the Corps. Perhaps she doesn't know she should ask about you at the Koscialkowskis. But I told her your address, Arrington Gardens."

"Harrington."

The address, 63 Harrington Gardens, now seemed the best address and the best name in the world. Who was Harrington anyway? Was he some lord, I wondered, a famous horseman and rider in the time of, well, at the end of the nineteenth century, in Victorian times? It was enough that he had existed and that the house where I lived might once have belonged to him. The golden liquid rocked in my hand, I asked for another. "Drink with me, please, Hania, have a drink, you do understand."

Hedder was watching this disapprovingly. The staff were probably not allowed to drink, and in addition, we were talking Polish.

"Good news, Mr Hedder. Very good."

"Oh, I see," he said without smiling.

"When did you see her?"

"The day before yesterday. She's living with friends, but I've got their address at home. I'll telephone you tonight just in case, but she'll probably get to you first."

She kept wiping glasses. I could see her fingers through the glass, like pink stems in white leaves, as the whole world spun in an assumed transparency.

"There's a chap in the room over there. I don't know who he is. Terribly glum. I noticed him when I came in.

I'll take him a beer, all right? What about you? What news?"

"The same. We haven't seen each other yet, but it'll probably be any day now."

So why was she still working here, I wondered. Did she want her husband returning from the war to see how she had coped, as if she were on duty, and to take her away from here? Perhaps.

35

I did not move from the house. I sat like a rock. I even asked Angus for cigarettes. I hardly left my room, keeping the door ajar to the corridor, where the indoor telephone kiosk stood. I phoned Marian Koscialkowski's house in Acton Town to say that I was leaving London for a few days, thus ensuring that no one would be in touch with me except for Mrs Drymmer.

I did not find Mrs Drymmer at the number Hania had given me, so I left mine and waited. I wrote about myself and my brother. I wrote almost endlessly so that nothing of these moments should be lost. I was arriving at the high point of my life and could hardly believe that fate was bestowing this on me. Arriving at such heights rarely happens, although at this time many people must have shared the experience. Everyone knew just one password, one sign of recognition which was sometimes passed on with only a nod of the head: 'survived'. And my reiterated surprise: Why is there no Church of God's Smile in the world? Or perhaps there is, only in my ignorance I...

Something of this must have seeped out of me because

in the night, dreams-not-dreams flitted over me, leaving their indistinct trace after I woke. I generally slept heavily, using sleeping pills. I very rarely dreamt and generally woke with my head clear. Yet the day after my conversation with Hania, I woke to a curious remembrance, fairly indistinct and very pleasant, something that tempted and encouraged me, yet slipped away every time I tried to grasp it. Until finally, and it was nearly noon by then, something on a white background loomed up out of these nocturnal blurs, neither card nor envelope, and a thin, light inscription in printed letters like on cheap visiting cards: J. Onlymercy. The phrase pried open my memory when I said it out loud. They were the words which, long ago, I had read in the cemetery in Chlebna on a miserable scrap of paper: 'only mercy'. The sentence, grown illegible, had borne a pale trace of a name, which I had been able to decipher as 'Jesus'. Now these scattered words had flocked together into a surname.

Strange that nothing wrenched or surprised me. I felt as if I had received a pleasant and valuable gift. And an idea: I would make a present of it to the parish at Devonia Road. I'd discard my previous project of a decorative vase, which was embarrassing me with its banality. In my imagination I saw something different: a votive picture, painted on glass but not pretending to be folk art - Lord Jesus Onlymercy. I wouldn't let Father Staniszewski, director of the Mission, into the secret of this picture's origin. Would anyone check that it's not an authentic place name in some distant land, but a sigh of a word, a pleading request for God's help for a person in need?

It was not going to be a large picture, twenty-five centimetres squared at the most, and it would depict the Sorrowful One, but in a somewhat adapted portrayal. With his right hand he was supporting his head bent down by the crown of thorns. His right elbow was resting on his thigh in the classic pose, but his back was covered with a cloak which, falling down by his side to the ground, rested on his knees in numerous wavy folds. In the very centre, he was holding a fiery heart on his knees in his left hand. Shown in the traditional way as a radiant heart, perhaps blazing as well. The rest of the background would be occupied by a motif of plants and shrubs. With birds in the branches.

I immediately sketched it on paper, with the feeling that if I did not do so at once, then I might never do it. With exaggerated precision, and more and more slowly, I drew the birds and then the shrubs, leaf after leaf, twig after twig, multiplying them beyond measure, then erasing them again, until a whole Tree of Expectation grew. Nothing soothes better than drawing leaves, any sort, plain or more elaborate, with lifelike venation though generally fantastic, not to mention the stalks.

I was halfway through the stalk on the leaf of a hornbeam, *ulmus*, when I heard my name being called from downstairs. It was the creaking voice of the owner of the house, who pronounced the foreign surnames of her tenants with some difficulty, and immediately after I heard other words, very loud:

"A Polish soldier to see you."

I leapt through the door and fastened myself with both hands onto the banister at the landing. Far away, downstairs, halfway along the entrance corridor I could see the 'Polish soldier' who was gesticulating, obviously unable to communicate in English. I examined him clearly and breathlessly. He had hands. He had feet. His head with a thick black mop of hair turned away from me was moving freely on his neck. His arms had normal human movements. He had pulled something out of the breast pocket of his uniform, had shown the woman, and was obviously trying to tell her something. He raked his fingers through his hair, he was having difficulty, but I was not going to help him. I wanted to look. Every movement as before, perhaps in this situation every movement was reflected against former times. The similarity had not been erased although I had never seen him in this uniform. He was like he used to be. The same. My brother. And finally, finally, I recovered my voice and called his name from my banister. Or rather something called it through me.

We threw ourselves onto the stairs, he up, I down. We reached each other halfway. There was probably a moment of subliminal consciousness, because I saw every detail as if I had become a telescope. Yet the feeling of reality was not failing me. I could hardly believe - it was reality that had to assure, encourage and convince me - that these arms were his, the smooth but slightly rough cheek, and the same eyes, perhaps a bit deeper under his brows, the same teeth and mouth that with a quiet breath said, "Daddy? He's dead, isn't he?"

"Mother and us. The people in Poland..."

He knew. He knew that I was abroad alone. But this was not a moment for information. We were incapable of describing or remembering anything at this moment. We were in the very eye of the cyclone. Years and ages will pass, but that moment froze, and I knew that it was the essence of what is most human. Then and for ever.

And so, mutually supporting each other, suspended, almost superterrestrial, we went up the stairs. It must have been our real legs we used.

In the following days, still unsatiated, unable to say everything there was to say, we talked feverishly, incapable of mastering the quantity and quality of matters so numerous and deep. All the more, because it was harder to find fortunes more contrasting than Bogumil's experiences and my gorgeous security in Bern. It pleased him, as if it were a good joke played on the whole world. He had been spared nothing, and he considered it a miracle that he had managed to drag himself to the Polish army created in Russia and was among the first seven in the First Signals Corps.

He did not speak ill of the Russians; everything was suffused with limitless commiseration. I liked the way he described everything, quick, precise, agile, naturally billowing with digressions, not in the least gloomy. At times he even laughed at incredible situations and dangers. They probably all talked that way, those who had survived and had someone to tell.

But none of this past was a subject for him. It had rushed backwards by now and was almost re-interred. His subject was the future. "What will happen to us now? After all, they won't leave us here in this England." He shrugged his shoulders, while I did not have the courage to tell him what I knew. I decided not to tell the truth; there would always be time for that. Anyway, I did not have to know everything. I myself was in England only on a temporary stop-over, and was close to take-off now. Let's be happy that we're alive. That we've met.

He had brought heaps of things for me. He was afraid that he would find me in a miserable London neighbourhood, in poverty, and only when he saw my street did he begin to have hope. "It's decent this Harrington Gardens, and the house is too." He laid out the wealth he had brought: whole rows of tins, meat, jam, fruit, even milk, a beautiful Italian silk blouse, cloth which I immediately earmarked for my wedding dress, pyjamas with blue flowers that I still have to this day. This artillery of care surrounded me on all sides, bringing relief to my siege, and immediately, as happens in situations like this, the differences between the observers and the observed were effaced, the objects suffused with our emotion lived with us, we with them, having them as eternal witnesses to our happiness which had 'overcome the gates of hell'. Those gates had been so close. When I wanted to wipe the glasses using a cloth with wild flowers and poppies, Bogumil closed his eyes without a word, then said, "Haven't you got a different cloth, those poppies..." He whispered it so quietly that I barely heard.

We walked through sunny London in summer, not able to sit still for joy. It was a different city too; I knew it by sight but not intimately. Now I wanted to look at it in the daytime and without fog. Food in restaurants, drinks in pubs, double-decker buses which the newcomer was unfamiliar with, and parks, benches, fountains, bridges, and parks again, houses, gardens, streets, lanterns, policemen, postcards, post-boxes, life to the power of n, because there are so many powers opposed to it.

But I did not take my brother to Battersea Bridge.

He had a wife. He had got married in Italy, in Rimini, to a nurse in our army, senior to him in rank, whom he had met while still in Russia. She had saved his life nursing him outside the hospital. She had heaps of virtues; he talked enthusiastically about her. She came from Lida. He showed me a wedding photograph, both in uniform, arm in arm, Poland, Poland, the lovely face of a very serious blonde, complete tranquillity and goodness. I was pleased. I was to meet her in a few days. Their military transport had been located in Diddington in former British army barracks. What, how, where, it all meant nothing to me; everything was becoming second-rate, third-rate. And suddenly easy, as if I had pushed my boat away from the shore at a stroke and sailed silently into the water. Into the water.

In the night, the first and second after Bogumil's arrival, I became aware that my boat was ready. Bogumil took a room on the same floor; my landlady was touched by such an explosion of joy between siblings who had found each other again. He slept there like a log. As for me, quite the reverse, despite walking the town all day long. As soon as I threw myself onto the bed, something rustled above my head, trundled and tripped next to me, toppled over, angular and heavy. "Don't you recognise me?" asked a strange object, "I am the cornerstone."

"What cornerstone?" I asked, certain that I was already dreaming, that I was falling asleep so soundly, but I was afraid of dreams. Then I understood, my senses returned. It was the large package prepared for Bogumil, and I had forgotten to give it to him. In the joyous confusion I had forgotten to give him my present. It doesn't matter, I'll do it tomorrow, even better, we'll be more lucid. It was no stone, but earth. A box of earth from our garden at home. I had received it from Poland and had divided it into two; half I had kept for myself, the other I intended for him in the event that he should survive the war and return. For that highly unlikely event.

I had added another division of spoils to the box, half that is, three bone buttons for pillowcases and a small photograph album. Then there was an expensive present but of foreign origin, a beautiful astrolabe, an unnecessary thing, decorative, with a quotation from Kochanowski which I had written on the rim: 'For as long as starry night, in ceaseless circle, follows the light of day'. A decorative object, but might it seem a tactless present now? Because what have we to measure now? The distance of the stars from the horizon? What and where is this horizon of ours? No. That is for later, when we reach a landing stage, when rebellions are extinguished and hopes arise once more - small blades of grass. Because now I will make sure that they grow. It is possible to cut defined ways of living from the absurdity of the world; people do succeed, they do, they do.

And I, had I not gradually quietened down, was I not beginning to get used to the thought that I would be a cosmopolitan, although knowing nothing of how my history would turn out or what I would manage or have time to do? My state of lamentation, my angers, jeremiads and rebellion had lasted nearly a year. Would it not finish with my living like a settler and knowing personal happiness? But homeland affairs, going more out of fashion every day, still hurled themselves at me with their own desperate delirium. Yet I would not show Bogumil that. Not him.

Strange that he seemed not to know anything about it either. He did have some illusions, I think. Had they discussed something in the army on the journey to England? Had they been told something? Was he pretending as well?

When this constriction of my heart which I called a cornerstone finally eased, I got up. I carefully opened the door to my brother's room. I did not want to wake him, of course, only to check if he was really asleep. Could he be just pretending to sleep as well?

He was asleep. His peaceful, even breathing stirred the edge of the sheet; his pillow had a tight bulge beyond his head; he had obviously fallen asleep at once, on the spot. The narrow strip of light from the corridor did not let me see anything more, but I knew for certain he was asleep.

As I quietly turned the handle, I felt as if I had clasped something new and beneficent. A quiet but distinct current switched on in me, not exactly like an engine starting up or water being struck with an oar. But something like that. A strange feeling, difficult to name. I am grateful for it. To this day.

36

Serenissima the most dazzling became the most dark, and not for the first time. That is probably why my dark Serenissima appeared again, because she was bringing her problems closer: I did not know what my brother would choose. Perhaps he would want to return, like Kostek? But now I knew how to talk about it.

Still, I was completely unable to remember the surname of the poet (seventeenth century? eighteenth century?) who exalted the liberty of the Republic which others so envied us until 'they seized it in the same way as Alexander, also called Paris, seized Helen'. He brought her to Troy in a beech boat, and the Greek envoys were dismissed empty-handed - because Alexander had received Helen from the gods, Venus herself had given her to him. Was he to reject such a gift? That would be an insult to the goddess. So let the gods take heed of what they do. After that, war was unleashed, Troy destroyed, and Helen was retrieved. Troy was utterly destroyed, as Warsaw was later, as Berlin was later. Cities and states fell. The vessel escaped unscathed.

I did not remember the poet's name and could not tell Bogumil about something so distant from the present moment. Other matters demanded to be told. I related to him the stages in my history, Lwówian, German, Swiss, English, and the fact that the one to come, the French, was likely to be the most important. When he asked how I coped in England, I did not admit to frailty and internal fragmentation, or to my complicated and difficult financial position (an expression which has always amused me), nor to my pathetic and furious deliberations. Quite the reverse, I appeared competent, making light of all difficulties; I was full of initiative and common sense.

I laid out my drawings done for Curtis, which saved my credibility. My script of the history of Polish literature for the YMCA also helped me. In fact I did not need any proofs; my brother did not subject anything to the slightest doubt. My person, so strongly anchored by opinions and moral positions well chosen and reasoned, must have seemed to him - just as I wanted it - settled and strong, well entrenched and bold. Perhaps in his tenderness there was even some gratitude - but I'll never know - for my being composed exactly like this. A battle unit. Because, as I told him: "The war hasn't finished for us, it's only just starting. Except with different means."

Whatever he thought, whatever he felt, he must not think that they had fought in vain, that disaster awaited them and ruin pursued them. He sensed I was - just as I wanted - a combatant. Aware of another game and other means, but not in the least disarmed. On the contrary, preparing for sallies and attacks.

I was prepared to deny everything, renounce and contradict everything, just so that I could radiate like that, with an artificial light borrowed from all sides, purely a reflection, just so that I could persist with certitude in this role as my brother's protector. I must formulate my thoughts in the manner of a mathematical equation but pretend that there is only one unknown.

"Do you remember that brilliant story of the man who gives a public assurance that he'll guess the right word on condition he's allowed to ask twenty questions which can be answered only with a 'yes' or 'no'? And he proved he could. Do you remember?"

Bogumil did not remember. He laughed; he was returning to the realm of disinterested mathematical problems. He did not note that his former interests, mathematics and Latin, had not protected man in any way. Mathematics served mainly for killing, while the ancient world and classical values no longer existed. He might not have thought about it. What seemed self-evident to me might not be so for him. All the better. Was it possible that the war had allowed some people to retain order, or at least an illusion of it?

He was a believer, even fervently so. How good! He possessed a treasure above all others, and I immediately threw it into my imaginary boat where I was storing supplies of everything that might come in useful. It contained various absurdities, absolutes, aberrations and alienations. The Allies were also included as a warning and lesson. I was stuffing both older and more recent experiences into it. I was burdening the hold even with useless things, for they might be exactly what turned out useful. Shortly, or in the distant future.

To this cargo was added the most unexpected news of all, real ballast, and I had done well deciding beforehand that my boat would carry everything.

"I haven't told you until now; I thought I'd tell you when we got to Diddington. But you'll pretend in front of Zosia that you're hearing it for the first time in our barracks, won't you? Because we live in a barracks, a very funny one, with a roof like a barrel. That's why we call it our 'barrel of laughs'. In a few months something new will be laughing there for the first time in its life. You've guessed. We're expecting a child."

We were sitting on a bench in Kensington Gardens. I was holding a twig of a shrub, and how strange that it neither blazed purple nor blackened nor turned to dust.

A child. I had never thought about it. That exiles, people without a country of their own and beyond its reach, would be having children! How could I not have foreseen it, never imagined it, as if we were castrati? It had seemed to me that they did not have the right, though I had never analysed this extraordinary notion. It seemed to me, although I had not thought about it very precisely, that we formed a particular species, something like a warrior caste, full of zeal and transported with new strength. We would do battle with the new hydra of totalitarianisms and stupidities, but we would not multiply. Something like the Knights of Malta, who did not proliferate, but attracted the cream of knighthood from many countries and whose members were governed by the idea of serving their ideal. Well stocked - for that we would need time - and having connections with the whole world, we would conduct parallel political relations and, although without a territorial base, we would become a real force, deciding directly or through careful diplomacy about alliances with the world, curing it of wild and sick ideologies. Ideologies which had so extirpated us and which continued to destroy us. We had to grapple with great forces, while here a child was going to be born.

A child. The world was still in confusion. The war had not vanished from cities destroyed and countries subdued. The ruins were still smoking, London looked like a toothless old man, Coventry and Warsaw and Dresden filled us with horror, while here a child was going to be born.

I could not let him see my reaction. After a few seconds I even made it appear the surprise of good news. That was better, that was the best I could do, indeed the only thing. I laid my hand on my brother's hand and stroked it. Some great emotions dispense with words, which is how he understood it. All the better.

"And of course we want you to be godmother. We're asking you to be godmother," he said firmly. "You understand it's very important to me."

I nodded, moved closer to him, leaned my head against the 'Poland' on his shoulder. Parentheses opened inside me, I felt good, very good. But I thought that in fact fate was making fun of me. A shade good-naturedly, if ironically. I could not resist the comic thought that everything was happening by means of a *deus ex machina*, in this instance the *ex machina* being my own *frater*. It was natural and simple, of course, that he would ask me to be godmother. Not realising what cursed fields I had faltered through, how I was dragging myself up from my own nothingness, what shores I had been approaching.

So I shall be holding this child of his for baptism. I did not even ask when or where it would be. Probably there in that Diddington place. I kissed him on the cheek, he kissed my hand, and we sat like that, hand in hand. I squeezed up to him; I almost wanted to dissolve in him like powder poured into liquid. He was merry and smiling.

"Do you remember everything that should be said?" He laughed. "Because, you know, with time people forget. Of course, people aren't often godparents, and the victim can't remember. The baby should shout. Ought to shout or cry. It's said to be a bad sign if a child doesn't cry while being baptised. It's even better to pinch it a bit, so long as it responds."

"I can pinch it."

"What else?"

"I remember that you say 'I renounce the Devil and all his works.' But I don't want to, I don't believe in Mr Unde, in the Devil, I mean."

"But there isn't a sentence like that about the Devil, as far as I remember. That's at confirmation, when you're ten or twelve. During baptism the priest only asks what you want from God's church and you reply: 'Faith'. Then the question: 'What does faith bring?' Reply: 'Eternal life'. Then the priest says: 'If you want eternal life, keep the Commandments.' There's nothing there about any Devil."

"I think that at the end I have to say the whole of 'I believe in God', don't I?"

"So what? If you don't remember it, I'll write it down for you, and you can learn it by heart. I remember it very well because I say it every day when I'm saying my prayers. Then I say, do you know what, 'Angel of God, my guardian dear', just like we were taught when we were children, remember?"

"I remember. Yes, I do remember that."

But not only did he remember it, like me, as a detail of earliest childhood. He believed in the soul, in the immortal soul, and people who believe so strongly are winners that deserve to be envied.

Then I remembered Hilo, the hero of my comedy. He was conceived *ex nihilo*, from absolute nothingness, and that was his claim to fame. He met with incredible situations, convinced that with a pedigree like his, nothing bad would happen to him. And when it did, he did not recognise evil, only negotiated with it. He negotiated. He negotiated with every opponent until his opponent was out of breath.

It was a comedy written in Bern at the time when I wrote nothing for publication or fame, simply for the pleasure in the word. It portrayed a world in which comedy was the only weapon given to man to lighten his fate.

But that was untrue. Comedy was not man's only weapon, and I was ashamed for having once thought that.

I remembered a small but significant detail, a childhood fault of mine: during holy days and the mass for All Souls', when reciting the litany to all the saints, I used to omit the names which started with the letter 'M', an abbreviation for 'Martyr', as well as such epithets as 'Virgin and Martyr'. My eyes would slide over these saints in order to stop at other ones who had the title 'Doctor of the Church', or even 'Prophet'. I could not pray to people who had been tortured physically, to those who in fact probably most deserved their sainthood. I was angry with myself for this, so I boldly decided to admit it at my next confession, which was on my tenth birthday. The priest was somewhat surprised; he was silent for a moment, fidgeted, and seemed confused or alarmed.

I felt sorry for him, I had not behaved correctly, I had simply been tactless. What had I said it for? What could he do about it? Besides, he had been hearing confessions all that afternoon and could well be very tired, while the chapel was still full of people. "But do you love Lord Jesus?" he asked at last, turning his face to the wooden squares that were worn and slightly polished from the confessions of sin by two generations. "Yes, I do," I replied like a good girl, sincerely ashamed of my behaviour and suddenly scared that when I grew up, I would be unable to restrain myself from saying unnecessary things.

And so when at last he gave me the end of his stole to kiss, I kissed it carefully, mindful not to touch the gold thread of the embroidered cross with my lips, since these threads are especially sensitive and easily lose their shine when touched.

I could not have foreseen what a terrible punishment would come upon me. When I grew up, the era of my youth and early adulthood was branded by cruelty to an unforeseen extent, and although personally so strangely spared by fate, I nevertheless knew and saw and felt the horrors of war, and those of peace as well.

But now my brother was sitting next to me, and I knew nothing else apart from the fact that he had survived. And that I might never learn the details of what he had undergone, what he had endured. That is something one does not tell even one's very nearest and dearest. I was chasing this thought away, erasing it in myself, but I knew that I would never be rid of it.

37

We had various matters to deal with. The day after Bogumil's arrival I received the long-awaited news from the Mission at Devonia Road that my various papers had at last arrived, even copies obtained from Lwów by my family of my birth certificate and my degree. All that remained to be done was for me to sign, which I could do any afternoon in the parish office.

At the same time a letter arrived from our mother, written in Polish and English, about our family house in Jaslo. Like the whole town, it had been burnt down by the Germans in reprisal for the rescue of Home Army prisoners from the prison there. The ruins as well as the whole of the garden and out-buildings could now be sold, and the letter contained instructions about the documents needed for effecting the sale. It did not contain a word of personal regret or reminiscence, as if it concerned something indifferent, or else burnt out of feeling. By a strange coincidence the window of my room facing the old well and the garden had survived, but no photograph was enclosed. Perhaps they did not have one.

We wanted to settle it quickly, as quickly as possible. I made an appointment with a lawyer recommended by Marian Koscialkowski's sister. I insisted that it concerned an urgent matter, and at the appointed time we seated ourselves, my brother and I, in front of the desk of the solicitor, Mr Sanders. Both of them, desk and owner, exactly fit the mental picture I had already formed about what an English solicitor and his office should look like. Both already aged although belonging to different epochs: the neo-Gothic window casements, the coloured panes pretending to be stained glass, the heavy curtains, old photographs on the wall, probably of well-known personages, and the indispensable brass vase with an eternally green plant, an everlasting feature of such places.

Yet the clients turned out to be exceptional specimens. I alone did the talking; Bogumil did not speak English. I expounded as briefly and clearly as possible the purpose of our visit. Then the solicitor, Mr Sanders, pushed his glasses further back on his nose and studied us for quite a while without a word, clearing his throat and wiping his nose, probably to gain time. From his words it transpired finally that the document we wanted was a serious matter, very serious, exceptionally grave, and that we had probably - bearing in mind our youth - not given enough thought to what we intended to do. Surrendering the rights of ownership to part of a house and property should warrant some form of compensation and should include conditions.

"No conditions," I explained again. "We surrender all rights with no compensation whatsoever, neither now nor in the future. The one and only owner of the house and the property becomes our mother who - if it has to be added separately - we authorise to manage affairs exactly as she pleases."

And unexpectedly the whole business started to drag on for a long time. The solicitor - we could read him like an open book - had never had anything to do with Poles; they were evidently not fully normal. English restraint and reserve are completely correct with regard to people from the Continent, especially from such little-frequented countries as Poland. Of course in the war there were these people, Poles, they even took part in the famous Battle of Britain. In wartime one has to meet various sorts of people, even make alliances with them, yet in peacetime these same people turn out not to possess any legal concepts; even the concept of property is not understood there as it should be.

He cleared his throat again and started a conversation about the situation in general: it may still undergo various political changes, and your business may take another turn, if...

"Even if it does take another turn, which unfortunately we don't foresee, our will is that the house should be the exclusive property of our mother so that she can sell it, which she cannot do without the consent of all her children. We're in a great hurry, Mr Sanders."

But Mr Sanders was not in the least sensitive to this hurry of ours. He pointed out that all rights to the house would be lost also by our children and the children of their children, once and for all, once and for all, and that none of us would ever...

"Nor our children. Nor the children of our children. Nor any of us, ever. Mr Sanders," I shouted at last in despair. "Our father was a lawyer; we know what we're saying. We understand what law is."

But now it turned out that "No one knows yet what legal norms are binding for foreigners who have the status of political refugees, and as for members of a former allied army, it's not yet completely clear. They don't have any rightful country, and a document of this nature cannot be drawn up immediately in this way. You'll have to wait. Furthermore, you should consider it very carefully once more and think the whole matter over again. Come back next week."

I rose from my seat, carried away with irritation. I sat down again and started to explain everything from the beginning, very slowly, surprised that I could find the cool blood and patience. The need for money was an urgent matter in this instance, and there must be a paragraph which, according to which, having looked...

And then we heard from behind the desk, when we were already standing up: "And what about the right to pre-empt?"

Pre-emption? But we could not buy it back. The authorities of the present government of Poland do not permit foreigners to own anything, let alone émigrés.

"But your mother, when selling the house, can reserve the right of first refusal to buy the house back if the new owner ever decides to sell it. Just in case."

We fell silent. This was a mirage which had flashed before us, such as appears to people in the desert. It appears, then either disappears immediately or else lasts for a very long time. The exhausted traveller follows it when he is on his last legs, usually dropping from exhaustion although he can see his goal in front of him.

To buy it back. To be able to return there. The foundations of the house were still there, the cellars too. And the ground where the garden had been, now wild and deserted. To rebuild it, renew it.

No, this was a dangerous *fata morgana*, a sorcerer's trick. Mr Sanders was operating according to English concepts, according to English possibilities that individuals could take decisions; he did not realise that over there these concepts and possibilities no longer existed. But maybe something will change, not everything has been finally settled there yet. If only we could have a say in the town's decisions. To allocate half the house for the town library, for instance, or for the county archives.

"So we'll come back next week, Mr Sanders."

We went out in silence, into the jostling, sunny streets. The huge wall of a red bus stopped in front of us, a bus stop. It was our bus, but we did not see it, gazing into the past, the future, into unknown sources and their murmur in the depths of our souls. The next bus arrived immediately afterwards anyway; it was also going in our direction and we got on. We would not achieve anything by standing here after all.

What about somewhere else? No, not that either.

And we sat down in the park again, saturated with warmth, with light, with silence in the shade of rhododendrons large as houses. We were rid of all our thoughts which - I could feel it - seemed to flow off us onto another plane and come to a standstill.

"Do you know what rhododendrons are called in Polish?"

"They're called rhododendrons, aren't they?" Bogumil moved, and the 'Poland' on his shoulder flashed. A butterfly passed between our heads, flew on, made a circle in the distance, returned, settled on a bush nearby.

"*Rozaneczniki*. Rhododendron comes from the Greek, *rhodon* a rose and *dendron* a tree."

We were smiling, with a smile that was at first faint and then more and more generous, although we did not really know why. A self-seeding smile. We were alive, others were not.

I was entering deeper and deeper into my role. In every simplest sentence, about any old thing, about nothing, about important matters or no matters at all, I was sure of my own rightness and was moving peacefully through this post-war storm which had been unleashed for us Poles. The old historic exiles from our cemetery disappeared. (Perhaps they only concealed themselves, who knows?) So long as they never appear again. There must exist some exorcisms with which they are warded off; I shall pretend that I know them. *Être c'est paraître*. I did not allow myself a single word of criticism of our terrible situation, as if being a match for it were normal. Very well, I shall be a match for it. I shall be godmother to the child, and because of that a complete suit of armour capable of warding off all blows in all future brawls will be given to me. After all, I had told my brother that the war was only just starting.

I again repeated to myself: I must seem to be strong, then I shall become strong, and others will believe me, I shall be useful. I will load my beech boat with everything I need. I shall reach shores new and old, easy and difficult, and I shall also be able to anchor it firmly and well. Beech is a strong, healthy timber that will endure everything; it hardens with age. The people who will tell us - they are already telling us - you don't bring your homeland on the soles of your feet, must be rebutted: if you're incapable of doing so, you're unworthy of your homeland.

A butterfly was flying past again, this time pale yellow, almost transparent like the shadow of amber. It was in trouble, its flight seemed to unravel a stitch in the air, then it looked as if it had become caught on something and could not extricate itself; it tugged itself down, levelled its trembling flutter, glided forwards on the faintest breath of air and disappeared into the light of the sky.

I could not see it any longer, but the spot where it had disappeared from my sight was pulsating in my pupil.

A little boy in a red sweater was running across the lawn with a butterfly net stretched upwards, exactly as in an eighteenth-century painting. He fell over, then quickly ran on in the deceptive hope of seizing his prey. His net was intricate, its sides were all covered with large artificial flowers - bait. Don't let yourself be netted, my pale yellow airman of the summer sky. The flowery net was reflected in the water of the pond like a white wreath. The child ran along the side, then dipped it into the water, where other children were sailing paper boats and small ships. Their hands disturbed the surface of the water, while the net described a lazy circle, once, twice, then stretched itself out immobile, as if with pleasure.

One of these boats was hit by a ball from the lawn. The boat swayed and toppled onto its side; water poured into its paper interior and the opposite side shone in the sun with deathly whiteness, gliding slowly and still more and more slowly. Two children ran up, pulled the ball to the side with a stick, unfastened the wet boat from it. Its creased shape fell near the stone edge of the pond, and the children ran off where they had come from and disappeared behind a wall of box shrubs.

I picked up the crumpled little paper boat and shook the water off it. Pressed between my tight fingers, it assumed a similarity to its old self. I determined that when it dried out, I would keep it. I would write today's date on it, and it would accompany me in my future odysseys.

It accompanied me long and faithfully. Many years later I gave it, as a symbol, to the son of the deceased Kostek, a young man who belonged to the movement called Solidarity, who left the country and immersed himself in the wave of new emigrants.

About the translator: Anna Marianska was born in London in 1950. She completed her university degree in English literature and linguistics, then taught English to children of Indian immigrants in the north of England. After returning to London in 1982, she was employed as a social worker with elderly Polish and East European refugees, and she became active in the Polish community abroad. She translates professionally for commercial and media clients, and is a member of the Translators Association of the Society of Authors. Her most recent academic translation is *The Fate of Poles in the USSR, 1939-1989,* a study of the deportation of Poles from eastern Poland and their subsequent treatment in the Soviet Union.

In 1992 Ms Marianska moved to Neubrandenburg in Germany.

DATE DUE

GAYLORD			PRINTED IN U.S.A.